NO ORDINARY JOURNEY

Colin tells his story

Colin Tinsley

NO ORDINARY JOURNEY

Colin Tinsley
6 Hawthorn Hill, Kinallen, Dromore,
Co. Down, BT25 2HY, Northern Ireland
Email: hopeforyouthministries@gmail.com
Web: www.hopeforyouthministries.org

Preface

C S LEWIS once said that "Children are not a distraction from more important work; they are the most important work". His words typify the story you are about to read. Options: there were several. Temptations: there were many. Distractions: they were omnipresent. But, if one thing outshines them all it is the love of Jesus Christ. Evident at the moment of Colin's salvation, it has remained evident through the twists and turns of life ever since. Colin Tinsley is a man who experienced the love of Christ for him. This in turn allowed him to discover the love of Christ for children all around our world. And it was this discovery, which has led him to where he is today. He found, surrendered to and labours in the most important work.

Prepare to laugh, be ready to cry. Prepare to share in moments of highest ecstasy and then in the very next turn be plunged to the very depths of despair. One thing is, however, undeniable: the very hand of God is traceable on every page. As you read, look for God's hand and blessing will surely enrich your soul as you behold the Almighty at work. Having done all this; be ready to respond to the challenge. In these pages you read of the power of one life, the importance of one decision and the value of one soul. I have known Colin for over 15 years now. Both he and Joanna have always been an example of Christian service, sacrifice, sincerity and support to me. I heartily commend his ministry and this book to you. Pray for him as he labours in this most important work.

An ordinary journey it certainly hasn't been, but if this book is the reason one person begins their journey then it will have been worth it all. This is Colin's story – all the glory to God.

Ps 37:5

Jonny Ormerod

Contents

INTRODUCTION

Unfinished Business

THE SALMON FISHING season had finally arrived. After a busy week, we packed the car and headed sixty miles south, to the little town of Elliston on the coast. Having moved to Australia for a two-year pastoral placement in a local church, we took every opportunity to explore our new surroundings. Sea fishing on the beaches was a massive attraction for the locals and I was eager to try my hand at it.

I borrowed a rod and other fishing gear from a friend called Billy who was an experienced fisherman. He talked me through the steps involved in catching a big salmon. Fish happens to be one of Joanna's favourite foods, so I was determined to catch a huge one to cook for dinner!

We parked up and gathered the fishing gear from the boot, then descended sixty metres down the wooden staircase to access the secluded beach at Locks Well. Jagged black rocks bordered the beautiful, golden sandy shoreline of the Southern Ocean. It was a perfect summer's day with not a solitary cloud in the bright blue sky and the noise of majestic waves crashing onto the beach was awesome. Although it was a notorious bay for sharks, surfers often risked life and limb for an exhilarating ride on the waves!

Joanna found herself a sheltered spot to relax and read her book, but as my mind was focused on catching a big salmon, I hooked up and headed straight to the shore. My biggest concern was if the rod would be strong enough to pull a large salmon in, or would the line snap due to the weight of the fish? After some time maintaining a firm grip on the thick, three-metre fishing rod without anything biting, I decided to wade out a little allowing the water to cover my knees. It was very frustrating as I could see huge salmon jumping out of the water not far in front of me, yet none of them were taking my bait.

After fishing for over an hour I still hadn't caught anything, so I waded out into deeper water, where the sea was now up to my waist. The water was warm and the rolling waves felt therapeutic as they gushed past, bobbing me up and down. When I glanced back, I noticed Joanna was quite some distance away as I was in much deeper water, with the waves brushing my chin. Gradually, I became aware of a strong undercurrent and the sand shifting beneath my feet. At that moment my thoughts turned from catching a fish to getting back into more shallow water, but it proved to be a considerable challenge. Before long I realised I was trapped, as the power of nature was sucking me further out into the ocean and below the surface simultaneously. I reckon even the strongest of swimmers wouldn't have been able to swim against such an angry current. Nevertheless, I tried not to panic and kept breathing whilst attempting to maintain a firm foothold on the bottom. I knew if my feet left the ground, within seconds I would be swept out into the ocean to face my doom. It was terrifying!

I yelled at Joanna to get assistance, but the boisterous waves crashing onto the beach drowned out my cries for help. I could see her sitting peacefully on the beach taking photographs of the scenery with her camera, completely oblivious to my desperate need of rescue. I knew I had gone out too far and within minutes I would be food for the sharks and great sea monsters. Finally, Joanna turned her camera my direction and through her zoom lens, she noticed my expression had changed and saw I was panicking. She rushed to the shoreline but was so far away, she could barely hear me, never mind assist me.

I remember crying out to the Lord for help and begging Him to save me from drowning. I was terrified and felt like a fly in a spider's web or a deer in the jaws of a lion. I was helpless, hopeless and powerless against the mighty power of the ocean. My life flashed before my eyes and I became conscious of just how little I had accomplished for God and humanity. Crying like a baby, I promised God if He would save me from death and Joanna from becoming a widow, I would serve Him fervently the remaining days of my life. Although already a Christian and ready for heaven, I had unfinished business to complete on earth. *Please save me! Help me, Lord!* I cried with all my heart and strength. *Keep my feet in the sand, because if they lift I am gone – gone forever!*

I could see Joanna standing almost frozen, panicking on the shoreline, pleading for me to come back to her. But the power and force of the ocean was too much for me. I was a fighter and knew I had to act quickly because I was tiring and before long my head would be underwater. At that moment it dawned on me the fishing rod could help. With all my strength I drove the base of the pole into the sand to get an anchor to hold on to. I steadied myself briefly, but after a moment it also became loose.

As I sighed and stared into the horizon I noticed a gigantic wave rising above all the others. *This is my only chance*, I thought. I needed to hit the crest of that wave and ride it to the shore. I prayed in desperation, *Lord, make this wave be like the whale in the story of Jonah and use it to dump me onto the beach!* I waited nervously until the crest arrived, then sprung up like a dolphin and for the next thirty seconds, I paddled furiously underwater with every ounce of energy I had. Finally, my hand hit something solid. I feared it was the body of a shark, but thankfully it was the sand on the beach. Thoroughly exhausted, I lay trembling with shock.

Although I didn't see Him, I knew God had heard my prayer and rescued me from the most precarious situation I had ever faced. When I gathered enough strength to sit up, right in front of me was a big sign with bold writing saying: DANGER! NO SWIMMING – DANGEROUS UNDERCURRENT! How stupid was I for getting so engrossed in catching my prized fish that I failed to see that sign?

Joanna took a few minutes to reach me because the tide had swept me at least a hundred metres down the coastline. She was so relieved I had returned from my 'swim', as she described it and gave me a big hug. Then she asked, "Where is Billy's fishing rod?" to which I quipped, "The salmon must have been so big it took the rod and all!" As we sat together on the beach reflecting on what had just happened and how the consequences could easily have been tragic, I felt God had given me a second chance and a new zeal for life. I remembered I had made a serious vow – a promise to God; that I would make my life count for Him – that I fully intended to keep.

CHAPTER ONE

An Ordinary Little Boy

AS I COMMENCE my story, it's worth mentioning how easy it is to assume that a missionary is someone from a privileged or highly-educated background or whose parents are full-time Christian workers themselves. On the contrary, God called me from a humble, rural family in County Antrim, Northern Ireland without claim to any of these credentials. If God in heaven can use me, then at the outset of this book I want to assure you He can use absolutely anyone.

As a young lad, bedtime was something I didn't really look forward to. However, once Mum's voice echoed throughout the house, "Time for bed boys", there was no discussion but rather a mad rush to get our pyjamas on. My six brothers and I would then jump into the two beds in our room and mess about and wrestle each other until we heard Dad's footsteps coming up the hall! Then we piled on top of each other like a litter of little piglets and pretended to be asleep when the door creaked open. Being full of fun himself, I'm pretty sure Dad grinned as he shouted at us every night to settle down and behave. Mum knew he had the voice of authority in our house, so he had to let her hear him scold us to pacify her, but then he quietly whispered, "That's enough boys, time to sleep."

Growing up in a small house with lots of children was serious fun. With seven boys going to bed at the same time, we dreaded being the first one to fall asleep, as you could waken up the next morning with a moustache or extended eyebrows scribbled on your face! A funny memory I have from my childhood is slipping across the field to our neighbours' yard to watch their TV through the window. On one occasion I remember knocking their door and asking the man to turn up the volume as we could not hear it. Sadly for us, he was very stern and closed the curtains instead. What a pity as cowboy films were our favourite! With childlike logic, I remember thinking, *how could I love my neighbour when he won't even let us watch TV through his window?*

One Easter, Dad bought a donkey to keep the grass short in the field directly in front of our house. My brothers and I came up with the most amazing game ever. When the donkey had his head down munching on grass, we sneaked up and jumped onto his back, then tried to stay on as long as we could. It was normally only a few seconds as he bucked us off instantly! On one occasion three of us managed to jump on at the same time before crashing off and landing in a heap on the ground. We giggled, laughed and roared at each other, such were the endless hours of fun. Another time I was running so fast, I leapt right over the donkey and landed just in front of him. Then his big long ears came down and he chased me around the field, much to the amusement of my brothers. Other times we dangled a stick with a carrot on it in front of his nose, which made him run around the field chasing the carrot, surprisingly it didn't get any closer, as we bounced about on his back and clung on tightly.

A few years later, Dad got pigs and when he let them into the fields to eat grass in the summer, we had the same competitions, only with the big sows! When we jumped on their backs they would run as fast as they could until we either jumped off or fell crashing to the ground as it was so difficult to stay on.

My brothers and I loved doing what boys do best – playing football, follow the leader, hide and seek, paddling in the river and other such simple games that children play. Mum never had a problem getting us out of the house to play, but it was a different story some nights trying to get us all back in again. We loved the summertime when the nights stretched on and it seemed they were never going to end. Sometimes Mum put us to bed, but we climbed back out the window and across the fields to play again. Another one of our favourite games was mischievously sneaking up to neighbouring houses, knocking their doors and then running to a hiding spot. The laughs we had seeing the looks of confusion on people's faces when they came to the door and found no one there still makes me smile!

Although I didn't understand it at the time, looking back now I realise I had a very simple upbringing as I advanced through my primary school years. Only a few rooms in our home had carpet, with the rest having concrete floors. We didn't have a telephone nor grid electricity, though a little mobile generator gave us light at night. Times were tough for Mum and Dad as they embraced the challenge of raising seven boys with huge appetites on a modest income. After the birth of my eldest brother Trevor, Mum stayed at home while Dad continued to work as a digger driver and farmer. When Trevor turned two, Isaac was born, followed by James, before the twins – myself and Edwin, then Derek and finally Matthew – seven boys, but no girls. From early childhood, our parents taught us always to be thankful and honour the Lord with our lives. Before mealtimes, we said grace, although it was necessary to cover your food when you closed your eyes or one of your sausages could disappear! Somehow, I got the blame most times!

We were quite self-sufficient and Dad kept a cow that he milked each morning and evening. Mum then used the milk to make tasty puddings such as rice, semolina, tapioca or custard. In late spring, she added delicious rhubarb that she grew in the garden for extra flavour!

Dad really loved the outdoors and often took us hunting in the fields for rabbits, hares, pheasants, snipe and woodcock. Then when darkness fell, we waited in the woods for pigeons to shoot. In the summer our focus turned to fishing in the local rivers. After periods of heavy rainfall, Dad often asked me to go and get worms from the dunghill to use as fishing bait. Then off we trooped along the rivers looking for the dark spots where fish would likely be. On one occasion, my dad caught seventeen rainbow trout! When we returned home, the excitement really began as we prepared ourselves for either tasty stew or fried fish. I also recall from my early childhood the brown automatic Mini Dad owned. On Sundays, all nine of us squeezed into it and drove to church, often tickling and nipping each other on the way. With Dad massively distracted by our boisterous behaviour, the overloaded Mini would shake and swerve from side to side as he drove along the road. It got comical, and looking back quite dangerous, as we flicked his ear and then he would shout and attempt to slap us in the backseat trying to work out who the culprit was. It was funny blaming it on the wrong person and seeing them get whacked! We burst into fits of laughter as Mum then yelled at Dad for nearly crashing. I'm surprised Dad never got pulled over by the police and accused of drink driving! In winter when it snowed, Dad put us in the link box of the tractor and covered us with a big blanket and then drove us to Sunday school and church. Even in a blizzard, our diligent parents made sure that we heard what the Bible had to say each Sunday.

Mum and Dad were Christians who really loved the Lord and their greatest desire was that each one of their seven boys would make a personal decision to trust Jesus as their Saviour and Lord. They did their best, as every evening we sat together as a family and read the Word of God. On many occasions I observed Mum and Dad on their knees, praying to God by their bedside. It amazed me how they could talk directly to God with such assurance that He heard them.

In the summertime when Sunday school was not on, my parents sent us along to local Holiday Bible Clubs, which we loved. I really enjoyed the games, but the missionary stories left me awestruck! As I listened to the intricate details, deep down I wondered what it would be like to take the message of the Bible to people in different parts of the world. It seemed like the most exciting and worthwhile job ever and a little seed of desire was planted deep inside my heart that one day I would be a missionary.

Although we were taught much about God and the Bible during our primary school days, none of us boys made a profession to be a Christian. Yet, the seed of God's Word had already begun to sprout in our lives, just like the Apostle Paul said about Timothy in the Bible, *"And that from a child thou hast known the holy scriptures, which are able to make thee wise unto salvation through faith which is in Christ Jesus" (2 Timothy 3:15).*

In addition to church and Sunday school, Mum and Dad faithfully sent us along to the local Boys' Brigade – an excellent Christian organisation catering for boys from the ages of four to eighteen. I loved all the different activities there on Friday evenings, starting with our uniform inspection, then drill and marching, followed by games and finally settling down for a Bible lesson. On Saturdays, we played football against other BB companies and each summer, our leaders took us away on a camping trip which became the highlight of my year.

While in the BB, and in particular during the process of obtaining my President's and Queen's badges, I developed teamwork and communication skills that would benefit me in adult life. My self-confidence also grew as I learned how to manage responsibilities. In the BB, I heard more stories about Christian missions at home and abroad. Again they captivated me, but by this stage, I reckoned only an extremely bold and supremely gifted person could become a missionary.

As we entered our teens, the prayers of Mum and Dad intensified. They pleaded with the Lord to protect their boys from danger, to keep them out of trouble and most of all, to save them and give them the desire to serve Him. Like many other Christian parents, my folks laid claim to promises in the Bible such as: *"Train up a child in the way he should go: and when he is old, he will not depart from it" (Proverbs 22:6).*

Throughout my teens on many Sundays as I sat in church listening to good preaching, I felt God often probe me and ask, *"What about you Colin, what about you?"* Like Moses of old, I replied, *"But God, there are so many others, who are more gifted, smarter and better looking."* I didn't have money, a good education, or experience. On the contrary, I had very little going for me. Little did I realise, a few years later God was going to save and use me in the future to bring His Word to thousands of people, especially children.

At that time, I could never have imagined serving the Lord in a full-time capacity, but I am proof the Lord is always willing to use anyone who is willing to be used. I was just an ordinary little boy with humble beginnings, but God had chosen me for His work. We were probably the poorest family in our church financially, yet in other ways, we were the wealthiest, as we were taught to love and respect our culture, country and most of all the Lord, whom we feared and extolled.

The Apostle Paul reminds us that God is not looking for ability, but rather availability. *"For ye see your calling, brethren, how that not many wise men after the flesh, not many mighty, not many noble, are called: But God hath chosen the foolish things of the world to confound the wise; and God hath chosen the weak things of the world to confound the things which are mighty; And base things of the world, and things which are despised, hath God chosen, yea, and things which are not, to bring to nought things that are: That no flesh should glory in his presence"* (1 Corinthians 1:26-29).

From a human perspective, I was a very unlikely candidate to be considered useful for carrying out the purposes of God. However, when we open the Bible we read that God told Samuel *"man looketh on the outward appearance, but the Lord looketh on the heart"* (1 Samuel 16:7). In other words, God doesn't always call the qualified, He qualifies the called. I was just an ordinary little boy who, deep down somewhere, had an urge that God would take whatever I had and use it for whatever He wanted.

CHAPTER TWO

A Higher Call

DESPITE HAVING COUNTLESS happy memories from my teenage years, I faced many challenges, most of which occurred at secondary school. After seven joyful years in a little rural primary school, I moved to high school in the town of Lisburn and was the only country boy in my class. At times I felt everyone continuously made fun of me over every little detail in my life. I was not able to rise above it and my response was to challenge those taunting me to a fight after school. Looking back, I think I had fisticuffs with nearly every boy in my class, as the bullying I faced was too much for me to bear.

On one occasion, in Home Economics I baked a cake for my mum. I spent a lot of time decorating it and was extremely proud of it as I knew Mum would love it. I carefully placed it in a tin and took it with me to my next class. I set the tin on the floor of the corridor as we stood outside our classroom waiting for class to start. A moment later, one of the boys in my class jumped on the tin and squashed the cake into a messy pulp. He laughed at me for making the cake and that time I didn't even wait until after school to teach him not to disrespect my mum. Despite the temporary satisfaction of settling scores, the constant rejection and isolation from my peers caused a deep-rooted anger to grow within me. I longed to be accepted and really struggled to find or form my own identity. I suppose I developed a 'chip on my shoulder', as people in Northern Ireland would say.

As I entered adolescence, I became very conscious of my appearance and believed the whole world was judging me. One spot after another appeared on my face and my hairline receded beyond my control. With hindsight, I now realise that everyone else in my class probably had similar thoughts, but at the time I felt I was their sole focus for mockery. How different things might have been if I'd understood the biblical principle of taking my eyes off myself and fixing them on Jesus.

As time went on, my anger and frustration increased so much I often lost my temper and shouted and cursed like a madman. Regrettably, the recipients of my angry and foul-mouthed tirades were often those even more vulnerable than I was – my younger brothers and to my shame, my own dear mother.

Mum's chosen method for disciplining us was the tried-and-tested punishment of the old wooden spoon. However, one night when I was sixteen and full of anger, Mum took it out of the kitchen drawer to scold me. Since I was physically the size of a grown man, I hardly even felt the pain when she scalped me. I mocked her verbally before grabbing the spoon from her and snapping it in two over my knee. Mum burst into tears, realising that one of her sons had become as cheeky and defiant as a boy could be.

I understood the fifth commandment to honour my parents and I guess deep down, I despised the way I was living and wished things could be different. However, I was too proud to admit it and went to bed all puffed up thinking Mum couldn't control me any longer. In fact, my older brothers rebuked me and told me I shouldn't have spoken to Mum so harshly. The entire time a war was raging within me. God was calling me and trying to get my attention, but I was stubborn and had a rebellious heart and was trying not to listen.

Much to my shock, a few hours later I was wakened by the bedroom light coming on and my blankets being pulled from me simultaneously. Dad stood at the side of my bed and asked, 'Did you give cheek to your mother earlier?" I was half asleep and before I could utter a word, Dad held me by the arm and gave me the biggest lashing I ever received. He repeatedly charged me, "Never speak back to your mother again!" I remember looking at him as I grimaced with pain. His eyes also had tears in them and I realised that Dad was hurting more than I was. I needed disciplined and it was his responsibility to do it. Never again did I take advantage of my mum and belittle her. As hard as it was, I was still under my parents' roof so I had to love and respect them.

My greatest release to divert my mind from the harassment I faced at school and my low self-esteem was to immerse myself in manual work on the farm. There was nothing I enjoyed more than pulling on my overalls each morning to feed the pigs and cattle before school. Then when I returned home, the first thing I did after throwing my schoolbag in the corner was to swap my uniform for farming glad rags. Farming was in my blood and living the country life was a natural desire of my heart. On many occasions, I sat up all night on the straw to help sows deliver their piglets safely. This was necessary because sometimes sows struggle adapting to motherhood and occasionally squash or even eat their own piglets. Those were long nights as I couldn't sleep for fear of rats roaming around looking for food. During those periods, I pondered how I had ended up such an insecure person after such a great start in life. Then my thoughts turned to the future and what I was going to do with my life.

In my mid-teens, I started my farming journey when Dad gave me a sow for breeding. Much to my dismay, she wasn't able to breed and bring me piglets. Dad kindly bought me another one and thankfully she gave birth to a litter of piglets. I fed them every day and watched them grow bigger and heavier until they were ready for the market – which meant a day off school! With a little money now in my bank account, I had great plans to expand my stock and go big-time! However, a few weeks after my sow delivered her second litter of piglets, circumstances took another turn for the worse.

Every morning when I entered the yard, the pigs would grunt and squeal knowing that food was on its way. On one particular morning though, my sow didn't grunt at all but just lay on the floor looking at me, surrounded by her little piglets. Before leaving for school I asked Dad to check on her later to make sure she was okay. As soon as I got home from school, I ran straight to the pig-house but my sow was gone. Dad met me in the yard and informed me she was already dead when he got to the pig-house shortly after I'd left for school. I was left completely shaken and stunned. I believed that farming was my clear calling in life, but twice in quick succession, my efforts to build a pig herd were met with failure. Although it baffled me at the time, when I look back I can trace the hand of God in my circumstances, making it clear that farming was not His plan for me.

It reminds me a little of the parable of the prodigal son. He set out as a proud, young man with plans to make a future. However, after some time he lost all his possessions, along with his hopes and dreams. The Bible tells us he was so hungry and desperate he was tempted to eat the pigs' food. Although I never lacked good food, the story taught me how God used adverse circumstances to get the prodigal's attention and lead him home to his father's house. In like manner, I believe the Lord used my circumstances to speak into my heart, which at that time was set on building a farm here on earth, with little regard for eternal things. Even though I took my seat religiously in church each Sunday, my heart was most alive on Saturdays when I was cleaning out calf pens or working for other farmers – gathering spuds, wrapping round bales or drawing in their grain. I loved every part of farming life.

A further painful memory occurred one Saturday morning when I took our tractor, a David Brown 990, into a field above our lane that we called 'The Hill'. It was a gradual slope overlooking Lough Neagh and for some reason, our manure spreader was there, instead of in the farmyard where it normally stayed. Dad asked me to take manure out to the fields, so I set off for 'The Hill' to hook on the manure spreader. When I reversed back to attach the spreader, its drawbar was too low for the tractor's hitch, so I jumped out of the tractor to prop it up a few inches. As I was wandering around trying to find a big stone to place under the drawbar, I heard a noise that resembled army Land Rovers coming up the road. To my horror, when I lifted my head I realised the noise was our tractor hurtling off down the hill! I raced after it as fast as I could, but as it gathered momentum it got further and further ahead of me. It was a considerably compact and brutish tractor and I reckon either the brakes slipped or I forgot to put them on. As it approached the ditch at the edge of the field, many thoughts raced through my mind. If I caught up and somehow climbed back onto it, could I turn the wheel sharp enough to avoid the ditch yet not topple the tractor over? Or if it hit the ditch with me on-board, would I get thrown off or crushed?

I didn't have an opportunity to find out because I couldn't catch it. Just before it crashed into the ditch, I dived to the ground and put my hands over my ears. When I finally had the courage to look up, everything was silent and the tractor was balancing precariously in the ditch, with one of the rear wheels off the ground still rotating slowly. To rub salt into my wounds, one of my brothers had observed the entire incident and immediately alerted my father. Many fears rushed through my mind – Would I ever be allowed to drive a tractor again? Would my brothers laugh and tease me about it for years? How cross would Dad be and would he scold me? I didn't have to wait long as Dad appeared moments later in his Land Rover. He jumped out and ran towards where I was sitting on the ground shaking my head in my hands. "Are you alright?" he caringly asked. "Yeah" I muttered, "and sorry about the tractor." I sheepishly replied. Dad butted in, "Awh! Never worry about the tractor, son. It's only a bit of metal – so long as you're okay." Tears welled up in my eyes at Dad's response. I had made a foolish and dangerous mistake. Dad had every right to be angry with me for being negligent, but he remained totally calm. At that moment, I witnessed first-hand, the response of a compassionate and forgiving father. After I apologised, he recovered the tractor and the incident was never mentioned again.

Reflecting on these early experiences and efforts to make a living at farming, it is almost comical how almost everything I put my hand to failed miserably. The hand of the Lord was clearly upon me, to show me His calling for my life was not in agriculture. A higher call was waiting for me, even though I didn't perceive it at the time. I often smile as I think of myself running around the farm trying to work things out, yet the entire time the Lord was gently whispering, "*It's not for you Colin, it's not for you!*"

CHAPTER THREE

Finding Christ

A T THE AGE of seventeen, I knew I needed to become a Christian, but it just was not something I wanted to do right away. I realised the Lord could return at any moment, but instead of getting ready to meet Him I decided to gamble with my eternal destiny and live a few years on the edge. On numerous occasions during this period of my life, I realised I was playing the fool and frequently considered seeking God. However, my thoughts always condemned me and I genuinely believed I was not in a good enough state for God to accept me. I was also full of pride and anger – characteristics I knew were not associated with a Christian!

I did make a number of attempts to sort my anger issues out in my own strength, but when I was put under pressure I burst into fits of rage before I could restrain myself. It reduced me to tears and I pleaded with God to help *me* sort things out so I wouldn't be so frustrated. Little did I realise I was warring with God because deep down, I had a stubborn heart. The Lord patiently waited until I proved to myself over and over again that I could not manage my emotions in my own strength. As I was full of pride, I wanted to make myself a better person and then approach God for salvation. After much agony, tears and turmoil, the penny finally dropped – God was the *only* One who could transform my broken life.

It was only after I surrendered my pride and stubborn will, that the Holy Spirit of God had the opportunity to work supernaturally in my heart. Not many days later, Sunday 25th June 1989 to be precise, I finally responded to God's call and made the most important decision of my life.

I had recently received my provisional driving licence, which meant I could only drive the car under the supervision of a licence holder. Mum appeared in the farmyard that afternoon while I was feeding the animals and asked me if I would drive her to a gospel mission in Lisburn that evening. Initially, I hesitated because I had already been to church that morning, but the opportunity to get another run behind the wheel was too good to turn down. The main speaker at the mission that night was a local evangelist called Noel Grant.

The meeting started in traditional fashion with a few hymns and announcements from one of the leaders. My mind was only thinking about getting through the next hour and hitting the open road again for home. Noel began to preach and even though I wasn't really paying attention, I felt myself getting restless and unsettled. His words confirmed what I already had discovered – I was living a life of rebellion and my anger problem was beyond control. My thoughts briefly turned to my brother James, who had become a Christian at Easter, a few months earlier. Since then, I had witnessed first-hand a massive change in his life and if I am honest, I was envious of him. Remarkably, in the course of Noel's message, he made a few comments that rattled me and addressed the urgency of my situation. "Young man…" he said. "…maybe you are a policeman or a soldier? What would happen if you get shot or blown up in a bomb? Young woman, if you had a car accident, where would you spend eternity?" Those words struck my heart like a dagger. I realised I was gambling my life away, attempting to enjoy the pleasures of sin for a season. I figured that waiting until I was older to become a Christian was a risk I couldn't afford to carry any longer. *"Boast not thyself of tomorrow; for thou knowest not what a day may bring forth" (Proverbs 27:1)* came to my mind. God the Holy Spirit was convicting me within and offering me another opportunity to come to Christ. I realised just how merciful the Lord had been for striving with me so long. Contrary to my previous thinking, God warns us, *"My spirit shall not always strive with man..."* *(Genesis 6:3).* This means we cannot decide to get saved whenever we want, as the feelings of conviction can suddenly go.

As I sat in that solemn meeting, I knew it was decision time and whatever spiritual state I chose to leave that meeting in, would dictate my final destiny. I was either going to spend the rest of my life on earth and all of eternity with Christ or without Him. There was *nothing* I could do to save myself. The Bible says: *"For by grace are ye saved through faith; and that not of yourselves: it is the gift of God: Not of works, lest any man should boast" (Ephesians 2:8-9).*

As Noel concluded his message, he explained how the Lord Jesus loved every one of us so much that He died to free us from our sin. Jesus took the punishment our sins deserved and all we had to do was sincerely repent and accept His offer of salvation. If we did, we could be assured of a home in heaven after we die and spend the rest of our days on earth fulfilling God's unique plan for us. I had no idea what that plan would be, but it was clear in my mind that God would accept me just as I was. I couldn't wait for the meeting to finish – not because I was desperate to get out onto the road again, but rather I wanted to talk to Noel about salvation. The Scriptures tell us: *"Neither is there salvation in any other: for there is none other name under heaven given among men, whereby we must be saved" (Acts 4:12)*.

After the meeting, Noel counselled me for a short time in the kitchen. He led me in a simple prayer where I, as a repentant sinner, called upon the Lord Jesus Christ and asked Him to forgive me and cleanse my heart. I entered the meeting as a rebellious and angry young man but left it bouncing with joy. *"Therefore if any man be in Christ, he is a new creature: old things are passed away; behold, all things are become new" (2 Corinthians 5:17)*. I was really thankful the Lord had been so patient with me for many years and I was desperate to make up for lost time.

When we returned to the main hall, everyone had gone except my mum who was waiting for me in the front row. Her face was red and wet with tears. This time she wasn't crying tears of brokenness over my rebellious lifestyle. Instead, they were tears of joy because God had answered one of her greatest prayers. We hugged and I apologised for my old lifestyle and all the grief I had burdened her with. She couldn't stop smiling and I knew she was thrilled! Dad was also delighted and shook my hand when I told him. He is a man of few words, though when he said, "That's good son!" I knew he was over the moon too. My mum, on the other hand, talked non-stop about it!

At that time I was employed in a warehouse and when I told my friends and colleagues in work I'd become a Christian, most of them were happy for me, but some were disappointed and snubbed me. They knew how other professing Christians lived and realised if I was serious about my faith, I wouldn't be socialising with them at weekends anymore. Others reckoned I was just going through a phase and soon would be back to my old ways.

One thing startled me when I witnessed to some acquaintances – some of them believed I already was a Christian just because I didn't smoke cigarettes, drink alcohol or take drugs! This is a tragic problem in the world, as the devil has fooled many sincere people into believing if they live a 'clean life' on the outside that makes them a Christian! If they would only read God's Word, they would clearly see that salvation is in Christ alone.

After my conversion, I had a great desire to pray and read the Bible more. I was amazed at how all the verses and Bible stories I had learnt as a child came back to my mind. Instead of dreading church, it became something I looked forward to. I even started taking notes of the sermon to review at home later on! I also started to attend the Bible study and prayer meetings regularly and began to pray publicly. I stuttered and stammered at first, but I was not deterred and kept on praying.

God was truly blessing my heart. My chief desire was to live for Jesus every day and serve Him the rest of my life. Even though I felt all I had to offer was energy and enthusiasm, I searched for opportunities to get involved in Christian work. Doors opened for me to assist in a children's meeting and give out gospel tracts on street corners. I was nervous and uneducated, but I just loved serving God! The Lord knew my boundaries and He was my strength whenever I felt stuck. One thing I was sure of; I had decided to follow Jesus and wasn't turning back.

A famous missionary, Hudson Taylor, once said these challenging words:

"God uses men who are weak and feeble enough to lean on Him. God isn't looking for people of great faith, but for individuals ready to follow Him."

I certainly needed to lean on the Lord if I was to accomplish anything that counted for eternity. Before long, I discovered there was a cost involved in following the Lord and I felt He was challenging me to see whether or not I was willing to pay it. All I could offer God was my life, but that is all He requires from us. Was I willing to go through with God and follow Him unconditionally the rest of my days? It's one thing to become a Christian; it is another to forsake all and follow Him. I had found Christ, but would I follow Him?

CHAPTER FOUR

The Stone Wall

AFTER BEING SAVED for a few months and spending time studying my Bible and serving the Lord, I began to think I could get the best of both worlds and live pretty much as I pleased. After all, I thought, I was seventeen years old and full of life and certainly didn't want to miss out on making the most of my best years. There were also many people who claimed to be Christians who seemed comfortable having one foot in the church and the other in the world, so why should I be any different?

Then came the day when I passed my driving test. It presented me with one of the best feelings ever – freedom! Finally, I felt in full control of my life as I could head far away from home and do whatever I liked without anyone at home knowing.

Rather than feeding my new spiritual nature and starving my old carnal one, I began to live on the edge and consciously allowed my old rebellious and stubborn ways to take control. One particular Saturday night, a friend Ian and I were out in the car with two girls for a spin. After driving about aimlessly for a few hours we got bored and mutually agreed to go to a nightclub. Immediately the Holy Spirit convicted me that going there was wrong, but I fought my conscience and attempted to justify it in my mind. I promised the Lord I would not drink or smoke and would even tell someone about Jesus while I was there. Besides, the fact I was driving would probably reduce the likelihood of an accident, as I definitely wouldn't be drinking. I was trying to justify what I was doing even though I knew fine rightly a nightclub was no place for a Christian to be, as there are so many temptations to sin.

On our way to the club, I noticed my fuel gauge was in the red, so our attention switched to finding a petrol station. Just when a garage came into view, the car began to chug and splutter before coming to a halt a few hundred metres from it. I knew we wouldn't be going anywhere for some time because it was an old Perkins diesel engine and would need to be bled. Ian and the girls left me to sort the car out and got a lift into the town. After some time, a kind man pulled in and offered to tow me home. I never made it to the nightclub and I believe this was to remind me of the fact that I was a new person. I knew that meant I had to change my friends, habits and the places I visited – but I didn't want to give them up just yet.

A month or so later, another friend called Robert asked me to go to a nightclub in Banbridge with him. I'm ashamed to say I didn't learn from the previous incident but again said a half-hearted guilt-appeasing prayer asking the Lord to give me an opportunity to witness there. Although I knew fine rightly God didn't want me going there, we got into my Mini and headed off to collect another friend. Laughing and joking as young lads do, we zoomed down the carriageway towards Banbridge, speculating how the girls would be queuing up for a spin in my bright red Mini with its white roof and wide wheels.

Midway between the two towns, we went over a little bump in the road and suddenly there was an almighty bang. My bonnet flipped open and crashed against the windscreen and none of us could see anything ahead! I rolled down the driver's window as fast as I could and stuck my head out to keep control of the car. When I pulled onto the hard shoulder and stopped the car, the two of us sat in silence, shocked to the core. I realised if we'd been travelling on a single-lane carriageway with on-coming cars, we could easily have been killed.

It was as simple as that. Was I going too fast? Was the bonnet not closed properly? Was it the wind? Or could it have been the providence of God that flipped the bonnet open to get my attention once again? We searched around the car to find something to restrain it so we could drive home. Fortunately, we found a few bits of baler twine in the boot, since the Mini was often used to take bales of hay down the road to feed the cattle.

The next infamous road trip was on Halloween night later that autumn. Whilst still in my backslidden state, Ian and I planned to attend a fancy-dress party in Banbridge, dressed up as Laurel and Hardy – me as the chubby one obviously! Since the nightclub didn't open until 11 p.m., we entertained ourselves by playing 'Knock-Door-Run.' This time instead of running between the houses on foot, we had my dad's Vauxhall Chevette and were able to jump into it and race down the country roads after knocking peoples' doors. One house after another got targeted and we laughed every time someone opened their door and walked about looking for their mysterious visitors.

When we reached the last house on the road, we parked in the shadow of the hedge and crept quietly up the driveway. We knocked the door as loud as we could, then charged down the lane and hid behind the Chevette. We waited a moment, but even though the house was lit up no one came to the door. Suddenly a car engine started and we knew by the speed of it coming down

My childhood

With Silver the pony

The seven Tinsley brothers!

Primary school

Edwin & me

Proud parents with their new twins - Edwin & me

Growing up

Ready for Sunday school

First year at Laurelhill High School

My first car - the red Mini

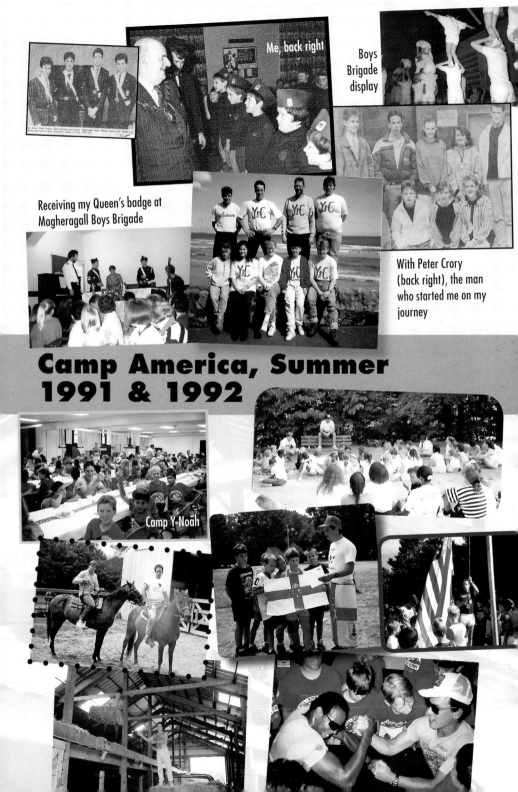

Me, back right

Boys Brigade display

Receiving my Queen's badge at Magheragall Boys Brigade

With Peter Crory (back right), the man who started me on my journey

Camp America, Summer 1991 & 1992

Camp Y-Noah

Meeting Joanna while travelling around Europe, summer 1993

Myself, Ian & Gary on the Berlin wall

At Grand Canal in Venice

The day I returned home from inter-railing

The window where we met

The photo Joanna gave me when we first met

Krakow Main Square at night

Letters

TO
COLIN TINSLEY
1 BALLYMACWARD RD
DUNDROD, CRUMLIN
Co. ANTRIM
BT 29 9JB   N. YRELAND
(PÓŁNOCNA IRLANDIA)

The heart-shaped potato & hay from the farm I posted to Joanna

Today is Sunday I'm just back from church a couple of hours ago. I go to church every Sunday morning and night. I enjoy it very much. I became a Christian when I was 17 years old. By doing this I simply excepted Jesus into my life by prayerfully saying Into my Hearth -Into my Hart - come into my hearth lord Jesus, Come into day come into stay, come into my heart lord Jesus. By doing this my Sins were washed away and my Night was turned to day Since Jesus came into my heart. I now own him as my Lord and Saviour. Hes my best frend. I gave him all my problems and pray to him often. It a nice felling, a personal love

Letter I sent to Joanna on 21st March 1994

Joanna's reply dated 7th April 1994

is Jesus, our Lord. It took a long time, and suddenly one day came. one of my friends came to visit me and we prayed together at my home. I felt exactly what I must to do. I felt I must invite Jesus to my heart. I felt I need him like nothing else. And that was it! I'll tell you some more about it. I hope it will be soon. I already would like to Ireland.

Our wedding, 1995

N. Ireland & Poland

Dad giving Joanna away

Brother Matthew as best man, niece Cherie as flower girl & Amy (our friend from USA) as bridesmaid

Prayer during the Wedding blessing in Krakow Baptist Church with Joanna's family

The early days of married life

My granny's house –
our first home

Our first Christmas
turkey, 1995

Camping

My 29th birthday!

Joanna with her mum in Donegal, 1997

Studying for Bible College exams

Preparing for children's work

Our mobile home

Joanna's artwork

Helping Joanna frame her paintings

First exhibition in Dublin

Painting in Australia

Painting in Donegal, Ireland

Nephew James helping me frame Joanna's paintings

Joanna in the studio working on bigger paintings

Preparing for exhibition

Joanna with her dad & step-mum, Elizabeth in the gallery

Dublin

Joanna beside her painting in the Galgorm Hotel

Exhibition in Belfast

Joanna showing Mayor of Lisburn (James Tinsley) & Arts Minister (Edwin Poots) her painting 'Summertime'

Joanna's older brother, Thomas visiting the exhibition

Joanna & her younger brother Maciek

My family, N. Ireland

Having fun!

When my brother, James, became Lord Mayor of Lisburn

All seven brothers

With Mum & Dad on her 75th birthday

My nephews & nieces in N. Ireland

Mum & me

My aunts & uncles

Dad & me

The Tinsley family at Mum's 80th birthday party, 2015

Joanna's family, Poland

Joanna with her family

Joanna's family in Poland

Joanna & her mum

At a wedding in Poland with my Polish nephews

Mum & Dad visiting Joanna's home town of Krakow, 2017

Krakow old town

My brothers' weddings

Isaac's wedding in Antrim

Trevor's wedding at Belfast Castle

James' wedding in Barbados

Edwin's wedding in Lisburn

Derek's wedding in England

Matthew's wedding at Stormont

Travelling adventures

Turkey

Vanuatu

Egypt

TURKISH BATH

Spain

Switzerland

Turkey

Austria with Joanna's family

Poland

New Zealand

Australia

New Zealand

Morocco

Gambia

New Zealand

Playing my favourite game, volleyball in Mexico

Australia

Cambodia

Shopping at the market in Gambia

Vancouver

Spain

Surprise meeting in Alaska with Lot (and his wife Janny) from Tasmania

Cambodia

Spain

Laos

Czech Republic

Cambodia

Italy with Joanna's brother, Maciek

London

Laos

Gambia

Mauritius

WRITING BOOKS IN DIFFERENT PARTS OF THE WORLD

N. Ireland

By the Mekong River, Laos

Mexico

Gambia

Krakow

Laos

Vietnam

Thailand

Cambodia

Books & tracts I have written

My collection of books & tracts

In a Christian book shop

Book launch at Lisburn Civic Centre, 2007

Book launch at Laurel Hill Community College, 2015

Book launch, 2010

Books presented as prizes to schoolchildren

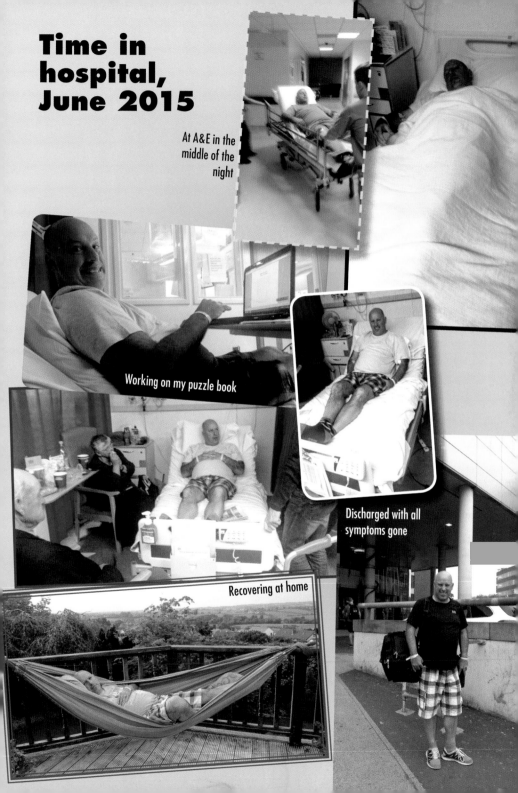

Time in hospital, June 2015

At A&E in the middle of the night

Working on my puzzle book

Discharged with all symptoms gone

Recovering at home

CELEBRATIONS

Larchfield ministry banquet, 2012

Ministry Banquet

'He brought me to the banqueting house, and his banner over me was love.'

Song of Solomon 2 v 4

Table names

Community service award, 2011

Larchfield Estate

Celebrating 15 years in full-time ministry, Gracehall

New Year's Eve, 2013

Gracehall, Moira

Hope for Youth Ministries 10th anniversary

Special praise service

Bringing in 2014 with games & fun

A donation has been made on your behalf to Hope For Youth Ministries to celebrate the marriage of **Gillian and David, 27th June 2013.** Psalm 27:1 The Lord Is My Light And My Salvation.

Wedding of Gillian & David

At the wedding of Rachel & Andrew

With Gary & Nigel

COLIN TINSLEY happy birthday

40th birthday

Stephen & Helen

Wedding of Rebecca & Philip

The Daily — WILLIAM & KATE — COLIN TINSLEY IS 40 TODAY. YES 40 TODAY!!

Wedding of my niece
Cherie & Jordan

Richard &
Cherith

Paul &
Cheryl

A donation has been made on your behalf towards

Youth MINISTRIES

To celebrate the marriage of
Paul and Cheryl on
29th August 2013

Please pray for Colin and
Joanna as they seek to
reach children with the gospel

The Lord is my light and my Salvation. Psalm 27 v 3

Amy & Dave

Wedding of
Judith
& James

Good times with Joanna

The window where I first saw Joanna

At our friends' wedding

Tasmania

Belfast Castle - celebrating after art exhibition

Asia

Czech Republic

N. Ireland

At Ballygally Castle

Krakow, Poland

Canadian Rockies

Our dogs Tas, Tolly & their puppies

the driveway, it was coming after us. We scrambled into the Chevette and sped off into the night, fearing they might catch us and recognise my dad's car! We rallied along the country roads at lightning-fast speed, taking roads to the right, then the left, as we attempted to shake off and lose our pursuers. After a few miles, we were sure no one was following us, but I still maintained my speed and kept one eye on the rear-view mirror.

On the approach to a tight left-hand corner, I dropped the car down a gear and just as I eased onto the throttle exiting the bend I realised I wasn't in control of the car. I later learned we had hit wet leaves on the road, but despite braking as hard as I could, a stone wall on the outside of the corner got closer and closer until we smashed into it. I remember the first words I cried were "Mummy, help me!" It's amazing how our mothers are often the first person we think of when we are in difficulty. Whilst still in a daze, I asked Ian if he was okay. "Yea, I think so" he replied, still rubbing his head. Thankfully, we both managed to get out of the car in one piece and although it was dark we didn't appear to have any serious cuts or broken bones. Thankfully our pursuers never appeared, but my fear turned to what my dad's reaction would be to me wrecking his car.

As we removed our Laurel and Hardy masks, I consoled myself with the thought that again I had avoided the place of temptation. When my dad came to rescue us, I was stunned that he didn't raise his voice or become angry with us for wrecking his car. Rather, he was thankful that neither of us was seriously hurt, such was his caring nature and big heart.

Regrettably though, I still didn't understand that while Christians live in the world, they should not live for the things of the world. The following week my brother Isaac asked me if I would drive him and his friends to that same nightclub in

Banbridge. Again my conscience told me not to go, but I crumbled to the pressure of 'people-pleasing' and agreed to drive. As before I promised the Lord if He would turn a blind-eye to me joining them in the nightclub, I would witness to someone about Him there. When we got inside, my brother's friend asked everyone what they wanted to drink. One after another they requested a variety of alcoholic beverages and when he came to me I said, 'I'll take a Coke, thanks!" With a bewildered look he probed, 'Why not a pint?" With everyone's attention focused on me, I explained I didn't drink because I was a Christian. Looking reproachfully at me, he retorted, 'If you're a Christian, what are you doing in here?" Talk about feeling embarrassed and ashamed of myself!

As the night progressed, everyone else seemed to be having the time of their lives but I felt empty and pathetic, sitting there with these so-called friends. I began to despise myself for not obeying the voice of God within me that begged me not to go. I realised I was being a fool and was only messing around with the Lord. I had started to run the race like an athlete out of the blocks but had fallen at the first hurdle. Right then, words of the Lord Jesus pulsated through my mind: *"No man, having put his hand to the plough, and looking back, is fit for the kingdom of God" (Luke 9:62).*

A few months earlier at the mission, I had valiantly put my hand to the plough, but now I was looking back to the things of the world rather than focusing on God's kingdom. I knew it was grieving the Lord to see me waste away my life in such dark environments when He had saved me for a purpose. Furthermore, as a new creation in Christ, it was only logical I felt a complete alien there. I knew I was living a sinful life that was dishonouring the Lord and I had become a stumbling block to others because of my shoddy testimony. The Word of God rebuked me as the Holy Spirit brought Scriptures I had learned as a child to my mind. Deeply sorrowful and convicted to my core, I recall leaving the place fighting off tears. I realised how the Lord had been striving for my attention and had spared my life in the recent car incidents, but in the end, it took the simple rebuke of an acquaintance to remind me of my calling. God was concerned about my unfaithful lifestyle that was dishonouring to His name. Although I took my place at church and youth group each weekend, my love for the Lord was far from what it should have been. I had relegated the Lord to second place in my life when He should have been first.

The penny finally began to drop and I realised that God had a plan for my life and was using circumstances to break my attachment to worldly pleasures. How easily the Lord could have let me go, but He was very gentle, loving and caring to soften my divided heart and mould me into the person He had called me to be. When I picked up His Word, He tenderly spoke to me and encouraged me to return. That night I repented before the Lord and told Him I was sorry for straying and living a double life. I made a commitment to come back to my first love and asked the Lord to forgive me, restore to me the joy of my salvation and help me to live the remainder of my life for Him. I knew the Lord had forgiven me because God's Word promises *"I will heal their backsliding, I will love them freely: for mine anger is turned away from him"* (Hosea 14:4).

I pledged to get serious with the Lord and stop playing the fool by sitting on the fence. I was a very slow learner, but thankfully the Lord was extremely patient with me. Similar to the disciples, who repeatedly let the Lord down on numerous occasions, I also knew His forgiveness and He restored me to a safe place. Very often we hesitate to give people a second chance, but thankfully God does not. The Lord in His mercy gives us many opportunities as we continually fail Him and let Him down time and time again. *"The Lord is gracious, and full of compassion; slow to anger, and of great mercy" (Psalm 145:8).*

For the next few years, life was more settled. I worked at Marks & Spencer's food store during the day and farmed in the evenings and at weekends. I applied for various jobs and at one stage I was offered three different jobs, one of which was with an insurance firm in England. I remember packing my case and getting ready to catch the boat to England when my dad asked, "Can you not settle yourself with a job here?" I knew by his tone of voice, his heart was concerned for me. He was aware that I could end up being like the prodigal son and possibly wasting my life in wild living. I just looked at him and said, "Yeah – you're right Dad." Immediately, I phoned the company and declined the job offer.

I continued to help with youth work in my local church and also volunteered at my local YMCA branch. When I was nineteen, I spent three months in the USA working as a volunteer at a summer camp called Camp Y-Noah in Akron, Ohio. The camp consisted of sports, horse riding and water activities by the lake in perfect summer weather. I loved it so much I returned again the following year! During those two summers I was completely in my element interacting with the kids and encouraging them as they completed the activities. I guess it was during those two summers that I caught the travel-bug, as after the nine weeks of camp each year, a couple of friends joined me to travel around America. We drove from New York to Florida, then the whole way across to California and back again!

The whole time I was there, I knew God was preparing me for something much greater. Of course, I didn't have any idea what it would be, but God was going to reveal the next step very soon.

CHAPTER FIVE

Joy and Pain

FROM MY EARLIEST memories, I have always possessed a great sense of adventure and it was that trait that led my friend Ian, cousin Gary and I to travel around Europe by train one summer. We visited cities during the daytime, then slept on a night train as it thundered along the track from country to country. Normally, this involved action-packed days and much-needed rest at night. I say 'normally' because one night will live long in my memory.

We were travelling from Berlin in Germany, to Warsaw in Poland and knew if we missed our early-morning stop, our next destination would be Moscow! We went to bed as usual and tied the door of our cabin with a piece of rope as we routinely did to stop anyone disturbing us or pinching any of our possessions. Before long we all fell asleep, but I frequently woke up to check the time in case we missed our stop. However, my light sleep was soon disturbed by something else. I saw the shadow of someone kneeling outside our cabin and I felt something was not quite right. I rubbed my eyes and flicked on the light. A knife, long and shiny, was sawing back and forth through the rope that kept our cabin door closed! An intruder was seconds away from entering our cabin so I jumped down from the top bunk and thumped Ian who lay beneath me. He woke with a yell and with that we heard footsteps scurrying up the corridor. Ian and I jumped up and chased him down the carriage, but he had too much of a head start and we couldn't catch him. At least our lives were safe and we were thankful that none of our possessions had been stolen. To this day I wonder what could have happened if he had entered our cabin and we had woken up to find him rummaging through our bags, not realising he had a knife! Praise God for His hand of protection as the thief didn't cross the doorframe of our cabin.

Shaken but not deterred, we arrived in Warsaw a few hours later. We expected to find a city full of spectacular landmarks from centuries ago but were surprised to find many modern, high-rise office blocks and a well-developed transport network. Later, we discovered the German Luftwaffe had dropped bombs and levelled the original city at the beginning of World War II. This meant even the oldest buildings were only fifty years old and were constructed on tight post-war budgets during communism. Since we visited all the tourist attractions there were that afternoon, we boarded the train again the following day and headed southwards to Krakow, another big city in Poland. We got talking to a few Americans en route and learned that the seventh-century medieval city was completely untouched by the war and the central square was the largest of its kind in Europe.

We disembarked the train late in the afternoon and booked into the first youth hostel we could find. Then we headed out to explore the sights and get some tea. It was 10th September 1993 and the huge cobblestone square was buzzing with thousands of tourists wandering around. Melodious street buskers played their accordions, guitars and fiddles and street traders enticed visitors into handing over their Polish Złoty notes at various market stalls. Surrounding the plaza, picturesque cafés and candlelit coffee shops released tantalising aromas into the air. Every few minutes, we would hear the jingle of bells as elegant horse-drawn carriages taxied love-struck couples around in style. The atmosphere and surroundings were surreal and reminded me of a movie scene.

We made our way through the crowds and chose a little café to eat in. The old Krakow buildings had tall rectangular windows and since it was a pleasant evening, they were opened wide. Slowly, my attention was drawn away from the conversation of my acquaintances to a window ledge where a girl stood. She was dressed in white with a red bandanna on her head. I was totally captivated and mesmerised by this figure. My movie scene progressed to a dream scene – one in which an angel had descended from heaven! None of my friends detected that I had disengaged from their conversation, nor had they noticed this girl who captivated me. During that brief moment, feelings arose within me I never knew existed. Some people talk flippantly about love-at-first-sight, but in my experience, it was the case. My heart was drawn irresistibly to this stranger who hadn't even noticed me. Nothing or no one could curtail my instincts, as this time I knew I had got it right. Such was the pull inside of me towards this girl, not even the enticing smell of freshly-cooked food distracted me.

Suddenly, she left the window and began to walk towards me. I knew I had to make a move immediately or forever hold my peace. So I left my friends, who were studying the dinner menu to make myself known to this girl. My heart beat rapidly as I walked straight towards her, still feeling as if I was in a dream. I initiated conversation in the most novel way: "Excuse me, do you speak English?" I uttered shyly. "Yes I do – can I help you?" she replied with the most inviting smile ever. *Sure, you can help me, I* thought inside - *you can tell me everything there is to know about you!*

To buy a little time, I asked if she could translate the menu for me. To my embarrassment, she pointed out it was also in English! We laughed at my mistake and this paved the way to develop the conversation further. My friends trudged over a few minutes later and were astounded to see me talking to such a beautiful girl. Their minds were a bit clearer than mine and they had no problems ordering food from the bilingual menu. We had great fun chatting and as the minutes passed by, my admiration for her grew deeper. I was totally mesmerised by her countenance, yet I couldn't pinpoint exactly what it was that instantly attracted me to her. It was like I was having the most beautiful dream ever and I didn't want to wake up. I had met someone who felt like the missing part of my life; her name was Joanna.

A few hours later, Joanna walked us back to our youth hostel and kindly agreed to give us a lift in her car to the bus stop at eight o'clock the next morning. We had planned to catch a tour to Auschwitz, the Nazi concentration camp where over a million Polish Jews were executed during World War II. When we settled down in our dorm that night, I remember taking a deep breath and reliving the previous four hours. I couldn't believe I was falling in love with a complete stranger, especially one that lived almost two thousand miles away! But I could not deny or crush those feelings that arose in my heart. I am living proof that love-at-first-sight isn't a myth and definitely can happen.

Even though I was oblivious to it, the Lord was leading me in a special way. A story in the book of Genesis tells how God clearly directed Abraham's servant to a particular girl as he searched out a wife for Abraham's son, Isaac. The servant prayed the Lord would lead him to the woman of God's choosing. Before he had finished praying, Rebekah appeared in the distance and walked directly to the well where he was praying. If I'm honest, finding a girlfriend was not a serious matter of prayer for me at that time and settling down with a wife was the last thing on my mind. However, the Lord knew more about my needs than I did.

The next morning, Joanna collected us in her little red Metro and dropped us off at the bus stop. We were devastated to discover all the bus tours were full. Sensing our disappointment, Joanna offered to drive us there if we put some petrol in her car. Without hesitation we obliged and forty-five minutes later we arrived at Auschwitz. I was looking forward to chatting more with Joanna as we toured about, but much to my dismay, she said she would wait in the café for us. As my friends and I wandered around the harrowing death camp, we felt an eerie silence and a remarkable sense of emptiness in the place. Even the birds seemed to avoid the area.

It was then that I understood why Joanna didn't wish to join us. These were her people – Polish nationals who were executed in many despicable ways. Some were poisoned in the gas chambers, some shot at the Black Wall or flogged at the 'Post', while others were simply overworked and starved simultaneously. The depravity of man to act with such cruelty to his fellow man disgusted and disturbed me. We heard how men would line up for work at one side, while their wives and children lined up opposite them. They believed they were queuing for communal showers, but instead of having the therapeutic feeling of warm water running over their skin, they were choked to death with poisonous Zyklon B gas. Their bodies were then dragged out and burned or buried in mass graves – often dug by their own fathers and brothers.

At the end of our tour, we met Joanna back in the café. She was very reserved and we grasped she didn't want to talk about what we had seen. I later found out that the Nazis burned her grandparents' house and they had to flee to the forest with their seven children for their lives. We got into the car and sat still for a moment, reflecting on the history of Poland and the chilling fact that these atrocities occurred only a few generations ago. Joanna then started the car and said, 'We don't have much time – let's go!' I bit my tongue and answered inwardly - *don't have much time? I have all the time in the world for you!* As we drove back towards Krakow, the heaviness we felt at Auschwitz gradually lifted. I was in my element and savoured each moment in the company of my new friend. I also clearly remember that it seemed in every village we passed through, there was a wedding taking place. *Was this a sign?*

Joanna was very talkative and informed us she worked as an artist. When we got near to our youth hostel, she asked if we would like to see her paintings at the nearby studio. As we were still shattered from our sleepless night on the train, Gary and Ian chose to catch a few hours' sleep and passed on the offer. Despite my physical tiredness, I was running high on adrenaline and certainly wasn't going to turn her offer down! We waved my friends goodbye and drove a few more miles and parked up at the studio. Although I didn't have the slightest clue about art, I tried to sound witty and appreciative of the detail in Joanna's paintings. I thought I was doing well analysing one particular picture until Joanna informed me it was sitting upside down!

After showing me her paintings, Joanna then invited me to peer through her photo albums. We glanced quickly through her childhood pictures, but I stopped her flicking through the album when we came to one portrait that really stood out. It was a beautiful shot of Joanna as she gazed past the camera at something on the horizon. It was a sentimental moment and I studied it for ages. "I would like this!" I said. "Will you let me have it?" Joanna thought I meant the picture but I wanted the heart, soul and life of the girl in it.

After viewing her paintings and photos, we took a walk in a pear orchard that was outside Joanna's studio. I mentioned that pears were my favourite fruit so as we walked around the orchard Joanna picked me one pear after another. I must have had about five of them! They were really ripe and the juice squirted all over my face but I kept on munching as she handed them to me and we laughed as we ate them. We came to a little bench so we sat down and continued to chat. I knew I had to make a move to show my affection, but every time I attempted to embrace her she moved, so I pretended I was scratching my head. It happened so many times she probably thought I had head lice! Finally, my moment came as we gazed up at the sky, amazed at its perfection and stillness. I slowly stretched my arm across the back of the bench and just as my hand was about to touch her shoulder Joanna jumped up. "What about your friends, Colin?" she asked. "We need to go and pick them up!"

By then, we had been away for a couple of hours. We motored back to the youth hostel and I ran in to get Ian and Gary. As I was half way up the stairs, I paused and contemplated what I was about to do – invite two lads to join Joanna and me on an evening out. One which had the potential to be one of the most romantic evenings ever! *I don't think so,* I thought. I was so desperate to hug Joanna I would have eaten another twenty pears if required and I wasn't going to miss this golden opportunity. I reckoned since they were still asleep they needed a good rest so I turned around and tip-toed back down the stairs and jumped into the car. 'They're too tired and need a good night's sleep" I informed Joanna. I chuckled at the thought of them wakening up and sitting on their beds waiting for their taxi driver and me to return! It was a pleasant evening and Joanna decided we would go for a walk along the river. As we passed a little shop, a song by UB40 came on the radio and caught our attention. The chorus goes 'Wise men say, only fools rush in; but I can't help, falling in love with you.' The track became 'our song' and in the years that have followed, we've lost count of the number of memorable occasions we have heard it playing. The feelings I experienced back then were so real. If this was love, it was incredible and I couldn't help falling for this girl.

The next day we were scheduled to depart. Joanna used the excuse of giving us a lift to the nearby train station to say a final goodbye. Ian and Gary gave her a hug, sincerely thanking her for being so kind to drive us everywhere. I didn't want to leave her and waited until everyone else had boarded the train. Then came the dreaded sound – the final whistle. Instinctively as she turned to me in what seemed like a slow motion scene from a movie our eyes caught each other and before we knew it we hugged and kissed each other, something we had never done before. Her lips were so soft and juicy; all I could think about were the pears in the orchard. My heart was pounding and felt like it was burning hotter than the engine of the train I was about to board!

At that moment I was filled with joy and pain. Joy at the prospect of a loving relationship with my 'dream' girl, but pain at the reality of leaving her behind; perhaps never to see her face again! Joanna slipped something into my hand while I presented her with a rose I found earlier and had carefully placed in my pocket. I jumped onto the train, which was already moving and popped my head out of an open window as it slowly took off. I remember leaning so far through the window, I nearly fell out as I waved towards Joanna until the platform disappeared out of sight. With a smile etched on my face, I finally took my seat beside the lads. They started to jeer and kept me going as guys do, but I knew they were sorry they hadn't seen Joanna first!

The train reached full speed and we left the grandeur of Krakow for the lush Polish countryside. I slowly opened the envelope and inside was the picture of Joanna – the very one I had sat and gazed at in the studio. *How would I ever meet this girl again?* I thought. I had to find her one way or another. I was confident we would meet again and someday in the future she would finally be mine. When I flipped over the picture, I noticed Joanna had written her address on it. I smiled to myself and thought, *I'm going to find you!* How that would happen I didn't know, but even if I couldn't find her, I believed she would somehow find her way to me. I was from Northern Ireland and she was from Poland. Two people brought up thousands of miles apart yet destined to be together. For the first time in my life, I had fallen in love. It was the most incredible feeling in the world!

CHAPTER SIX

The First Letter

OVER THE NEXT two months, we crossed one border after another and set foot in twenty-four countries across Europe. While exploring the southern coast of Spain, we even sailed south across the Strait of Gibraltar to rummage around Morocco in North Africa. Yet, no matter how far away from Krakow we went, the Polish girl remained close to my heart – I must have studied her picture a thousand times!

One thing disturbed me though – I never witnessed to her about the Lord or told her I was a Christian. I assumed that she wouldn't be a Christian and wouldn't be the slightest bit interested in becoming one. In my determination to get to know her, with much regret, I avoided telling her the best news in the world. As the weeks progressed, my heart yearned for Joanna even though we did not have any further contact. For better or worse, communications and technology in the early 90's weren't as advanced as they are today. There were no mobile phones, Facebook, WhatsApp or social media messaging services.

As my mind imagined a future with Joanna, I realised I needed to tell her how I felt about her, but more importantly about my love for God. So the week I returned home, I wrote a long letter to put Joanna straight about my Christian faith and explained in detail what happened to me that night, on 25th June, four years earlier. I described how I came to the Lord as a repentant sinner and thanked Jesus for taking the punishment my sins deserved when He died on the cross. At that moment He forgave me, saved me and came into my heart to stay forever. I honestly didn't expect a reply and if she did respond, it would likely be a 'nice to meet you' type of letter.

The Bible explicitly tells us we should never be ashamed of being a Christian. I had a deep peace in my heart I was doing the right thing, regardless of how Joanna might receive the news. Jesus said, *"For whosoever shall be ashamed of me, and of my words, of him, shall the Son of man be ashamed" (Luke 9:26).* I had to be faithful to the Lord and tell her the truth – that being a Christian was the most important thing in my life. I could not deny it and I would never apologise for being a follower of Christ. Jesus warned, *"But whosoever shall deny me before men; him will I also deny before my Father which is in heaven" (Matthew 10:33).* The Bible also makes it clear a Christian should never enter into a relationship with an unbeliever. I knew I needed to clarify the matter sooner rather than later.

About three weeks after I sent the letter, I started to feel like a response was on its way. At this time, I was working at Marks & Spencer and every afternoon during my lunchbreak, I rang home and asked Mum if any letters had arrived for me. The answer was always negative, until one day Dad answered the phone. He informed me that a letter had come from the Pope with my name on it and he was going to throw it in the fire. Puzzled I asked, "What do you mean the Pope?" He retorted "It has his picture on the envelope." It suddenly dawned on me that the Pope was Polish and the stamp would have his face on it, just like we have a picture of the Queen on ours. I begged him not to put it in the fire and said it was from 'that girl' I met in Poland. "What girl?" Dad asked with bewilderment. "Please do not open the letter or do anything with it," I pleaded and then hung up the phone.

I must have checked my watch a thousand times that afternoon as I was desperate to know what the letter said. Once home-time came, I jumped into my red Mini and sped home. I might as well have been on a motorbike going round corners and flying over the hills as I leant across the car to keep all four wheels on the ground. I screeched to a halt in our yard, jumped out and ran into the house. "Where is it?" I shouted with excitement before even saying hello to anyone. "Where's what?" Mum sarcastically joked. She passed me the envelope and after hearing the commotion, Dad then joined us in the kitchen. They both stood there staring in expectation like it was exam results arriving. It was obviously much more personal and I felt that the next five minutes would change the course of my life one way or another, depending on what this letter contained.

I left them in the kitchen and withdrew to the privacy of my room to carefully tear open the envelope. As I did so, powerful emotions rose up within me that I still find difficult to explain to this day. Impassioned thoughts rushed through my mind – *How did this situation ever come about Lord? Why are you making this happen, Lord? Would You really tease me if this isn't what I want to read, Lord?* With my hands shaking, I straightened out the hand-written letter and began to read it meticulously. Deep inside, I started to well up and tears appeared from nowhere that continued to flow as I read the letter. Joanna began by saying how nice it was to meet me and spend time together. Then she said how pleased she was to hear that Jesus meant so much to me. "I have a similar story to tell…" she continued to write. "All my life I have been searching for God and tried many ways to find Him, but on Easter Saturday this year I got saved by trusting in the Lord Jesus Christ after some friends witnessed to me at university."

My heart was overjoyed and thrilled at what I was reading. The way things were unfolding was beyond my wildest imagination. I laughed out loud through my tears as I realised Easter was five months before we met and Joanna had made a commitment to follow Jesus without any influence from me. And it got better! Joanna wrote: "Every day for the last five months I have prayed and asked God to send a man into my life who loves the Lord." I shouted with all my strength, "PRAISE THE LORD – I'M YOUR MAN!" I ran back down to Mum and Dad and said, "Guess what? The girl I met in Poland is a Christian – saved and born-again, just like me. Hallelujah!" My mum and dad looked at each other in bewilderment wondering what on earth I was on about. It was only at that moment I realised I had never told them about the girl God had brought into my life, who unbeknown to me, was a born-again Christian.

After receiving this news, I knew God had a plan and I could see it unfolding right before my eyes. I had never been so excited and felt I was walking on air. In the preceding months, I had prayed many times that God would place me right in the centre of His will. Instantly I realised the entire time I was in it! At precisely the right moment in God's amazing plan for my life, Joanna appeared on the scene.

People often ask, how do you know if you are living in God's will for your life? My answer is *you just know!* God will implant an incredible sense of peace and contentment in your heart. You will stop searching for anyone or anything else to satisfy you. You have now found the good, acceptable and perfect will of God. For some people, finding a potential partner for life can be easy, but that does not automatically imply they are God's choice for them. For others finding a life-partner is a challenging and frustrating experience, possibly requiring them to wait a considerable amount of time before the Lord brings someone into their life.

Six months before I met Joanna, I had a girlfriend whom I had known for several years. We had dated for three months and she was a lovely, sincere Christian girl who taught in Sunday school. I blindly assumed the relationship was in line with God's will for my life until I shared my desire to become a missionary with her. She was honest and told me she didn't like travelling and then a few days later, she ended the relationship! At the time I was devastated, but looking back I realise how disastrous it would have been for us both if we had stayed together with different callings on our lives. I am so glad I was bold and told her the direction I believed the Lord was leading me, as just six months later I met Joanna in Krakow – God's ways are perfect! He brought Joanna along when I wasn't looking or expecting to meet anyone. She was indeed a beautiful gift from the Lord and if I'm honest, she is probably more than I deserved.

In the months that followed, letters began to flow back and forth between Northern Ireland and Poland with an ever-increasing frequency until we were writing at least once a week. In school, I was never enthusiastic about writing and avoided it at all costs, but after years of neglect I definitely made up for it! I reckon I wrote more in my letters to Joanna than I did in all my studies at school. Unlike today where we have Skype, emails and Facebook, in those days all our communication was through pen, paper and envelopes. The only difference was the envelopes I sent to Poland had the Queen on them, whilst the envelopes I received had the Pope on them!

At this time in work at Marks & Spencer, I was assigned to serve customers at the checkouts. There were periods each day when things were quiet and I was able to scribble down thoughts that came to my mind. Then in my room in the evenings, I would develop my ideas and construct them into poems for Joanna. Some days, I would literally have dozens of little thoughts jotted down. We also shared Bible verses to encourage and build each other up in our faith – after all the Bible is the ultimate book when it comes to inspiration and motivation. I also took lots of notes at church on Sundays and sent Joanna a condensed transcript of the sermon!

The situation was entirely new to both of us as we had only met in person for a couple of days and these letters were our only means to learn more about each other. Deep down in our hearts, a bond was being formed and space was being created in each of our hearts for another person. As time went on Joanna told me she believed she would never find a suitable husband in Poland – but found it funny how she met me there, even if I was only visiting as a tourist! Even to this present day, there are very few Christians in Poland, let alone single, eligible men for Christian girls to marry. I am still troubled and feel burdened by this and it makes me realise how blessed we are in Northern Ireland with a relatively large evangelical population. I found myself often thinking *this country really needs the Lord!* Isn't it amazing how God created within me both a love for a Polish woman and her people as well! As time went on, we began to see the bigger picture of God's plan for us to return many times, to reach her people with the gospel.

CHAPTER SEVEN

A Match Made in Heaven

FALLING IN LOVE with a stranger changed my entire outlook on life. It was the most incredible feeling ever and work colleagues repeatedly asked me why I was constantly smiling and ever-cheerful. I kept them in suspense and told them the postman was making me happy! They hadn't a clue what I meant, not aware that he was my link to Joanna.

The following summer, Joanna planned to have an art exhibition in Germany. In a letter around Easter time, she suggested continuing her journey westwards to visit me in Northern Ireland. This was no meagre proposition and confirmed to me just how serious Joanna was taking our relationship. It would be a huge challenge for a young woman to drive almost two thousand miles alone, from Poland to Northern Ireland.

The letters went back and forth every few days until early June when Joanna set off on her journey across Europe. After a week without any letters from the postman, Joanna called our home telephone on a Friday evening and informed me she had made it across the English Channel and had arrived in London. It was the first time we had spoken since saying goodbye at the train station in Krakow nine months earlier. With hindsight, I guess it was strange I never once thought about asking Joanna for her telephone number in any of my letters; though if I had, it would have been an expensive and risky experience with my brothers listening in on another line! I was thrilled at the prospect of Joanna arriving in Dundrod a few days later.

Then on Sunday, as usual, I rose early to help Dad tend the animals before church. As soon as we got cleared up, I headed straight to the bath so I would smell and look my best for my special visitor. As I relaxed in the bath, I contemplated whether it was wise going to church that morning. I reckoned Joanna would arrive late afternoon, but if she turned up while we were all away to church, it would be a disaster. It wasn't as simple as firing off a text or calling her mobile, as we would today. She had my address and home telephone number, but I had no way of contacting her.

Before I made a decision regarding church, I heard a gentle knock on the front door. *Surely that couldn't be her at this time of the morning?* I thought. Then someone opened the door and a voice spoke. "Hello, does Colin Tinsley live here?" I couldn't believe it – she had arrived in Dundrod and I was stranded in the bath of all places! I listened intently as my brother James teased Joanna. "Sorry. No Tinsleys live here. I think you are lost!"

When I heard those words, I sprung out of the bath like a jack-in-the-box and pulled on my jeans and a jumper without drying myself – they stuck to my skin like glue! Without even glancing in the mirror, I swung open the bathroom door and ran up the hall. There she was – dressed in a cream dress and wearing white shoes. As our eyes connected, it seemed everything went into slow motion. She manoeuvred past my brothers and made a beeline for me. We embraced tightly and at that moment I knew the summer of 1994 was going to be the best one yet.

As each day passed, our relationship blossomed. Joanna didn't have to return to teach at Art College until September, so she was able to stay on our farm in Northern Ireland the rest of the summer. We set up a makeshift studio in an old barn so she could continue to paint, but Joanna preferred to help Dad with farm work most days! She learned how to drive the tractor and shake hay in the fields. Then at mealtimes, she often helped Mum prepare dinner for us all.

In the evenings when I got home from work, we often set out on long romantic walks in the countryside or got in the car and went for beautiful scenic drives. Joanna became my best friend and effortlessly slotted into my life. I felt I had reached a higher place in life – one I never even knew existed. There was a spring in my step and a lightness in my spirit. Even though my life was already full and happy, meeting Joanna raised it to an entirely new level.

One very funny memory I have from that summer was a phone call Joanna made to her dad. We had helped a cow deliver her calf in the barn earlier that evening and Joanna was eager to tell him all about it. In her excitement, she somehow couldn't remember the Polish words for calving or calf. She tried to tell him a mummy cow gave birth to a baby cow in the barn, but whatever way she translated it, her dad believed we had helped my mum give birth to a baby in the barn!

After a wonderful summer, September came and Joanna had to return home. Being a gentleman, I volunteered to drive Joanna all the way back to Poland in her car. It took us three days driving through England, Holland and Germany to reach Krakow in south-east Poland. For the first time, I met Joanna's family and was able to stay two weeks with them. It was quite humorous because I couldn't speak a word of Polish and her parents didn't understand English, so all our conversation had to be translated by Joanna. We spent most days visiting Joanna's friends and relatives, then in the evenings we explored the city of Krakow. The weather was perfect and most nights we walked around the leafy suburbs and parks before grabbing a coffee at one of the little cafés in the city square.

Despite feeling like I was truly living the dream, I realised as each blissful day passed, the day of my departure drew nearer. Somehow we had managed to spend three wonderful months together and our relationship had developed from being long-distance pen pals to being a closely-knit couple. I didn't want those times to end but the inevitable faced me. I knew I had to be clear to Joanna and her family about my feelings towards her before I returned home.

On our final evening together, Joanna's family arranged a special supper and invited close relatives and special friends along. I wished to share a few words during the meal so I took Joanna's brother Maciek to the side and asked him to translate them into Polish. When an opportune moment came, I rose to my feet and motioned for her dad to stand up so I could address him. I wished to say, "Please sir, should the opportunity ever arise, can I have the hand of your daughter in marriage?" Immediately, Joanna and her brother burst out in hysterics laughing. Her dad, who only spoke Polish and French smirked a moment, then shouted "Absolument, absolument!" which is French for 'Absolutely, absolutely!' They later informed me I had mispronounced the words 'please' and 'daughter'. Whilst keeping a very straight and sincere face I had addressed her dad: "Pig, can I have the hand of your turkey to marry?" Thankfully, he had a good sense of humour and saw the funny side.

Twelve hours later, I had hugged and kissed the girl of my dreams goodbye and was in the air, flying home to Northern Ireland alone. As I stared at the back of the seat in front of me, I was overcome by a mixture of emotions. I was totally in love with the girl of my dreams, but I had no idea when I would see her again. I tried hard to be strong, but tears of joy and sadness flowed simultaneously beyond my control. I was in a mess and had no idea when I would ever see Joanna again.

During the next few months, the letters resumed and often little gifts were exchanged, as our relationship continued to mature. On one occasion when packing potatoes at work, I came across two potatoes joined in a perfect heart shape. I thought it would be a romantic gesture to buy them and send them to Joanna. She sent a letter in reply saying she had no idea why I was sending her a deformed potato. She obviously didn't see it the way I did!

Looking back, those were difficult days, as my heart ached from being separated from the girl I loved and wanted to spend my future with. The evenings seemed long and lonely. The Lord had given me perfect peace about Joanna. It was completely His doing, right from when He orchestrated circumstances the day we met, when I visited Krakow. True love has no boundaries!

Even though I had no idea what my future held, I realised God had a plan for my life and Joanna would definitely be part of it. I could not sit in limbo any longer, so one Sunday afternoon in February 1995, I sneaked the phone into our living room and rang her. After exchanging pleasantries, she went into overdrive excitedly recounting her weekend in detail to me. 'Joanna, Joanna!" I authoritatively butted in. "What, Colin?" she replied. I knew some of my brothers could burst into the room at any moment and as much as I wanted to hear her talk, I had to stop her. I had called for a specific reason and after taking a deep breath, I shyly asked, "Will you marry me, Joanna?" I exhaled slowly, releasing an enormous amount of pressure that had built up over the previous four months. It was a proposal long overdue and it seemed time stood still as I eagerly awaited Joanna's response.

In the weeks previous, I had spent hours imagining what her reaction to my proposal would be. Instead of hearing screams of ecstasy down the phone in excitement, which I had imagined, the line went eerily quiet. Thoughts raced through my mind. *Had the line dropped out at the crucial moment? Was Joanna so overcome with emotion that she couldn't speak?* Finally, I heard her crystal clear. "No, Colin." *No?* I repeated under my breath. I was totally stumped and momentarily stopped breathing. I had no plan B as I had not expected that response. I had prayed specifically and God had shown me this was the girl for me. Suddenly I heard her say, "Sorry, Colin I mean YES!" Perplexed, as I thought she was making a joke out of something so serious I impetuously retorted, "Why did you say *no* then?" She explained, "To agree in Polish, you say *no*. I was so excited I forgot to translate it into English! The word means the opposite in the two different languages…" I was baffled, but she assured me she definitely meant yes and was delighted I had finally asked.

The Bible tells us *"Whoso findeth a wife finds a good thing, and obtaineth favour of the LORD" (Proverbs 18:22)*. I had a solid assurance, conviction and confidence that this was of the Lord. He had provided a woman for me in the most extraordinary and astonishing way. Almost two thousand miles away, was a beautiful city girl and there in little Dundrod was I, a rugged country boy, yet God in His sovereign providence brought us together. His plan was for us to become husband and wife, so together we could love and serve Him all the days of our lives. My previous frustration was replaced by a real zeal for life and a heightened sense of purpose.

Just over three months later, in May 1995, Joanna arrived at Belfast International Airport with her suitcase in one hand and a wedding dress in the other. We were really excited to see each other as it had been nine long months since we last embraced in Krakow airport. When we got to the car, we sat for ages catching up, completely oblivious to the fact that every fifteen minutes we sat there, it cost another few pounds. Finally, when our stomachs started to rumble we decided it was time to get dinner. I was shocked when we got to the carpark gate and the attendant informed me I had been parked for three hours and handed me a ginormous bill! I pleaded sympathy with him and explained I was arranging my wedding. He laughed and said, "Yeah mate, try a better excuse next time!" "It's the truth!" I begged, but my pleas fell on deaf ears. I had planned to take Joanna for fish and chips but we ended up going home and made sandwiches instead.

A few days later, I approached my minister and asked him if he would officiate at my wedding. "Who to?" he smirked, thinking I was winding him up. "Remember the Polish girl I told you about? I am going to marry her," I explained. His expression then changed to a puzzled frown and he wisely inquired. "Is she a Christian girl, Colin?" "Of course she is!" I assured him. "She is saved and really loves the Lord." Our wedding date was set for 25th August 1995. We booked a hotel for sixty guests and organised everything within a few weeks. We had saved up enough money to pay the bills and Joanna sketched a charcoal portrait of everyone who helped at the wedding as a gift to them. Both of us had a love for horses, so on our big day, we rode a majestic horse bareback to the hotel – Joanna sitting side-saddle while I took the reins. It was a perfect moment and reminded me of the truth in God's Word, *"Therefore shall a man leave his father and his mother, and shall cleave unto his wife: and they shall be one flesh" (Genesis 2:24)*. It was His perfect plan and will for our lives. It is wonderful when two people meet, fall in love and then get married with Christ at the centre of their marriage.

Soon after our wedding in Northern Ireland, we packed our bags and journeyed to Poland by bus to repeat the ceremony. Finally a married couple, we spent our honeymoon travelling all over Poland visiting Joanna's family, before making the long trip back home to Northern Ireland in her little red Metro car. However, this time Joanna was there to stay and a new chapter in our lives had begun. Where it was taking us, we had no idea, but we were in love with God and each other. We knew God loved us and believed He would sustain us regardless of what life would bring our way. It was a match made in heaven and that is what mattered most!

CHAPTER EIGHT

The Call of God

SETTING OUT ON married life after such an exciting and long-distance courtship was an incredible experience. Even to this present day, when I think how two complete strangers, living in different countries could meet, fall in love and get married in less than two years, I am still amazed! We were truly blessed by the Lord and as we grew more in love with each other as the days went on, we felt a greater sense of purpose for our lives.

Entering marriage did present many new challenges for us just like any other newly-wed couple. After organising two weddings and paying for flights and boat journeys on our honeymoon, our thoughts turned to setting up a family home together. We didn't have enough money to put down a deposit on a house, so for six months, my cousin offered us the use of my granny's old house which he had inherited.

No one had lived in the old country cottage for years, as it didn't have a bathroom or central heating. When we needed a wash, I brought an old bath the cows used as a drinking trough in from the field. We filled it up with water and placed it in front of the fire in the living room to heat it up. I remember one night just after I had jumped into it, my whole family arrived round.

As they peered through the window, they laughed and jeered at me relaxing in the bubbles in front of the fire! Like a lightning bolt, I grabbed a towel, sprung out of the bath and darted upstairs to get dressed. My brothers and I laughed as we emptied it using buckets and reminisced about the day Joanna arrived when I was also in the bath. It may have been a humble dwelling but looking back, it was all good fun and made us appreciate life's little luxuries in the future.

In addition to getting accustomed to married life, Joanna also found the first six months exciting as she adjusted to life in a new country and culture. Apart from my family and a few close friends, she didn't know anyone else in Northern Ireland, so she enjoyed meeting people and building new friendships. She continued to paint but sought opportunities to improve her English and gain a better understanding of Northern Irish culture. One of her ventures was volunteering as a care assistant to help elderly people with their housework and to take them on shopping trips.

In addition to my job at Marks & Spencer and helping Dad on the farm, I got some part-time work as a van driver, delivering bread and buns for a local bakery. The long hours were tiring, but the opportunity to earn some extra money to help us get our own home with central heating and hot water motivated me. As my dad often said, it was a case of 'welcome to the real world!'

We saved hard all winter and in the spring of 1996, with a little help from my parents, we bought our first home. It wasn't made of bricks and mortar but was a twenty-year-old static caravan. We placed it in a field beside my brother's house on the Sheepwalk Road in Stoneyford, near Lisburn. We had offered our lives completely to the Lord and were willing to serve Him in whatever way He wanted, so we didn't think it was wise to take on a lot of debt that would require us to work long hours to keep up our repayments.

After a few weeks, we transformed the caravan into a really welcoming and cosy abode. Sadly though, in the process of moving, we were burgled and most of our belongings, including our wedding presents and pictures, were stolen. It was very distressing as many items had sentimental value attached to them and none of them were ever recovered. So we literally only had each other as all our money was spent and everything we had accumulated in our married life had been taken from us. Thankfully family and friends helped us with the basic necessities that we needed for everyday living. The mobile home remained our residence for the next three years. During that time, Joanna grew more accustomed to living in Northern Ireland and I was delighted to see her make lots of new friends through church and work. My brothers and I built a studio onto the side of the mobile for Joanna to paint in. There were lots of windows and a big skylight in the roof to maximize the level of natural light, which is vital for painting. We really appreciated how God had provided so much for us in a relatively short period of time.

As we both had a great sense of adventure and loved the great outdoors, in the summer months one of our favourite pastimes was to go camping. Many Friday evenings after I got home from work, we packed the tent into the boot of our car and headed off for the weekend. I recall one weekend we headed south-west and ventured into County Sligo. It was dark by the time we reached our destination and since we couldn't find a campsite to pitch our tent on, we looked for a level field. Finally, we found one and parked the car up, then erected our tent in the moonlight. The grass was really short and soft, so we looked forward to viewing our surroundings the next morning.

It didn't take us long to fall asleep after such a long drive to the west coast of Ireland. We had a really peaceful night's sleep until something whacked against our tent just after daybreak. I assumed it was a few youths in a tent nearby lobbing stones at us. After rubbing my eyes, I pulled my boots on to chase them away. When I unzipped the tent, I couldn't believe my eyes. We were pitched in the middle of a golf course and our tent and little Metro car were like sitting ducks on the fairway for golfers to aim at! I'm sure they had some laugh when they got to the tee of that hole. We didn't wait to explain ourselves, but packed up in record time and sped away into the distance!

On another occasion, we were camping in a field near the Wicklow Mountains and woke early to find a cow staring into our tent! The funniest incident of all though occurred another night in County Wicklow, but this time our tent was pitched on the beach at Magheramore. It started out a very romantic experience with the background noise of waves breaking onto the shore. However, in the middle of the night, our tent began to leak water. That was nothing unusual as it was an old tent, but this time it was from the bottom and not the top! The tide had come in further than we expected and we had a difficult task getting out. We even had to get a tractor to tow our car out as it also ended up getting stuck.

Towards the end of 1996, I got promoted to mid-level management in work and Joanna's artwork business was really starting to flourish. She was exhibiting her paintings at art galleries, such was the demand for her work. In her entire career, those three years were her busiest and most profitable. Although life was great and I was very content juggling work at M&S, the bakery and helping Dad on the farm, I felt God was calling me to something higher. By the spring of 1997, God had put a strong desire in my heart to serve Him and I could not get away from it – nor did I want to. In contrast to my years of rebellion when I tried to quench the voice of God, this time I searched the Scriptures diligently to find His leading in my life.

As strange as it may sound, even before I became a Christian I was aware the Lord had a unique plan for my life. Without a doubt, I believe it was God who planted the little seeds of desire to become a missionary in my heart many years earlier at BB. Regrettably, I had acted selfishly and wasted many years living for myself. Then after I did get saved, I tried to excuse myself from answering the call by convincing myself there were many others who were far more capable and qualified than I was. In primary school, I was held back in primary six and missed my final year because they deemed me a slow-learner and things didn't improve any at high school as I left with no exams to my name. I also believed that I was too shy to stand in front of people.

However, as God spoke clearly to me through His Word, all those fears that previously gripped me began to dissipate. It seemed that every time I read my Bible, a particular verse in the passage made reference to serving the Lord. I felt obligated to show my appreciation to the Lord, not by giving Him money but giving Him my life. Deep within my heart, the Lord was beginning to shake, challenge and uproot me. I was involved in various ministries in my local church as well as other youth programmes, such as the YMCA in Lisburn. Despite serving the Lord most evenings during the week, I felt the time had come to leave secular employment and step out in faith to serve the Lord full-time. He had given me the perfect missionary partner in Joanna as she loved travelling and had no ties to Northern Ireland except for me. As a couple, we were open to going anywhere in the world that the Lord would lead us to.

At that time, I also read many autobiographies of former missionaries. Their stories fanned the flames that were flickering inside me. Hudson Taylor, the founder of the China Inland Mission (now OMF) once declared:

> *"The Great Commission is not an option to be considered; it is a command to be obeyed."*

The Lord Jesus gives us a direct command to fulfil this Great Commission: *"Go ye therefore, and teach all nations… to observe all things whatsoever I have commanded you" (Matthew 28:19-20).*

God needs men for His work and even if others were unwilling to do it, I was ready. Before his death when taking the gospel to the Auca Indians in Ecuador, Jim Elliott said:

> *"He is no fool who gives what he cannot keep to gain what he cannot lose."*

This world's goods are a perishable commodity of bricks and mortar. Whenever I compare this to the eternal value of reaching souls for Christ, there is no comparison. John Wesley, the famous English preacher once proclaimed:

> *"You have one business on earth – to save souls."*

Although that was exactly how I felt, I wondered how it could ever happen. I had no idea how the Lord was going to use me, but deep within my heart, I knew that God had a plan. I just wanted to follow Him by faith like the patriarchs, reformers and missionaries of previous generations.

Once again, I realised that I needed to respond promptly to the Lord's leading. Joanna trusted me completely and we prayed together every day about our immediate future. She had peace in her heart and both of us were very excited at what the future could hold for us. The Lord brought many specific verses before me, through my devotions and in meetings I attended. Various circumstances, common sense and the confirmation of God's Word focused me on attending a Bible college in Northern Ireland, which offered two-year and four-year courses on its syllabus. Just like any other vocation, I knew if I was to be effective in the ministry, I needed to undertake formal training. The Bible tells us the importance of studying the Word of God for everyday living, yet how much more would it be required if I was to minister to others? My desire was to get through college as soon as possible and start the work of reaching souls, so I opted for the two-year course.

With such aspirations running through my mind, I began to find work at Marks & Spencer less engaging. Even though I was promoted and had greater responsibility and a good wage, I felt I was only giving God the leftovers of my daily efforts in the evenings. Around this time, one of the senior managers approached me on the shop floor one afternoon and asked me to go upstairs to the boardroom as the management team wanted to talk to me. Five of the finest and most respectable business people I have known faced me and one of the men gently said, "Colin, we have noticed your joy is gone and you don't seem to be as focused on the job as you used to be. Is there anything wrong or can you explain to us why this is the case?" I paused for a moment, pondering how I should respond to their question.

I asked if the meeting could be adjourned until Monday to which they agreed. I knew they genuinely wanted to see me happy as well as more engaged in my duties. Although I had a good idea what I was going to tell them, I believe when faced with important life-changing decisions, we should think things through thoroughly and count the cost. It's easy to make rash decisions without considering the consequences. We read in Genesis 22 how God instructed Abraham to offer Isaac as a sacrifice to Him in a location three days' journey away. That gave Abraham time to commune with God and resolve in his mind what decision he would make.

In the springtime of that year, we were given three small lambs to graze the field our mobile was in. A few months before, we had butchered one of them for lamb chops and kept the skin. Joanna used it as a little rug by her bedside to pray on. It happened to catch my eye and made me think about the story of Gideon in the Bible. He was seeking confirmation from God whether or not he should lead the nation of Israel to battle against their oppressors, the Midianites. We read in Judges 6 how he laid a fleece outside one evening and asked God for a sign - that if it rained, his fleece would be dry and if there was no rain, his fleece would be wet.

Without telling Joanna, I took the fleece and put it outside late one evening. The weather forecast was giving a certainty of rain that night so I asked the Lord to prove the matter by keeping the fleece dry. I could hardly sleep that night as the rain pelted down on the roof of our mobile home. Early the next morning, I woke up and crept over to the door and gently opened it to see if the fleece was still dry. I couldn't believe my eyes as the fleece was nowhere to be seen! I put my boots on and headed out into the rain to see where it was. It had also been a very windy night and the fleece had been blown right across the field and was stuck in a hedge. When I came back, Joanna had wakened up and asked me what I was doing with her fleece. I was too embarrassed to tell her so I just said it needed a wash!

I realised I was being silly and didn't need a sign through a fleece like Gideon did. Unlike Gideon, who lived at a time when only a few books of the Bible were written, I had a complete Bible and the clear command of Christ to go. God had already confirmed it through His Word and I had an intense desire to serve Him. As Joanna and I sought the Lord's definite leading that weekend, He gave us much encouragement and extinguished any lingering fears we had of stepping out in faith to serve Him. He promised to sustain us through verses such as this one found in the book of Joshua. *"Have not I commanded thee? Be strong and of a good courage; be not afraid, neither be thou dismayed: for the LORD thy God is with thee whithersoever thou goest"* (Joshua 1:9).

Monday morning arrived and I took my seat in the boardroom. I agreed that for a number of weeks, I had been unsettled and was struggling to focus on my duties. When asked for an explanation, I stated that I loved working for the company, but for a number of months I had felt a burning desire to serve the Lord in a full-time capacity and wished to submit my resignation immediately.

The management team were quite shocked and genuinely disappointed that I wanted to leave the company after six years. As they had witnessed a change in me during the previous few weeks, they knew it was not an impulsive decision, yet they reminded me about the bonuses and benefits I would be giving up. I just smiled and assured them that the Lord would look after me. When they accepted that I was not going to change my mind, they thanked me for all my efforts over the years and wished me all the best for the future. The peace that filled my heart as I left that office and walked back to the shop floor was incredible. I knew I had been obedient to God's call and memories flooded back to the day I proposed over the phone to Joanna.

At twenty-five years old, I knew I was in my prime and knew if I was spared, the next forty years would pass by like the blink of an eyelid. I only had one life on this earth and I wanted to make every day count for God. I remember the words of Jesus challenging me. *"I must work the works of him that sent me, while it is day: the night cometh when no man can work" (John 9:4)*. The book of James also states: *"For what is your life? It is even a vapour, that appeareth for a little time, and then vanisheth away" (James 4:14)*.

It didn't take long for the news of my imminent departure to spread around the shop floor amongst my colleagues. I had great working relationships with the majority of them so there was a tinge of sadness on both sides. Most of them admired my decision and wished me well in my studies and a few reckoned I was crazy giving up a steady job with good prospects.

Prior to submitting my application to attend Bible College, I asked our minister for advice on how I could prepare myself for the course. He kindly agreed to visit our home and listened to me share how I felt God was leading me into the ministry full-time. Then we discussed the course itself and he gave me some examples of how I would be taught to use the Greek language to gain a clearer understanding of Bible passages. I struggled to follow him, as the only Greek I knew was a man who worked in a takeaway in Lisburn! Languages were not my thing but Joanna can speak a few, so she enjoyed that part of the conversation. He then passed on a lot of wisdom based on his time at the same college and also a few practicalities, like waiting until I had completed my course before we considered starting a family. A few days later, I submitted my application and following an interview, I was accepted. I was going to be a student at the Whitefield College of the Bible, near Banbridge in County Down.

A few weeks before college started, I finished my regular jobs so I could attend my lectures and fully engage in studying outside of class. Joanna didn't have a regular job but planned to remain at home and paint to help pay our bills. I was excited at the prospect of living by faith and completely trusting the Lord to meet our every need.

Only a few days after our minister's visit, we got a huge surprise. I was sitting reading a book in our mobile and could hear Joanna talking on the phone in the hallway. As there was nothing unusual about that I wasn't attentive to the conversation going on. Then she walked in before me with her hands over her face and exclaimed, "Colin, guess what? I'm going to have a baby!" I clearly remember my immediate response: "Are you serious?" This was possibly the greatest news I could hear and with a huge grin on my face, I jumped up off the sofa and gave Joanna the biggest hug ever. We both jumped up and down and kissed each other as we were overjoyed at the news a receptionist from the medical centre in Lisburn had delivered. During the next few days as the news sank in, it really felt like someone was filling up my insides with joy. The thought of having children and starting our own family was very exciting and it was not long until we were discussing potential names for the baby. I suggested if it was a boy we should call him "Colin Junior!" Joanna joked she could not possibly cope with another Colin. "Imagine the messing about and water fights you would both have?" she laughed.

However a few weeks later, at the beginning of September Joanna began to have sharp pains and after a few days, we decided it would be wise for her to get checked out in the hospital. The nurse examined Joanna and intuitively seemed to know what was wrong. They said Joanna's pregnancy had complications; an ectopic pregnancy had occurred and required an immediate operation. It was so serious it could possibly have resulted in the death of Joanna and the loss of the unborn baby. At that moment, our lives were thrown into turmoil and our joy was replaced by a dreadful sense of grief. After the operation, the doctors met me and broke the sad news that Joanna had lost her baby, but she was in a relatively stable condition. I rushed to Joanna's bedside and felt so sorry for her, as she lay asleep, still under the anaesthetic.

A few days earlier, before we knew there were any complications, Joanna's mum had arrived from Poland to visit. Since she didn't speak any English and I didn't speak any Polish, it was difficult when Joanna wasn't with us. The doctor said Joanna needed to stay in hospital for a week, so each evening I dropped her mum off at our mobile home and drove back to the hospital to stay by Joanna's side. Our wedding vows returned to my mind as I remembered the part about being together in sickness and health. We were in this together and Joanna's health was more important than anything else and I wanted to be there for her.

When Joanna got discharged from hospital, the doctor insisted she continued to rest, as her body had become frail and run down. Kind friends of ours offered us the use of their holiday home in County Donegal for a week. We graciously accepted their offer so Joanna could recover from her operation and it would also give us peace to reflect on the situation and come to terms with the emotional trauma we had experienced. Joanna's mum was able to stay another week, so she came with us. During that week, Joanna and I spent a lot of time praying together and especially thanking the Lord for saving Joanna's life and requesting that He would restore her to full strength again. Slowly, day by day this prayer was answered and she grew stronger and stronger. At the start of the week, Joanna was so weak that I had to carry her in my arms to the beach, but gradually her strength returned and she was able to walk to the seashore herself by the end of the week.

After a few days observing Joanna and I reading the Bible and praying together, her mum started to ask Joanna questions about our faith and how being a born-again Christian differed from her religious upbringing in Poland. Joanna spent hours that week talking to her mum about her need of salvation. She explained what the Lord Jesus had done for her on the cross and how her life had been transformed since she accepted Jesus as her Saviour. On the Thursday evening, as we all sat in the cottage, I noticed Joanna had started to cry as she spoke with her mum. I held her hand and asked what was wrong. She tearfully whispered, "My mum wants to get saved." Together the three of us knelt by the fire; then I led her in a prayer that Joanna translated and her mum received Christ as her Saviour. I'll never forget how passionately Joanna hugged her mum as joy filled her soul knowing they were now united in Christ forever.

We may have lost our baby, but God in His sovereignty had a plan. In the midst of pain and trial, her mum had come to Christ and joy filled the house. Over the years, Joanna's mum has become a wonderful encouragement to her and they have great joy sharing Bible verses from their Polish Bibles with each other. Even before I had attended one college lecture, the call of God had begun in our home, but it was about to spread much further afield in the years ahead.

CHAPTER NINE

Light of the World

AFTER SPENDING MOST of September shedding tears of grief over the loss of our unborn baby and tears of joy over Joanna's mum getting wonderfully saved, I headed off the last week of the month to enrol at the Whitefield College. I found it a challenge keeping up with the pace of my lectures and it reminded me just how long it had been since I was at school. In truth, I guess I never really knew how to study properly, but with the help of my tutors and dogged endurance, I finally got the hang of it. I recall a funny moment in an English class when the lecturer asked me what a clause was. I told him the only clause I knew was *Santa Claus* which gave everyone a laugh!

During my time at college, I got many opportunities to preach at various churches across the country. When doing the children's talks at these services, I often used an object lesson to illustrate the gospel. One Sunday, a church in County Down invited me to speak at their annual Children's Day services. I decided to tell the story of the lost sheep so I asked a farmer if I could borrow a little lamb for my talk. I wanted to make the point that the children needed to give their lives to Christ and then follow Him for the rest of their days, just like a lamb follows its shepherd.

When I got up to speak, Joanna went to the car and brought the little lamb in. It stood right in front of me and looked directly at my face, then followed me closely as I began to walk around the front of the church and even up and down the aisles! It was a perfect illustration of keeping our eyes upon the Lord and following Him wherever He takes us. At the end of the service, I went to the door with the lamb in my arms for all the children to shake its leg as they left the church. I believe that was one Children's Day that none of them ever forgot!

On another occasion, I was asked to speak at a children's meeting in a church in County Antrim. My message that day was based on the passage in Luke 13, where the Lord compared His protection for His children to a hen protecting her chicks. To get the children interested and engaged, I told them I had a surprise in the box. I invited them to guess what it might be, but even after giving them nearly a dozen hints, none of them guessed correctly. When I lifted the hen out of the box, the children gasped in amazement and squealed with excitement.

However, the noise frightened the hen and it began to flap its wings wildly, so I held it tight to fold them in again. As I did, it dropped something that landed on my foot that smelt putrid! The children didn't notice as I was behind the pulpit, but the stench was so strong I could hardly breathe for the next ten minutes as I spoke to them. After the children's meeting, the minister's wife was horrified because her husband had to speak from the same pulpit later on that night. She must have spent half an hour scrubbing the floor between the meetings! Sadly, I haven't had any further requests to speak in that particular church!

As well as taking part in church services on Sundays, I also received frequent requests to speak to teenagers at Youth Fellowship meetings. One meeting will live long in my memory and the story begins first thing that particular Friday morning. After Joanna and I read the Bible together, I vividly remember Joanna praying that the Lord would be our shield and shelter. She asked Him to protect us as we travelled and that the devil would be unsuccessful in any of his efforts to harm us.

The book of Ephesians teaches us the devil gets angry when Christians go out to serve the Lord in the power of the Holy Spirit and Paul instructs us to resist the devil in Jesus' name. Satan knows very well the mighty power of the gospel – how it can lead blinded people out of his kingdom of darkness and into God's kingdom of light.

I decided to teach the young people about spiritual warfare that evening and prepared a lesson that afternoon. After evening tea, I kissed Joanna goodbye and travelled the short distance to Hillsborough where I was to speak.

Little did I realise at the very moment I was speaking to the teenagers, Joanna was going through a perilous situation at home where she faced great danger and possible death. As I was totally unaware of her predicament, I stayed on after the meeting and joined the young people for a time of food and fellowship.

Around ten o'clock, the young people's parents collected them and not long afterwards, I packed up and headed home. When I swung the car into the entrance of our mobile home, I saw Joanna sitting on the doorstep wearing her red coat. My immediate thought was *that's lovely of her sitting out waiting for me at this time of night!* When I got closer, I realised she was crying and her coat was covered in mud. I jumped out of the car and ran over to find out what was wrong. She mumbled something as she threw her arms around me and hugged me with all her strength. I couldn't make out what she said through her sobs so as she trembled in my arms, my mind started to speculate – *had she slipped, been robbed or attacked?* After a few minutes, she finally relaxed a little and told me what happened when I was away.

About eight o'clock, she decided to take the dog for a walk, which she did most nights and since the country road we lived on was very quiet, we often let the dog off his lead so he could run about freely. He was well trained and usually very obedient, but for some reason that night was different. Without warning, he leapt over a fence into a field of sheep and began to chase them frantically. Joanna shouted at him to come back but when he ignored her calls she climbed over the fence and chased after him. Joanna didn't realise also in that field was a big herd of cows and a large bull. The sheep were terrified of the dog and ran ahead of him down the field. Above the barking of the dog and the bleating of the sheep, as Joanna ran after the dog, she heard the thump of hooves in the distance. Just when she turned her head to see where it was coming from, she was knocked crashing to the ground. The herd of cows trampled over her and ran on down the field. However, the bull stopped and gored at her for a moment with his big head before pursuing the cows. These animals were enormous and easily weighed half a tonne each. Joanna recounted how she was terrified lying on the ground staring up at their bellies and watching their hooves pass inches from her face. She said she felt like a lamb in the jaws of a lion ready to be crushed at any moment. Despite her screams and cries for help, no one was within earshot to come to her assistance.

When the ordeal was over, she lay alone in shock trying to comprehend what had happened. The dog returned and licked her face to get her attention. Slowly, she sat up to assess her physical condition and managed to hobble over to the gate and down the road home. When she made it to the mobile, she discovered the keys had fallen out of her pocket during the tumble. As I listened to her story, I recalled hearing about other bull attacks that ended in tragedy. Amazingly, when we examined her bruised body she didn't have any serious injuries.

As we reflected on the day during our devotions that night, our minds went back to how that very morning Joanna had prayed for God's protection. We thanked God for protecting her and saving her from an awful death. As I lay in bed that night, I realised that the cows had attacked Joanna the very moment I was speaking to the young people in Hillsborough about divine protection from attacks of the enemy. The devil tried to hinder me through this incident and subconsciously tempted me not to take on more speaking engagements in case something similar would happen in my absence. We were not for backing down or shying away from the work, but it was a timely reminder that we needed to keep close to the Lord and rely on His protection.

The Bible reminds us, *"Be sober, be vigilant; because your adversary the devil, as a roaring lion, walketh about, seeking whom he may devour" (1 Peter 5:8)*. Even though Satan is a powerful foe, we should not fear his work. Being saved means we have the all-powerful Christ dwelling within us in the form of His Holy Spirit and we read in God's Word *"Greater is he that is in you than he that is in the world" (1 John 4:4)*.

The Lord Jesus Christ had protected Joanna from serious harm that night. The next day, I took her to a doctor for a thorough examination and he was amazed she had not sustained any serious injuries. Within a few weeks, the bruises disappeared and Joanna was reminded she had been spared for a purpose – painting for God.

Since moving to Northern Ireland, Joanna had become known to many as 'the artist from Poland.' Whenever she first informed me she was an artist, I assumed it was just a hobby and not a career. At that time, she was preparing to commence her final year at university where she was studying fine art. Although I didn't know much about the subject, I could tell she was passionate about painting and exceptionally gifted at it. As I mentioned earlier, one of my first priorities after moving into the mobile was to build Joanna a studio. It proved to be a wise move, as the entire time I was at Bible College she was able to sell paintings to pay our bills.

One day, we were informed about an art competition in Dublin. I applied on Joanna's behalf and she was invited to send two paintings down for the judges to critique. On the final day of the competition my mum, Joanna and I headed down to the glitzy awards ceremony. At the end of the evening, the overall winner was announced but it appeared that they weren't there to claim their prize money! We thought it was crazy how someone who submitted paintings that made it through to the final shortlists didn't even bother turning up.

The next day, our phone rang and a lady from the gallery in Dublin informed Joanna she had won the top prize and they were sorry that she had not been there to receive it. We were baffled and can only assume that Joanna didn't pick up her name as the speaker had a strong Irish accent and Mum and I were busy talking since we didn't understand what the judges were describing in each piece of art. Joanna was astonished and thought I had got a female friend to call her as a joke! She even called the gallery back to check. In addition to receiving the prize money, the two paintings were sold – one to the Royal Hibernian Art Gallery and the other to a private collector.

The following week, a man named Pat, who owned an art gallery in Dublin, rang Joanna and asked her if she would be willing to exhibit some paintings on a regular basis. Although she already had some on display in The Charles Gilmore Fine Art Gallery in Belfast, she was happy to send some others down to Dublin. He was delighted with her work and asked if she would take part in another exhibition. Immediately, she got to work and painted morning, noon and night. Soon, both galleries offered Joanna solo exhibitions meaning she could exhibit thirty to forty paintings at a time. She was becoming a well-renowned Irish artist and clients from all over the island were coming to view and purchase her paintings. In those years, Joanna was in her element and lived her dream in the world of art.

One day, a couple from Dublin rang Joanna and asked if they could visit our home to see more of her paintings. They were captivated by her work that was on view in the gallery and Pat had told them about a large canvas Joanna was painting of two men in a field harvesting corn. When they arrived, they were very inquisitive and asked Joanna what inspired her to paint it. She explained to them that the fields are white unto harvest but the labourers are few and linked in the message of the gospel. They were looking to buy their son a painting for his eighteenth birthday and Joanna was hoping to make a sale as she needed money to buy more paints and canvas. Without giving a reason, they left without buying it. Despite our disappointment, we were thankful for the opportunity to witness to them about the Lord. Amazingly, two days later they called back and bought the painting. We hugged each other, delighted that the Lord had honoured our witness.

When painting, Joanna can turn something dark into something full of light, as only artists can do. Her paintings mean something to everyone but only she knows what's really going on as the picture unfolds and develops. If anyone looks closely at any one of Joanna's paintings, they will notice there is a 'ray of light'. Joanna told me that every time she paints it reminds her of her life – how for many years it was very dark and she was always searching for light in the world. Then one day she found Jesus who claimed: *"I am the light of the world: he that followeth me shall not walk in darkness, but shall have the light of life" (John 8:12)*.

Joanna's art pieces are a reminder that the Lord carried her through those dark nights of pain and suffering as a result of her failed pregnancy. She blossomed in the world of art and her greatest desire was that people would see Christ in her work. It should not come as a surprise that Joanna's favourite Bible verse is *"The LORD is my light and my salvation" (Psalm 27:1)*.

Those days were times of plenty when many people were well-off and desired exquisite art for their homes. I remember one day, Joanna and I were down in the art gallery in Dublin to speak to Pat. In the corner of my eye, I noticed a woman walk in and stand in front of one of Joanna's paintings for about thirty seconds. She turned around, walked straight to the counter and handed over her credit card and bought it. We were amazed how quickly the paintings were selling and on several occasions, Joanna struggled to meet the demand.

However, in 2008 when the credit crunch hit, there was a sudden slump in demand. People's priorities switched from splashing out on luxuries to putting food on their tables and meeting mortgage repayments. More than ever, we needed to keep our focus on the Lord and prove that He could look after us – the same way He provided for Abraham, Isaac and Jacob.

CHAPTER TEN

Christians in the Caribbean

WHEN I FINISHED my course at Bible College, I was offered an opportunity to work at a local church in Hillsborough. I was delighted to accept the offer and immediately got stuck into the work – assisting with youth activities, preaching in the pulpit, one-to-one pastoral ministry, and accompanying the minister on hospital and home visits.

A few months into the placement, Joanna and I realised how vital the work amongst the children was, but felt we lacked the skills to minister to them effectively. We brought this concern before the Lord and doors opened for us to attend a twelve-week Children's Ministry Leadership Course at the CEF (Child Evangelism Fellowship) European headquarters in Switzerland. We still weren't sure what the Lord had in store for us, but we reckoned that a few months sitting under the teaching of experienced children's evangelists would be time well spent. I remember being inspired by these teachers and lecturers who loved the Lord and teaching children. One of them in particular comes to mind, Henry Berry – he frequently said, "When you catch the vision, don't lose the vision!" I remember thinking, *Lord, give me such passion, love and vision for the souls of children.*

When we returned from Switzerland, my minister told me about an opportunity to pastor a little church in Jamaica for a year. He thought it would be a great experience for us and would bring some stability to the congregation out there. My heart rejoiced at the thought of it and I couldn't wait to tell Joanna.

As I drove home, my mind went back to a time when I was only five or six years old at Boys' Brigade. I remembered entering a colouring competition where we were challenged to bring a beach scene in Jamaica to life. As I meticulously worked with bright yellow and green crayons to colour the coconut trees and golden sand beach, I dreamed about visiting that land when I was older. I envisaged meeting the locals, climbing coconut trees and swimming in the Caribbean Sea. To my delight, twenty years later this dream was about to become a reality. When I told Joanna about the opportunity, she was as thrilled as I was. The prospect of finally having a ministry to pour our lives into was exciting. Even though we had just bought a permanent house in the village of Kinallen, near Dromore in County Down, we were happy to rent it out to cover our mortgage payments while we were away. We recognised that everything we owned came from the Lord, so we didn't let our attachment to it hold us back.

A few months later, we packed our suitcases and bid our friends and family goodbye. When we arrived in Jamaica, we were stopped at immigration because we had not purchased return tickets – as we intended to stay as long as we were required. To gain entry, we had to purchase the cheapest return tickets we could get, as we had no intention of using them! Once sorted we met Mark Telford, my dear friend from Bible College who had come to collect us in the church minibus with a group of young people from the church. They were buzzing to see us and gave us a heart-warming welcome. It never ceases to amaze me how Christians all over the world, regardless of culture, have a bond towards each other that surpasses skin colour, accent, dress or social status.

For some time, Mark had been responsible for pastoring 'Let the Bible Speak Church' in Little London, Westmoreland. However, he felt the time was right for him to return home, so we had his company for a week to ensure there was a smooth handover of the work. As he drove us across the island to our base on the west coast, I was awestruck by the scenery. There were breath-taking, jagged mountains, lush green rainforests, cascading waterfalls and beautiful coral beaches. The heat was intense but the sun radiated energy into my being and I couldn't wait to get stuck into the work. There was a big grin etched on my face during the entire journey as my heart poured out silent praise to God for granting us such an opportunity to serve Him, in what was surely one of the jewels of His creation.

The sub-tropical climate was delightful, with constant sunshine all year round. Temperatures reached the mid-thirties during the day and rarely dropped below twenty Celsius at night. Although there was always a refreshing breeze since it was a small island, I still sweated profusely in the high humidity and often changed my shirt three or four times a day! At night-time, the mosquitoes came out in force and were a real nuisance. Many nights, I pranced around the bedroom like a madman trying to swat them and often I woke up with a sore ear after slapping insects that bit me during the night!

On our first Sunday, the congregation held a special commissioning service and formally welcomed us into their church. There was no passive settling-in period but rather it was straight into the work – preaching the gospel and teaching the people from the Word of God every week. We are instructed to *"Preach the word; be instant in season, out of season; reprove, rebuke, exhort with all longsuffering and doctrine" (2 Timothy 4:2)*.

After a couple of months, I had preached all the sermons I had in my archives from my college days and previous speaking engagements in Northern Ireland. Preaching was relatively new to me and although I loved spending time engrossed in the Word of God, I found structuring sermons very time-consuming at the start. With more experience and obviously the Lord's help, I was able to offer the people fresh sermons each Sunday.

From the outset, our vision was to develop the gifts and talents possessed by the church family so they could be self-sufficient when the time came for us to leave. A few young men in the church had a gift for preaching and a willingness to serve, so it made sense to give them regular opportunities to gain experience in the pulpit. This assistance with the preaching commitments gave me time to focus on evangelism in the community. In ministry, the proclamation of the Word of God is the core activity – whether it's teaching to exhort and challenge Christians in their faith, or evangelism to warn and prayerfully win the lost for Christ.

The church made the most of the sublime climate and regularly organised BBQs and picnics for the church family. It was a great way to build and nourish friendships; particularly between the different generations. Everyone got stuck in and the fellowship was great. I always found it hilarious when the kids ran about shouting *"Me belly full man!"* when they were satisfied after eating. Looking back, I really believe it was these informal events that helped make the church such a closely-knit family that genuinely cared for each other. In relaxed settings, people often opened up and talked about issues and struggles in their lives and then others would pray for them.

The public schools in Jamaica were very open to the gospel and a few weeks after arriving, we were taking assemblies at eight o'clock almost every morning. The Lord used these openings to nurture an intense love and burden that was growing within us for reaching children for Christ. He opened my eyes to look on the fields that were white and ready to harvest. When an adult comes to Christ, often their best years are behind them, but when a child accepts Christ as their Saviour, an entire life is available for God to use for His purposes. Furthermore, children are very open and receptive to the gospel; plus their joy, laughter and fun make it a pleasure to work amongst them.

We built up a great rapport with the kids in the area and often when they saw us coming in the church minibus, they would run to school with excitement. We gave a lift to as many of them as we could fit in, and our hearts were filled with joy as they sang lovely songs about Jesus. The principals regularly told us that they had almost full attendances on the days we ministered in their schools as the children didn't want to miss our visit! I relished the opportunity to teach them and was really encouraged by how reverently they listened to the Word of God. To hear them singing and reciting memory verses was a real joy and we found it an amazing way to begin each new day.

None of the congregation had vehicles, nor a licence to drive one. I had such a desire to build the congregation that I became a taxi-driver preacher! I spent about nine hours each week ferrying people to and from the various meetings.

In addition to the morning and evening services each Lord's Day, we had Sunday school and youth group. The young people were a tremendous encouragement to the older folk with their love for the Lord and zeal to get involved in church. As a treat, on Saturday afternoons we took them down to swim in the river. The memories we have of jumping in and playing games with them will remain with us forever. At the end of the night, I reversed the bus into a shallow part of the river and they cleaned it inside and out, so it was shining for Sunday morning. We gave encouragement by informing them that even washing the bus was a service for the Lord.

One thing that struck me about the church in Little London was how the older generation cherished having these young people in their midst. They had the wisdom to recognise that if they held onto them, years later they would be the spine of the church. Thus, we were encouraged to invest as much of our time as possible into their lives and try to be good role models.

Once a month, we took the young people on an outing to another part of the island. On one of these trips, we experienced an immediate answer to prayer when we got caught up in a tropical storm. Due to its location in the Gulf of Mexico, the weather in Jamaica can change suddenly and thunderstorms can hit without warning. On this particular day, a severe storm arose and the young people were terrified. We immediately stopped the bus and everyone began to pray simultaneously that the Lord would protect us and keep us safe. A few minutes later when we had finished praying, we opened our eyes and looked up to see a clear blue sky and the sun shining again. The youth were amazed at how God had answered their prayers in such spectacular fashion!

During these outings, many young people approached us to discuss delicate issues in their lives or to ask us to pray for them. On one outing, we had the joy of leading a teenage girl to the

Lord. What joy she received as she gained assurance that she was a true born-again Christian!

Towards the end of our placement, I organised a residential camp at another part of the island. I built up the young people's excitement by announcing we would have donkey races there. However, when we arrived at the campsite, I was gutted to discover the nearest donkeys lived eight miles away. Not wanting to disappoint the young people, I removed the seats from the bus and put the donkeys in the back. As I drove back to the campsite, I witnessed some extremely bemused expressions – the local people had never seen a white man cruising about with donkeys in a church minibus! I just beeped the horn and waved at everyone who stared!

During our time in Jamaica, Joanna and I felt a firm conviction that we ought to be obedient to Scripture and get baptised as believers. Baptism by immersion was something that neither of us had previously considered nor felt challenged to do. In the book of Acts, when Philip the evangelist was sent by the Lord to a desert place, he met a government official from Ethiopia sitting in his chariot reading the Scriptures. Philip helped him to understand the passage from the Old Testament and explained how the prophecy referred to Jesus. The Ethiopian then asked Philip the rhetorical question, *"what doth hinder me to be baptized?"(Acts 8:36)*. Once he testified that he believed in the Lord Jesus Christ as his own and personal Saviour, he met the requirement for baptism.

Baptism is an outward expression of an inward possession. We were not ashamed of being saved and belonging to Christ, so it was a natural desire for us to express it publicly. Around this time, a Canadian pastor called Frank was visiting us for a few days and we asked him to baptize us in the beautiful Caribbean Sea. He agreed and we shared a wonderful time together and felt a great sense of peace and joy knowing we had obeyed a clear command from the Lord to believe *and* be baptized.

After Frank left, I had the privilege of wading out into the beautiful waters of the Caribbean many more times to baptize new believers in the name of the Father, Son and Holy Spirit. On many occasions, there were many tourists nearby who observed the baptisms and found them very touching.

At the end of our time in Jamaica, the church family organised a special farewell service for us. The most touching part of the service for us was when the young people said it was the best year they had ever experienced in the life of the church. Their parents thanked us immensely for caring for the children and investing so much time in the youth of the church. It was quite emotional leaving, but our time there had come to an end and it was time to move on to our next destination – wherever God would lead us.

CHAPTER ELEVEN

Down Under

WHEN WE RETURNED from Jamaica, my home church in Lisburn offered me a position in ministry where I was to shadow the senior minister for a while and then assist him with visitation and preaching. I was also encouraged to support other churches beyond Lisburn with their children's missions and Bible Clubs. I loved this aspect of the work and witnessed many children professing faith in Christ. This blessed my heart and encouraged the congregations in the various churches I visited.

After twelve months in Lisburn, another door opened to travel. We were invited to fulfil a two-year pastorate at a church in Australia. It was located in a small farming town called Lock, one hundred miles north of Port Lincoln, on the south coast of the island. Having served for a year in Hillsborough, Jamaica and Lisburn, we were delighted at the timing of this next assignment in the southern hemisphere. Each of the previous placements were steep learning curves and required us to rely heavily on God. I had learned much from the experienced ministers I served under in Hillsborough and Lisburn, so I was eager to put what I had learned into practice and help others in a church where there was no pastor.

The time soon came for us to fly the ten thousand mile journey to Australia. When we touched down at Adelaide International Airport, we saw a haze rising above the tarmac and parked planes glistening in the sun. Climate-wise, it was similar to Jamaica but the infrastructure and buildings were far more modern. We got through immigration swiftly this time as the visa system was a bit more sophisticated and they accepted that many travellers were staying for a couple of years. A family from the church collected us and drove us to the house that would be our home for the foreseeable future. One of the first topics of conversation was warning us about redback spiders and various snakes we might encounter! They advised us how to avoid them and what emergency action to take if we got bitten, as the venom was poisonous and could be deadly if not treated immediately.

It was information of great benefit, as just a few days later when I was clearing out the garden shed at the back of our new house, I noticed one of those small creatures sizing me up! I almost froze at the thought of it flinging itself at me. Suffice to say, action was taken immediately to remove it. On another occasion when we were out with some friends, one of them suddenly shouted, "Don't move!" As soon as I stopped, he grabbed a snake by the tail and flung it around and killed it before it bit me. He informed us it was poisonous and if any of us had been bitten we would have been in grave danger!

The locals were extremely friendly and helped us settle in quickly, which we appreciated, given how far away we were from our home. Many evenings, they took us out for drives to show us around and advised what spots were worth visiting. One of these trips was to Locks Well beach where they told us people fished for salmon. As I shared in my introduction, the return visit we made to do some fishing could easily have been my last fishing trip!

Another recreational pastime popular with the locals was spear fishing and on a few occasions, I was invited to join groups heading out at night to try it. Armed with a bright spotlight in one hand and a spear in the other, we waded out into the sea until the water was up to our knees. When we shone the spotlight into the water, the fish would be attracted to it and then we could spear them. Some of the fish we caught were massive! One night when there were dozens of fish swimming around our ankles and we were really engrossed in catching the biggest ones, for a joke someone shouted "Shark!" – We dropped our gear and bolted to the beach while those in on the joke nearly keeled over in fits of laughter!

In contrast to Jamaica, where we had the benefit of Mark showing us the ropes for a week, in Australia we were completely on our own from the start. It was a small country church and most of the congregation were farmers. I loved visiting their farms as I set about getting to know them. One owned ten thousand sheep and another had a hundred thousand acres of land – large-scale in comparison to Northern Ireland! During the harvest season, it was normal to see five combine harvesters in one field going up and down for hours cutting the crops.

The people in the church sincerely loved the Lord and supported the Sunday meetings, Bible studies and prayer meetings very well. I enjoyed the pulpit ministry and preached every Sunday. Joanna even rediscovered how to play the piano and she was put on the rota to play on Sundays in church – she had been taught as a child but hadn't touched a piano for years. Since there were only a handful of children in the church, we asked the local primary school if we could hold children's meetings there. They welcomed us with open arms and gave us permission to conduct a weekly meeting in their hall, which was very well attended.

At the beginning of December, just before our first Christmas 'Down Under', the council asked me to speak in the town hall as part of a big festival they had organised. It was a wonderful opportunity to share how Christ Jesus came into the world to save sinners and I felt a great liberty preaching that night.

The church had a commendable vision for evangelism and was in the process of planting a new church in a little town called Elliston some sixty miles away. Every Sunday after our church service in Lock, a few of us drove over and led a service in Elliston in the afternoon. In the middle of the week, we returned for a children's meeting followed by a Bible study for adults. A fond memory I have from our first Sunday at Elliston was a man called Shane giving his life to the Lord. To this day, he is still rejoicing in his salvation and serving God.

Another highlight of our time in Lock was the annual children's camp that a farmer from the congregation hosted on his land. The church invited all the local children along, so we had a great opportunity to preach God's Word each morning and evening. After the evening meetings around the campfire, the children amused themselves hunting and chasing wombats, which came out at night to feed.

In addition to the snakes and spiders, kangaroos are another animal greatly feared by the Australians. Not because they are vicious, but because they have a habit of hopping out in front of vehicles driving along the road at night. These creatures are the size and weight of a young cow, but instead of running away from car lights like a cow would, they seem to be attracted towards them! One night while driving home alone in the dark, five of them sprang out of nowhere and headed straight towards me. I swerved and managed to avoid the first four, but the fifth one changed direction at the last second and hit me. The impact caused severe damage to the front of the car and shattered the windscreen. My greatest fear was one of them ending up in the passenger seat beside me!

One other time, I recall driving along a dusty road with my friend Roger, who pastored another church nearby. Ahead of us, the road was getting dusty and we had to keep using the windscreen wipers to see where we were going. When we travelled a bit further and looked closer, we saw a kangaroo a few hundred metres in front of us. Roger sped up and since it was going in the same direction, we pulled out and drew alongside it. The race was on! We couldn't believe how fast those animals could hop and the race continued for several miles until the kangaroo suddenly leapt over the hedge and out of sight. There was dust everywhere, inside the car and out! The bodywork was a lovely shade of orange and the headlights and number plates were completely hidden. We laughed so much we had to pull over.

As time went on, we felt the Lord re-emphasise the importance of children's ministry to us. We felt it was our responsibility to show boys and girls the way of salvation before the things of the world caught hold of them. We even got involved in community life and sports clubs to befriend and reach as many locals as possible.

All too soon though, our two-year pastorate came to an end. The church organised a special farewell service for us on the

Sunday before our departure. It was hard to leave folks we had grown to love and who had become a massive part of our lives. When you arrive in a foreign country and don't know anyone, you really appreciate the small things people do for you. Those dear people did a lot for us and made a lasting impression that we will always cherish.

Unbeknown to the congregation, just a few days before our farewell service Joanna received some devastating news. She had become pregnant again, but for the second time there were complications very early on and she had a miscarriage. We had been so excited about the prospect of arriving back to Northern Ireland a year later with a baby, but our hopes were dashed again. During the farewell service, Joanna was quite teary and emotional. Everyone assumed it was because she was going to miss them and while this was certainly true, none of them knew about the heartache she was going through inside. The church was packed to capacity that Sunday as many of the locals came along to express their appreciation for our work and ministry within their town.

Although we had parted from the church, Joanna and I decided not to return home immediately, but rather spend an extra year travelling around Australia and ministering in schools. During our final month at Lock, I contacted over a hundred schools and booked assemblies and Bible Clubs in them. We planned to drive westwards to Perth on the coast, then two and a half thousand miles around the coast clockwise to Darwin in the Northern Territory. After Darwin, we would head east to Cairns in Queensland and then drive down through Brisbane and Sydney, to Melbourne. We had the goal of speaking at least once in every coastal town and city in Australia, as that's where most of the people live. The centre of Australia is so remote and dry that no one lives there apart from miners.

We bought a camper van for the journey and packed in one hundred thousand children's tracts to distribute in the schools and churches that we planned to speak in. As we were going to be a permanent presence on the road, I got the van covered with bright, fluorescent transfers that would be visible to other drivers day and night. On the front, we had *Jesus saves for all eternity*; and on the back, the verse *"For whosoever shall call upon the name of the Lord shall be saved" (Romans 10:13).*

Off we set and visited one school after another in our new vehicle. The decorated campervan caught everyone's attention. Many people beeped their horns and waved but a few gave us rude gestures. That didn't bother me – I just waved back and prayed that someday they would get saved. After all, it wasn't me they were offended by, but the message of the gospel. It was a great vehicle in many ways as it was practical to cook in, yet comfortable to sleep in. However, the climate was so sublime, many nights we just slept outside in swags, which are sleeping bags with mattresses in them and lay under the stars!

We kept on schedule and fulfilled all the commitments we made around the vast country. Before heading home, we spent the last few months helping a local church in Tasmania, an island three hundred miles south of Australia. We helped them with their youth work and organised Bible Clubs, beach missions and other outreaches in their community. They made the most of having a fresh face in their midst and asked me to preach at most of the Sunday services and the midweek Bible studies.

During this stint, Joanna suffered yet another miscarriage. Having children was one of our strongest earthly desires, so we continued to pray fervently that the Lord would give us a family of little boys and girls to call our own. We went for medical checks and the doctors reported we were both very healthy and they could not understand why there had been complications. We accepted God's plans were maybe different to ours and realised these matters were ultimately in God's will and control. Many times we wept together because the repeated pain and disappointment was very hard to accept. Yet in it all, we learnt to rest and trust God completely and not permit the sadness to make us resentful or bitter towards our circumstances.

In preparation for flying home, we advertised our campervan that had reliably taken us all around Australia. Remarkably, a buyer came forward with an offer that was more than we had paid for it a year earlier!

Whilst travelling around Australia, I read a book about a Scottish missionary called John Paton. In 1858, he left his home in Scotland to bring the gospel to the cannibals of Vanuatu (formerly known as the New Hebrides Islands) – eight hundred miles north-east of Australia. I was really amazed and challenged by his life story. Before he even set out he wrote:

> *"The opposition was so strong from nearly all, and many of them warm Christian friends, that I was sorely tempted to question whether I was carrying out the Divine will, or only some headstrong wish of my own. This also caused me much anxiety and drove me close to God in prayer"*

One quote that really struck me and gave me an insight to his outlook on life was in a response to a senior elder Christian who was trying to dissuade him from going:

Switzerland CEF training 2000

CEF Centre Kilchzimmer

Henry Berry, who was our inspiration during the training

Practical training at US Army base in Germany

Jamaica 2000-2001

AIM HIGH

LET THE BIBLE SPEAK MISSION

With Brian & Pastor Frank

Youth trip

Our baptism in the Caribbean Sea

Our weekly visit to the infirmary

Holiday Bible Club

Purchasing a new bus for the church ministry

Jamaica

The mission station

Donkey race at camp

Youth Camp

Camp leaders

Sunday school

Driving many hours every week

Our Jamaican congregation

Australia &
Tasmania
2002-2005

Lock, where we pastored the church for 2 years

Where will you spend
Eternity?

Except a man be born again,
he cannot see the kingdom
of God. John 3:3

Next 96 km

Beach mission

Australia

Time out with Roger

Weekly Bible Club in Lock

Weekly Bible Club in Elliston

Camping

Lock & Elliston friends

Australia

Joining the local tennis club

Getting ready for the wombat hunt!

Preparing a Bible story

Children's devotions

Joanna shearing a sheep

Children's camp

Jesus said, I am the RESURRECTION, and the LIFE: he that believeth in ME ...h he were dead, ...ll he LIVE:

Aboriginal school

Locks Well

New Year's Eve 2004

Fishing for salmon in dangerous waters at Locks Well

⚠ **Crocodile Safety**

WARNING

Estuarine (saltwater) Crocodile attacks can cause injury or death. These animals are known to move into this area undetected.
- Do not enter the water when closure signs are in place.

Freshwater Crocodiles inhabit this area. They can become aggressive and cause injury if disturbed.
- Do not approach or interfere with these animals.

Breakfast in the camper van touring Australia

Northern Territory

Kulgera 18
Erldunda 94
Alice Springs 293
Darwin 1780

Our big trip around Australia in 2004

Sydney

Aboriginal territory

MARRARA CHRISTIAN
SCHOOL
PRE-SCHOOL TO YEAR 9

NORTHERN TERRITORY
CHRISTIAN COLLEGE
YEARS 10 TO 12

ADMINISTRATION CENTRE
ALL VISITORS
PLEASE REPORT TO RECEPTION

Cairns
Christian
Centre

C157 Beulah 6
C137 Paradise 5
(Sheffield C136) 12

Early morning in the
camper van

Tasmania church

Tasmania 2005

Vanuatu 2004

Port Villa

Tanna Island

South Africa 2008

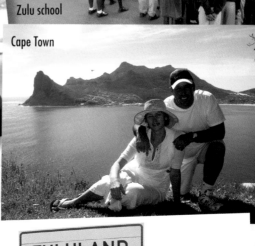
Zulu school

Zulu children

Cape Town

Swaziland

ZULULAND DISTRICT

UPHONGOLA

KEEP A SAFE DISTANCE FROM ELEPHANTS

Camp

Zulu school assembly

With Pastor Paul

Church in Johannesburg

Zulu house

Israel 2012

Arabic school

Jerusalem

Morning devotions

Druize school

With Samuel & Fadi

Our team

Nazareth

On Mount Carmel

Sharing our experience

Dead Sea

Garden of
Gethsemane

Isle of Man 2011

Bible distribution with Roy & Sharon

Lithuania 2013

Lithuanian & N. Irish leaders

Joanna scoring a goal!

Camp

Philippines 2013

With Uncle Noel

Our team

Street evangelism

Youth Camp

Church Camp

Distributing food

Helping administer aid after typhoon

Super Typhoon Yolanda
2013

Church rebuilt with the help of our friends

India 2014

Youth meeting

Our team

The orphanage

Children's meeting on the street

India

Nepal 2014

Himalayas

With Amos

This girl was the only Christian in the entire school

Dangerous roads

Rice fields

Nepal

Distributing children's Bibles in Nepali language

Canada 2014

N. Ireland beats Canada at Volleyball

Camp

Team devotions

Little Mountain
Bible Chapel

MEETING SCHEDULE
INFORMATION

KIDS ADVENTURE WEEK
COLIN TINSLEY FROM IRELAND
AUG. 5 TO 8   930 TO 1200
AGES 5 TO 12   WELCOME

Trips to Asia 2012-2016

I just told the elephant a joke!

Hong Kong 2013

School in Cambodia

Laos

6 hour boat journey

Vietnam

Asia

Floating shop in Vietnam

Team 2013

Bags full of Bibles

With my friend Stephen

Getting the Bibles ready

Joanna prays
with a new
believer

Team 2015

Heading for the duck market

Joanna eating live ants!

Taxi in Laos

On the Mekong River

Bibles safely delivered!

Kenya 2002

Kenya 2016

Our team 2016

High school in
Githurai, Nairobi

Primary school

Kenya

School assembly

Visiting mission station

Visiting people at their home

N. Ireland beats Kenya at volleyball!

Team devotions

Teaching an object lesson

"Mr Dickson, you are advanced in years now and your own prospect is soon to be laid in the grave, there to be eaten by worms. I confess to you, that if I can but live and die serving and honouring the Lord Jesus, it will make no difference to me whether I am eaten by cannibals or by worms. In the Great Day, my Resurrection body will rise as fair as yours in the likeness of our risen Redeemer."

They set off in February and finally reached their appointed island of Tanna in November. Before the end of March the following year, he had buried his wife and new-born son who both caught a fever. He battled on for four long years under incredible circumstances of constant danger until he was driven off the island in 1862. In Australia, he remarried and returned to another island called Aniwa. Over the course of the next fifteen years, he saw the entire island turn to Christ! Since it was only a short flight away, we decided to visit Vanuatu for a week before heading home. We bought tickets and flew there in a tiny, eight-seater plane, which was an unforgettable experience in itself – landing on a cordoned-off section of the beach!

During our short stay, we visited ten different schools to preach the gospel. John Paton left such an influence that even today, the islands have many wonderful Christian people who love God. Such was the openness and respect towards the Bible, one school principal asked me to stay an entire day to teach the children more about God. This parting memory of our time 'Down-Under' really convicted me I should invest all my efforts in reaching children with the gospel.

On the flight home, when I looked down at the turquoise blue ocean and saw the coast of Australia disappear out of sight, I reflected on what we had accomplished there and what God had taught me. I had no idea where our next calling would be, but it was clear to me that my gifts and natural abilities seemed to be most effective when ministering to children. We were willing to go anywhere and do anything God would lead us to, so long as it was going forward and building the Kingdom of God.

As I faced an unknown future in the ministry, I gained much encouragement by reading about great men of faith in the Bible. When Moses was leading over two million Israelites through the wilderness towards the Promised Land, they reached the shores of the Red Sea and he was unsure where to turn. Pharaoh's army was rapidly approaching from the north and impassable mountains lay to the south and west. He sought the Lord and was told to 'go forward' towards the sea. By faith, he advanced and it was only then that the Lord opened a path through the sea for Moses and the people to pass through. How I desired and needed such faith! We didn't have any idea where the next part of the journey would take us, but the Lord knew and we sought to 'go forward' at His leading.

CHAPTER TWELVE

Headache, Heartache and Hope for Youth

WHEN WE RETURNED to Northern Ireland, the belief that God was calling us to continue in the sphere of children's ministry intensified. Since I was a member of my local church, I asked for a meeting to be arranged with the mission board so I could share how I believed the Lord was leading me into full-time children's work. I also wanted to seek their advice and see if they would be willing to support me in my venture.

They listened attentively as I gave an overview of our experiences working with children overseas and how I believed such an effective ministry could be replicated at home. I told them how, as a young boy, I loved Boys Brigade camp and wanted to organise similar camps for children at Tollymore Forest Park. And then, with Joanna coming from Poland, I explained we felt obliged to take teams of young people out there to help reach thousands of Polish children with the gospel.

They gave me permission to visit different churches on deputation to share my vision and agreed that if enough people responded and committed to supporting me financially, it would be confirmation of my calling. Therefore, I made contact with dozens of churches and spent the next twelve months speaking at one or two meetings each week in the evenings, sharing what God was doing in my own life and encouraging folks in their daily walk and witness. Over the course of that year, I also met school principals, took assemblies and taught pupils in their classrooms about God. As well as doing ministry in schools, I also conducted a number of Bible Clubs in churches and led my first children's camp at Tollymore. Over sixty children attended it and we had an amazing time.

During that year, I met regularly with the mission board to give updates on my work. They were quite happy with how the project was going and also pleased that I had met my financial support target. However, they insisted that I would not be able to take any teams to Poland until such a time as there was a church from that denomination planted there. Joanna and I still felt we owed a huge debt to that land and really believed God was leading us to serve Him there at some stage. I knew I was not a church planter but rather a children's evangelist who assisted local churches, so we took the matter before the Lord in prayer.

Towards the end of my year on deputation, life took another unexpected turn for us. I was up in Kilkeel one morning speaking at a school assembly, before attending a special week-long prayer meeting believers had arranged nearby. Just before I went into the prayer meeting I called Joanna and when she answered the phone, I knew something was wrong. Through her tears and difficulty in finding words, she told me she had lost another baby. My eyes welled up with tears as I felt the weight of Joanna's grief just talking to her on the phone. That was her fourth miscarriage and it was looking almost certain that we would never have little kids to call us Daddy and Mummy. Joanna cried and cried down the phone and I was totally devastated. All she wanted was a baby and yet it seemed for us, it was never going to happen. I just felt like a broken and helpless man.

At the time, we were already extremely perplexed over what direction my ministry was going, then this added pain landed on our laps. I was completely confused and felt torn apart inside, but I had to remain strong for Joanna's sake. Despite our brokenness and a general sense of uncertainty in life, every time we read the Bible or prayed, we were convicted beyond measure that God knew all about our situation and was in complete control.

The men on the mission board were very sympathetic at this time, but understandably they needed me to let them know where I stood. As I pondered over my options I could see many advantages of committing to work within the church, such as support, encouragement and access to all kinds of resources. However, there were also many benefits of working as an independent ministry, but potentially many limitations too. More than ever before, I knew I needed to seek God's guidance to determine what direction He wanted me to go.

Remaining in the church would definitely have been the more comfortable option, but I could not get away from the calling I felt towards Poland. Initially, I didn't think that starting and maintaining my own ministry would be possible, but the more I thought about it, my mind kept going back to the days after I first met Joanna. On the surface, everything told me pursuing a relationship with her would be impossible, but deep down inside I just felt it was right. I knew God had a unique plan for my life and since He had shown me His power and providence before, I was willing to step forward in faith. Perhaps because at that time I felt so low, I reckoned I didn't have much more to lose. The loss of my credibility or pride was pretty negligible after losing a potential son or daughter.

Despite not having any definite future plans, I sent a letter to the church mission board thanking them for the opportunity to volunteer under their leadership and explained how I believed God was calling me in a different direction. It was difficult parting from the great people and established ministry there, but God's call is often one of sacrifice.

Now over ten years later, I realise I needed to be free before the Lord could lead me to the next step of my journey. It was a daunting time in our lives as many people questioned, and a few scoffed, at what we were doing. The idea of starting something on our own, without any guaranteed support, was a significant step but we were sure the Lord was in it. He repeatedly brought verses before us such as, *"Be strong and of a good courage, fear not, nor be afraid of them: for the LORD thy God is with thee; he will not fail thee, nor forsake thee" (Deuteronomy 31:6).*

After making this bold decision, I was not permitted to fulfil the bookings that had previously been made through the church. In fact, for over three months I didn't receive a single booking to speak. With so much time on my hands, I spent hours each day reading the Bible and praying to God about His plans for me. The more I read, the greater the peace and assurance I had about my future and some promises changed my confusion into a sense of expectancy.

Joanna was a tremendous source of strength and encouragement at this time and often helped me stay calm by assuring me she was one hundred percent behind me whatever way the Lord led us. In the meantime, she kept herself very busy painting pictures to display in the galleries to pay our bills and keep a roof over our heads! In faith, I started to write my first three books: a word search book, a crossword book and a sword drill book. During this period, many friends rang and called at our house to offer advice and guidance, which I really appreciated. The Bible says: *"Where no counsel is, the people fall: but in the multitude of counsellors there is safety" (Proverbs 11:14).*

Finally, after three long months, I launched out in faith on 1st May 2007 and established 'Hope for Youth Ministries'. We put in place a committee of wise and trustworthy Christian friends and applied to make the ministry a registered charity. We also sorted out statutory things like public liability insurance and child protection training for volunteers. It was a whirlwind of activity but after taking that first step, I felt a huge sense of relief – just like after I proposed to Joanna. With a new identity and clear focus on the work, I was chomping at the bit to get back into the schools again.

I remember reading about William Carey, who is regarded as the 'father of modern missions'. After spending many years spreading the gospel in India, he encouraged people to:

"Expect great things from God and attempt great things for God."

Another famous missionary, Hudson Taylor, also claimed:

"God's work done in God's way will never lack God's supply."

We were completely relying on the Lord as we had no formal support from churches or any other Christian organisations; nor did we receive any grants or funding from the government.

We just held on to the promises of God, that He would supply our every need. Our sole focus was to reach children for Him.

I also read memoirs from George Whitefield, one of the preachers during the Great Awakening in the USA. He encouraged believers to:

> *"Fight the good fight of faith and God will give you spiritual mercies. Press forward. Do not stop, do not linger in your journey, but strive for the mark set before you."*

I knew I needed to keep focused and *"press toward the mark for the prize of the high calling of God in Christ Jesus" (Philippians 3:14)*. All I needed to do was honour God and work hard serving Him. Even if some people didn't agree with me, it was definitely better going alone with God than receiving the praise of men and lacking the blessing of God. Sadly some people did distance themselves from me, but it was a sacrifice I knew I had to make if God was to have complete control of my life.

Before long, the phone began to ring again and churches booked me for speaking engagements, particularly children's missions. I also contacted schools to request opportunities to speak at assemblies or do Bible Clubs. Using the banner of 'Hope for Youth Ministries' gave me much greater acceptance in the schools and before long, I saw the wisdom in what God had prompted me to do.

The principals have a great responsibility for the children who attend their school and wisely are very cautious who they invite in, especially when the visit is of a spiritual nature. To be completely transparent, I launched a website so principals and parents could see exactly what we do and how we go about it. It isn't about promoting the ministry to build an empire, but rather to have a vehicle to reach the children for Christ – and it works wonderfully!

Those early days were exciting as we had a blank canvas and sought to find the most efficient and effective way to do children's evangelism in Northern Ireland. Little did I know that in the future, He was also going to lead me to more countries around the world than I could ever have imagined. There would be difficulties, hurdles and challenges along the way but God was going before me. If God was for me, who could be against me? Below are some quotes by missionaries of old, which really inspired me at the time I stepped into this new venture. I hope they encourage you if you are embarking on some form of service for God.

C.T. Studd (missionary to China with Hudson Taylor):

"If Jesus Christ is God and died for me, then no sacrifice can be too great for me to make for Him."

"Only one life, 'twill soon be the past, only what's done for Christ will last. And when I am dying, how happy I'll be, if the lamp of my life has been burned out for Thee."

"How could I spend the best of years of my life in living for the honours of this world, when thousands of souls are perishing every day? Let us not glide through this world and then slip quietly into heaven, without having blown the trumpet loud and

long for our Redeemer, Jesus Christ. Let us see to it that the devil will hold a thanksgiving service in hell when he gets the news of our departure from the field of battle."

Amy Carmichael (Missionary to India):

"Make me thy fuel, flame of God."

D.L. Moody (nineteenth-century evangelist in the USA):

"If God is your partner, make your plans big."

Leonard Ravenhill (English evangelist who focused on prayer and revival):

"Any method of evangelism will work if God is in it."

Christ Himself commanded us: *"Go ye into all the world, and preach the gospel to every creature" (Mark 16:15).*

CHAPTER THIRTEEN

Misunderstood

B Y THE AUTUMN of 2007, invitations to do Bible Clubs in schools and churches were coming in at a steady rate. I was busier than ever and more importantly, children were getting saved. I was also greatly encouraged by feedback folks gave me, telling how the missions in their churches had really warmed people's hearts for evangelism and refocused their vision of reaching local children for Christ. Also on some occasions, I heard how children who attended the missions came along to the regular children's meetings, which was a big answer to prayer.

A group of praying Christians is an essential part of the work and the Bible reminds us time and time again that it is God's chosen way of building His kingdom on earth. There was one particular children's mission that will always remain in my memory – firstly because I witnessed God answer persistent prayer and send His Spirit down in a powerful way; but secondly how there was an unexpected reaction in some quarters.

The story begins when a group of Christians approached me and asked if I would speak at a children's mission they were planning. They told me how their fellowship had been praying for over a year and there were two specific things that they had asked God to do: firstly, to fill the hall with boys and girls; and secondly, to save many souls.

As an evangelist, this was music to my ears. It is fantastic to labour with folk who take the work of God seriously and pray with expectancy and faith. The week before the mission, I visited some of the local schools in the area and gave the principals invitations to pass on to the children. Then on the first night of the mission, an hour before the club was due to start, I drove around the nearby housing estates with loudspeakers attached to the roof of my van inviting kids along. Children appeared from everywhere and were really excited. The ice-cream van stopped and the driver smiled and said, "I may wait until you are finished shouting because they can't hear me!"

Minibuses had been organised to collect the children at designated bus stops and it was thrilling to see them waiting on the buses, waving their parental consent slips. When the time came to start the mission, the hall was completely packed. The children enthusiastically sang the choruses and listened attentively to the lesson. After the quiz, I invited anyone who wanted to find out more about Jesus or becoming a Christian to speak to myself or any other leader at the end of the meeting.

Then I handed the meeting over to one of the organisers and sat down behind him in the pulpit. While I had my head bowed as he closed the meeting in prayer, a little nine-year-old boy came forward and poked my arm. He whispered, "Colin, I want to become a Christian!" After the leader finished praying, I got his attention and signalled to him that the boy wanted to give his life to Jesus. He shook his head and whispered, "You're the speaker and the children should talk to you." In the moments that followed, I had the joy of leading the young lad to the Lord. No other pleasure on earth can be compared to the feeling one feels when they witness a child asking the Lord Jesus Christ to forgive their sin and save their soul.

Praise God, on each of the four evenings that followed, more children put their trust in the Lord Jesus for salvation. On some evenings, there were over half a dozen of them counselled for salvation! Amazingly, each night most of the children who came forward didn't even know the others, as they lived in different estates and attended different schools. The boldness of the children made a big impact on all of the leaders and helpers. Everyone who was there recognised a special presence of the Lord in the meetings, but that should not have surprised us after all the prayer that had been offered up. Indeed the two specific prayer requests had been answered: The Lord did indeed fill the hall with boys and girls, and twenty-four of them got saved.

However, when God works powerfully in a place, it often isn't long until opposition raises its head. After word spread throughout the local area, other Christian groups began to question whether the children were genuinely saved because they had never witnessed so many conversions in missions they had held before. Obviously, it is necessary to ask for more details before believing such claims, but many believers scoffed when they heard the news without investigating further or asking those who were there. Surely all believers should rejoice in the news of lost souls getting saved, just as we know heaven does. The organisers were challenged that since twenty-four new children hadn't joined their Sunday school or children's meeting, the children must not have been genuinely converted. Rather than rebuking the scoffing and reaffirming what they had witnessed God do before their own eyes, a few of the helpers also started to doubt.

If I am honest, I was shocked and felt a sense of despair because some of the people who had prayed for this mission were now questioning the work of the Holy Spirit in the hearts of the children. When I enquired if anyone had visited the children to meet their parents and invite them to Sunday school, their answer was negative. In this day, it is completely unrealistic to expect children whose families do not attend church, to come along to children's meetings without some form of personal invite – and even then, children cannot force their parents to take them. Despite the adverse circumstances many children face as young Christians, the Holy Spirit is more than capable of sustaining them in their faith until they are at an age that they can go to Scripture Union in secondary school or youth meetings.

Two years after that mission, I was in a primary school in the same town doing a Bible Club. On the second day, a young boy in primary seven came up to me and asked if I remembered him. I admitted I didn't and explained to him how hundreds of children ask me the same question every year. Undeterred, he began to tell me how he had attended a mission in the town a couple of years ago and I spoke to him on the first night. He explained how he wanted to become a Christian during the story and when everyone sang the closing song "I am a C-H-R-I-S-T-I-A-N", he realised he needed to invite Jesus into his life. He recounted how everyone else went to the back of the hall to go home, but he went up to the front by himself to speak to me. With excitement in his eyes, he said, "You prayed with me and I became a Christian that night. I was in primary five then and next year I'm going to big school." I was delighted to hear his story and shook his hand.

I have learned that winning souls comes at a price, especially when the souls are those of children. Many times in the work, I have felt misunderstood and unappreciated, but it saddens me more when people oppose the ministry by doubting the experiences children have with God. I firmly believe that children are quite capable of understanding the simple message of God's love for them. Referring to the conversion of children, the famous Baptist preacher C.H. Spurgeon was quoted as saying:

> *"A child of five, if properly instructed, can as truly believe and be regenerated as an adult of fifty years." "A child who knowingly sins can truly believe."*

These children knew and admitted that they had sin in their lives and wanted to turn from their sin to live lives that glorified God. I know many other children who have been saved at the ages of three, four or five and ten years later are still going on well with the Lord. D.L. Moody once said:

> *"Wherever the gospel gets proclaimed, there should be an expectation of immediate results."*

I completely agree with him and every time I preach the Word of God, I expect to see children respond and I am disappointed if they don't. It isn't about my ability as a speaker, but rather the power of God's written Word. I believe *"the word of God is quick and powerful, and sharper than any two-edged sword" (Hebrews 4:12)*. It is powerful and effective – even in the life of a little child. Back in the sixteenth century, Francis Xavier, a Jesuit missionary in the Roman Catholic Church said:

> *"Give me a child until he is seven and I will give you the man."*

He reckoned that if he was given the opportunity to teach a child until they were seven years old, they would have sufficient knowledge and understanding so they would never drift from the

Roman Catholic faith. In the same way, we have seen young children profess faith, yet many people doubt they can have a genuine experience with God!

Statistics gathered by Child Evangelism Fellowship (CEF) state that eighty-five percent of individuals who are Christians claim they were converted before the age of fourteen. It is a fact that the older a person gets, the harder their heart becomes and the stronger they are tied to things of the world. These factors reduce the likelihood of older people getting saved, but thankfully, on frequent occasions, the Lord does soften the hearts of seniors and some do get saved in later life. Regrettably though, they have wasted many years where they could have served God and taken opportunities to be a witness for Him. They also miss out on His amazing love, divine protection and faithful provision.

Never doubt what God can do in the heart of a child. Some of the greatest evangelists were child-converts and millions of children are still being converted to Christ today. Many famous Christians and missionaries trusted in the Lord as children of primary school age. Bible expositor, Matthew Henry was converted at the age of six; hymn-writer, Isaac Watts at nine; and evangelist, Stephen Olford came to Christ on his seventh birthday. D.L. Moody was also quoted as saying:

> *"If I could relive my life, I would devote my entire ministry to reaching children for God."*

...Did he say this because children can believe with simple faith or because adults have too many entanglements in the world? Perhaps both!

CHAPTER FOURTEEN

When God Shows Up at School

W HENEVER WE TALK about school Bible Clubs, people who have not been involved in the work often wonder what exactly we mean, so I will endeavour to explain...

In the early days of Hope for Youth Ministries, my aim was to speak at an assembly in a public school each morning and then focus on five-day missions in churches in the evenings. However, before long, a number of the schools asked me if I would come in and spend longer with a single class of pupils as it would assist the school to deliver the religious studies part of the curriculum. After doing this for a few months, a number of teachers suggested to their principals I could do five-day Bible Clubs for the entire school. I met those principals and told them what format I used for the evening missions in churches at the time. I explained there was singing, memory verses, a Bible story and finally a quiz. One principal was quick to realise that through a Bible Club, children encounter almost every other academic subject!

...In every Bible story, there is a location such as Jericho in Israel – that's geography. All of the stories in the Bible are actual events, from the creation of the world until the life of Christ – that's history. There are more songs about the Lord Jesus Christ than any other person in the world – that's music, and when we add actions to them – that's physical education. When we teach stories such as the Ten Commandments or let the children calculate the scores of the quiz – that's mathematics. And so, after a bit of tweaking, the school Bible Clubs evolved from those simple beginnings into the mainstream focus of our ministry today. In the first year of Hope for Youth Ministries, I undertook about ten Bible Clubs in schools – then twenty the following year; followed by forty and so on until we have levelled off at around one hundred each academic year. Typically, the number of children attending a school Bible Club varies between fifty and five hundred, depending on the size of the school. We love going back to particular schools again the next year but it is important to continually look for new doors of opportunity to bring the gospel message to new children.

One of the reasons that children love the school Bible Clubs is because they are so interactive. With experience, we have learned that children like to move and fidget, so during the singing and memory verses, we get them to stand up and do actions. The secret for maintaining children's attention is to keep the Bible Club moving and let the children release all their energy during the singing and memory verse. Then, when it is time to teach the precious Word of God, the children sit reverently and are fascinated as we tell, teach and apply the stories of the Bible. Many of them have never heard about Moses splitting the Red Sea, Elijah going to heaven in a chariot, Daniel in the lions' den or any of the miracles performed by Jesus in the New Testament. I am convinced that children love Bible stories far more than anything they ever read in novels or watch on television. As well as the true stories being full of action and emotion, the children's hearts are touched when we bring in the story of salvation and explain that God desires to know each one of them personally.

Immediately after the lesson, we do a quiz to re-emphasise the central truths of the lesson. These are normally very lively with lots of interaction and competition. After the children get their prizes and the winning team is announced, we close the Bible Club with a song and prayer.

As the children leave, we give every one of them a gospel tract along with an activity worksheet and picture to colour in for the chance to win a prize the following day. On the rear of the worksheet, there is a space for the children to ask any question they have about God or the Bible. As the week progresses, we take some time to read out and answer the important ones. Sometimes, so much time is spent answering questions that we don't even have time for a quiz! An added benefit of inviting questions is that it helps me to grasp where the children stand spiritually, so I can tailor future lessons if certain truths need to be emphasised.

Whilst in many ways every Bible Club has the same format, each one of them is unique. I would like to share some vivid memories that stand out in my memory.

The first occurred during a lunchtime Bible Club at a school in Banbridge. It was the summer term and the kids were free to play outside, but each afternoon the majority of them scampered down the corridor and into the assembly hall. On Wednesday afternoon, we started the club by singing some of the choruses as we normally do, but we could sense there was a special atmosphere in the hall. The children sang with great gusto, yet between the songs, there was peculiar silence and you could have heard a pin drop.

A couple of volunteers taught the memory verse, so I stood to the side and watched on. I knew something unique was happening, but could not put my finger on it nor, to this day, try to describe it. The meeting just flowed really smoothly and those of us who spoke at the front felt a real clarity in our thoughts and boldness in our words. After the story, many children began to ask questions specifically about salvation and becoming a Christian. It thrilled our hearts to see several of them respond to the gospel challenge. As volunteers at the side of the hall counselled children and led them in prayer to the Lord, I was reminded just how powerful the Spirit of God really is.

On another occasion, Joanna and I, along with one of our volunteers, Cheryl, visited a school in Larne. As the children sang, at the beginning of the Bible Club, a child came forward and asked to speak with Cheryl. She moved to the side of the hall and began to talk to the child. Before they had finished talking, another child came over and waited to get speaking to her next. It was Cheryl's turn to teach the memory verse and bring the main lesson that day, but since she was counselling the children, Joanna and I stood in and kept the programme going. Almost like clockwork, right throughout the story as one child left Cheryl to sit down, another rose from within the gathering and made their way over to the side of the hall. The other children and the teachers seemed completely oblivious to what was going on, but God was moving and working in the hearts and lives of the children, as one after another, they put their trust in the Lord.

At another Bible Club in County Antrim, I was assisted by Cheryl and William. Just like in Larne, as soon as William started the singing, children began approaching Cheryl, wanting to give their lives to Jesus. I was sitting within earshot having a final glance over the lesson I was about to present. It was beautiful listening in on the sincerity of their questions as one by one, the children came to know the Lord. Their repentance was really genuine and even though they maybe didn't comprehend everything, they understood that the Lord Jesus was the only One who could take their sin away. Cheryl still refers to this club as the one where she never even got taking her coat off – as she was so busy ministering to children. After we packed up, we sat in the car park and shed tears of joy and praised God for His favour. We felt truly humbled that we were being used by God in such amazing circumstances.

Teachers at that school also remarked that whatever was happening in that Bible Club was making their children joyful and better behaved in class. They would say, "It's the most exciting thing that has ever come to the school." We would smile and say, "God is good all the time, and all the time God is good!"

In Portavogie one year, as we were packing up on Friday, a teacher asked if she could book us again for the following year because the children enjoyed it so much. She also confessed how the Bible Club made the children joyful, better behaved and more focused on school. I asked her if she had any idea why. Her response was remarkable: "The children told me that Colin said we should do everything in life as if we are doing it to please God!"

Another incident that sticks out occurred in a primary school on the Donegall Road in Belfast. I was in full-flow teaching a Bible story to over two hundred children when a little boy rose up and came to the front and said something to me. I assumed he was asking permission to go to the toilet, so I pointed him to the door – but he just stood there! He got my attention and looked directly into my eyes and said with conviction, "I want to become a Christian, Colin." I asked if he could wait until the end of the lesson, but he vehemently shook his head from side to side. I directed him over to one of the volunteers who counselled him and then led him to the Lord. The whole time, I kept telling the story and not one child was distracted by what was happening at the side of the hall. At another school, the Bible Club finished at home-time and a few kids wanted to get saved so we waited behind to chat with them. As we were counselling them, a football coach came in to set the hall up for after-school football. I hardly noticed him, but one wee girl waiting at the door shouted over, "Excuse me mate! You're gonna have to wait outside cause my mates are getting saved and that is more important than football!" The man was taken aback and gingerly turned around and walked back outside. It is amazing how earnest and bold some of these children are and how they take a commitment to Jesus so seriously.

At a lunchtime Bible Club a few miles from that inner-city school, we met a little girl called Bobbie. She was a troublesome girl with quite a difficult background and if I am honest, we did wonder what hope there was for her. The first day, she continually interrupted the meeting and distracted the other children. However, we persevered and the next day she got totally fixated on God and how He loved her so much, even though nobody else did. At the end of the meeting, she remained behind to talk about her salvation and after we went over the gospel message again, she accepted Christ as her Saviour!

The next day, we had barely started the Bible Club two minutes until she interrupted the meeting again. "Excuse me, Colin," she butted in. "I need to say something". Then, with everyone's eyes and attention focused on her, she shared how she got saved and how happy God made her feel. Next, she went round the group pointing to one child after another and asking if they were saved yet. Some of the children put their hands up and then Bobbie pointed at one girl and told her to take her hand down. She exclaimed, "You're not a Christian because you still have sin in your heart!" I bit my lip and let her continue. "And if any of you are not Christians already, you should become one today!" Suddenly a teacher walked into the room and Bobbie turned to her. "Excuse me, Miss! Are you a Christian? Because if you're not, you can be!" Wee Bobbie told us she was going to tell all the children, teachers and even the principal that she had become a Christian – such boldness from a new-born babe in Christ!

What alarms us most about city children, more so than those from the country, is that very few of them attend Sunday school and the majority of them have no idea who Jesus is. I believe this is why so many of them respond immediately to the gospel. If they have not been brought up in a family who attends church, most of them are living in ignorance, just like the Philippian jailer was in Acts 16. We read how the jailer responded immediately to Paul and Silas' simple presentation of the gospel and with these children, it is no different. There is a saying, 'the same sun that melts the wax, hardens the clay' – sadly, many folks who were brought up hearing the gospel message week in, week out, have become hardened to it. Yet, for many of these children, the story of redemption is such an extravagant gift offered to them, that the obvious response is to grab it with both hands and get saved. It is unfortunate that many Christians do not believe such incidents are even possible, but the Bible clearly tells us that *"whosoever shall call upon the name of the Lord shall be saved" (Romans 10:13),* – and this includes children.

When working with children, we do have plenty of funny moments too! One day I told the story of Naaman from 2 Kings 5 – how he dipped in the River Jordan seven times, his leprosy disappeared and his skin became like that of a new-born baby. In the quiz, one of the questions was "What did Naaman's skin look like after he washed in the River Jordan?" A little boy put his hand up and said "A new-born baby's bum!" It sounded so funny and the children giggled for ages.

On another occasion, after teaching the story of Zacchaeus the tax collector, a question in the quiz was "What was Zacchaeus' job?" A young boy in primary one raised his hand and shouted, "A taxi driver!" I thought he was joking but when I looked at him, he was so earnest – I didn't have the heart to tell him he was wrong as the whole school was laughing. The simplicity of a child amazes me and makes me laugh every day. Another day, my final question to the children was "What do you have to do to go to heaven?" A little boy instantly shot up his hand and when I asked him for the answer, with a sincere face, he said, "Die!" It wasn't exactly the answer I was expecting but it had an element of truth in it!

There are numerous instances of similar things that have happened in schools and it would take many pages to mention. So many children have been won for Christ or been touched by the Spirit of God through the outreach of Hope for Youth Ministries. To help the children grow spiritually, we have produced literature which we distribute free of charge. One of our most used books is called 'Stepping Stones' and is primarily for those who don't have the privilege of being taken to Sunday school or children's meetings. It is packed full of Scripture and practical teaching on how to live the Christian life as a child. We give one of these books to every child who professes faith, as well as a Bible if they haven't already got one at home.

Occasionally, older children write down on their worksheets that they would like a Bible. We do not announce, advertise or offer them as gifts, so such children obviously have an earnest desire to learn more about God when they ask for a Bible themselves. At one school in Dungannon, there were fifteen different nationalities represented and many of the children asked for a Bible. One of them was a girl from Lithuania who had been saved and said she had no other way to learn about God than to read the Bible herself. At another school in Lurgan, many Roman Catholic children were amongst those who requested Bibles.

One thing we have learned is that God is not bound or limited as to how and when He works. Some months He saves over a hundred children and other months just a few. We may not understand the moving of God's Spirit, but our responsibility is just to keep on preaching the unchangeable gospel message and relax in the knowledge that the results are completely in God's control.

Despite my many faults and limitations, sometimes extraordinary 'God-things' take place beyond our control. As I have already said, it really is amazing what happens when God shows up at school.

Here are some examples of what I or others have said about the school Bible Clubs:

"God has been present in this school like never before. The children have been touched and moved towards thinking about God in a very particular way. Can you please come back and do this again for the children because they loved it."

A school principal

"On Wednesday after the Bible Club, a child in my class came up to talk with me. I thought there was a problem, but they asked me if I would pray with them and help them become a Christian. So right there in the classroom, we prayed and the child received Jesus. It is the first time in my twenty-seven years of teaching I have ever experienced this. God has moved

this week and that child is not the only one – it's beautiful."

A school teacher

"Some of my small girls at hockey training last night were telling me how they became Christians in school! Keep powering on Colin!"

An encouraged hockey coach

"Brilliant week in Richhill, Colin. We were blessed and it was wonderful how many children testified of how they got saved. I'm delighted our wee Samuel was one of them!"

Samuel's mum

"Isaac was buzzing after school today. The Bible Club made his day and he can't wait until tomorrow. He said it was totally AWESOME! Keep up the fantastic work. 'Jesus, all for Jesus.' Thanks."

Isaac's mum

"I was encouraged on Friday when I went to a school assembly and the principal brought me into his office and put his hand on my shoulder and prayed for me before I spoke to the children. Pray for the teachers and principals in our schools who seek to maintain a strong Christian ethos and are open for assemblies and Bible Clubs."

Colin Tinsley

CHAPTER FIFTEEN

Floods of Revival

KELLS IS A little country village near the town of Ballymena. Those familiar with church history will recognise it as the epicentre of the great spiritual awakening that took place in Northern Ireland back in 1859. The origin of the revival has been traced back to the old schoolhouse in the ancient village, where a young man called James McQuilken and his three friends met to pray in September 1857. They had recently started a children's meeting but all of them felt very inadequate and inexperienced for the work, so they sought God and asked Him to bless their efforts.

For a couple of months, the four of them studied the Word and prayed without any visible results. Two other men later joined them and on New Year's Day 1858 the first conversion took place. Over the course of that year, many other young men joined them in prayer until there were over fifty of them crammed into the little schoolhouse. They pleaded that God would pour out His Spirit upon their community, beginning with the children's meeting many of them helped at. The attendance rose steadily until the building was overflowing with children! Many of the children who attended got saved and by the springtime of 1859, dozens of adults in the area were also putting their trust in Christ on a daily basis. It is estimated that over one hundred thousand people put their trust in Christ over the course of that blessed year alone. The high number of evangelical churches still meeting in the area today bear testimony to the revival – all because a few young lads had a burden to see children in their village saved.

In the years since the revival, many evangelists have held gospel crusades in this 'Bible-belt' area and witnessed hundreds of people come to Christ. Sadly though, in recent years the town of Ballymena has been blighted by drugs and substance abuse and scores of people in the area have died prematurely as a result. It is a huge problem that is rife all across the country and sadly most of the casualties are young people. Thankfully, there are many wonderful Christian ministries who help folks bound by addictions, but anyone involved in such work will testify that only a small percentage of addicts ever break the habit.

What has all of this got to do with children's evangelism? Well, the best way to reduce the number of drug addicts and tragedies as a result of their misguided behaviour is to reach children with the gospel! If a child gets saved early in life and grows up following the precepts of Scripture, they will realise their body is the temple of the Holy Spirit and they are commanded to glorify God in their bodies *(1 Corinthians 6:19-20)*. Rather than willingly destroying their bodies by dabbling with drugs, they will desire to look after their health so they may serve God all their days to the best of their ability. Furthermore, good Christian company will help keep them away from those who take drugs, and if they ever are offered some, the Lord will give them strength to resist the temptation.

It's worth noting that whenever God pours out a blessing, whether it's over a town, a church congregation or even an individual's life, the enemy often tries to destroy what God has done. Scripture is right up-to-date when Jesus exclaimed: *"the thief cometh not, but for to steal, and to kill, and to destroy: I come that they might have life and that they might have it more abundantly"* (John 10:10).

Despite the efforts of the enemy to completely extinguish the fire that has been burning since 1859, I have witnessed first-hand that God is still working in the area. A few years ago, I was invited to a school in the Ballykeel area of Ballymena to conduct an after-school Bible Club. On the first day, while I was setting up my equipment in the assembly hall, I had an unusual feeling that God was going to do something special that week.

Gary, a good friend who lives near Ballymena, came along to assist me each day that week. His boss kindly agreed to let him start work a couple of hours early each morning so he was finished in time for the Bible Club. After the lesson on the first day, a number of children approached us and enquired about getting saved. They were very sincere and really wanted to please God with their lives. On Wednesday, Gary was meant to be leading the meeting but from the moment he entered the hall, children surrounded him and asked him one question after another about the stories, memory verses and God's way of salvation. Such was the commotion, he didn't even make it to the front of the hall the entire time. I led the meeting in his place and when I glanced over I could see tears of joy in his eyes as one child after another settled the matter of salvation with God. The meeting continued as normal for all the other children, but those who were under conviction responded to the challenge of having peace with God and the assurance of eternal life.

As the week progressed, the blessing of God intensified further. The teachers told us that the children talked about the Bible stories all day and sang the songs during class and outside in the playground. Many of them came up to the front and told their friends when they put their trust in Jesus and their experiences since. Some were saved at home, others in Sunday school and some at the Bible Club that very week!

In the staffroom, the teachers also discussed the Bible Club and the impact it was having on the children. The last few days, some of them sat in and even the principal came along to witness what was going on. We asked one of the teachers, who we knew was a Christian, to play the piano and sing a song. She began playing and softly sang, 'Shine Jesus Shine.' The presence and power of God filled that assembly hall and all the children joined in the singing. It was a beautiful moment, which left us all speechless. Our eyes filled up with tears as we sat in the presence of a benevolent God accomplishing His divine purposes. I whispered to Gary, 'How do you explain that?' He just shook his head, with tears in his eyes and whispered, 'You can't!'

On another occasion, we were invited to Kilkeel by the local Baptist church, to conduct a children's mission in a barn on the perimeter of the town. The church had originally planned a mission for adults, but then someone suggested having a special week of children's meetings as well. They decided to have the children's meetings in the barn at 6:30pm and have it vacated in time for the adults' meetings, at which the church's pastor, Mr George McConnell, would speak.

The week before the mission, I went up to Kilkeel early one morning to meet the pastor and some of the men organising the mission. We prayed together and discussed some of the practicalities over breakfast. Then we visited the local primary schools to take the morning assemblies and invite schoolchildren to the mission. We had no idea what God was going to do through the venture, but we had high hopes and a great sense of expectation that God would save many souls.

On the first night of the mission, the leaders panicked because there weren't enough buses to lift all the children. At one stop in Annalong, there were over thirty children waiting to board a fifteen-seater minibus! Knowing that additional journeys to neighbouring villages would delay the start of the meeting, the men got straight onto their mobile phones to arrange additional transport. A local bus firm obliged and within minutes they had a bus and driver on the road bringing children to the mission. Such was the community spirit in the town that the owner refused to take payment for the bus or the driver's time.

After a short delay on the first night, we had over a dozen volunteers from surrounding areas lined up at the front of the barn. The music started and the volunteers led the children in gospel choruses and taught them the actions. They were all really enthusiastic and the singing was so loud, I'm sure the residents of the local housing estates heard every word!

Midway through the Tuesday night meeting, a breakthrough came! In a period of about five minutes during the story, without any prompting, a number of children got up individually and went to the helpers sitting around the edges of the barn for counsel. This scenario continued throughout the week and much use was made of a smaller barn next door, where the pastor and volunteers counselled and prayed with children. A common trait was that they all wanted the matter dealt with immediately and couldn't even wait until the meeting was over.

Back in the main barn, the buzz and excitement continued as we faithfully preached the wonderful, life-saving message of the gospel. Many of the worksheets we sent home with the children to colour in came back with the 'I have a question' box at the bottom filled in with the words, 'How can I become a Christian?' When such questions are asked, we cannot ignore them but are obligated to follow each child up. Again, the van shelves were emptied as many Stepping Stones books and Bibles were given out to children who made a profession of faith. Praise God that over thirty children were counselled for salvation over the course of the week. The local church was fired up for months after and followed the children up with invitations to their Sunday school and children's meeting.

It's very humbling to be standing at the front, teaching a Bible lesson and observing children praying with volunteers all around the hall. It brings much joy to my heart thinking about all the children who have got saved over the years, but then when I consider the many who haven't it really burdens me. For many of those who haven't, the reason is often that they've never received a clear presentation of the gospel. This is why we cannot slacken but must keep going on and reaching out – Jesus reminded us that time is short and *"the night cometh, when no man can work"* *(John 9:24).*

Another memorable week in the ministry was the second week of June 2012. We headed to the south Tyrone area and conducted Bible Clubs in primary schools in four different villages. The first school we visited each morning was Denamona Primary in Fintona. When we arrived on Monday morning, I didn't know a single child, but as the week progressed, the children built up such rapport with me it was like we'd been friends for years! Some of the children prayed and thanked God for how I was able to come to their school to tell them about Jesus. If there's one thing that can melt a man's heart, it's the sound of a child talking to the Lord. We were experiencing a real outpouring of God's Spirit.

There was no modern music, fancy clothes, drama or anything else but the focus was solely on the Word of God.

When I was leaving the school on the Thursday, I noticed many of the children were sitting in little groups in the playground. Initially I thought they were playing a game, but when I looked closer I realised they were praying. The next day some of them told me they were praying for the Bible Club and that God would speak to children who were still not saved. They were in touch with God and wanted to see Him save their friends. After the final club in Aughnacloy, which was at the end of the school day, a mother who was collecting her daughter asked the teacher if she could come in to speak with me. She told me she couldn't thank us enough for visiting the school. Her daughter was already a Christian but that week, four of her friends had got saved and she was planning to invite her friends over to study the Bible together. Although we didn't know anything about those four girls getting saved, the Lord was speaking on long after our voices were silent. I often wonder how many more children there are out there who have trusted the Lord in the privacy of their own bedrooms, living rooms or on their mother's lap. It may be hundreds, perhaps thousands? I have no idea, but the Lord knows, and one day, I will meet them all in heaven. I look forward to them saying, "Hey Colin, thanks for coming to my school because that's when I first heard about Jesus!"

Below are some of my memoirs and others' accounts of the missions mentioned above:

"A great start to a week of Bible Clubs in the Ballymena area. Four men are helping me today – thanks so much to Andrew Thompson, Mark Millar, Paul McIntyre and Gary Adair. Cheryl McIntyre even popped in during her lunchbreak to show her support!"

Colin Tinsley

"Another amazing week reaching the children in Coleraine, Ballymena and Cullybackey. It is always very special to see the looks of appreciation on the faces of the children when the Bible Club comes to their school. Heaven came down to the little school in Ballymena and eleven children trusted Christ. Seeing is believing! The children love these clubs! God is good and I just love reaching these kids with the gospel."

Colin Tinsley

"The powerful move of God that we are currently witnessing has come to Kilkeel and over thirty children were counselled for salvation. Great help and leadership from Pastor George McConnell and the team of helpers from Kilkeel Baptist. One of our volunteers, Cheryl McClintock, has taken the full month off work and has been a tremendous help to us. She has personally led over a hundred souls to Christ during this time. Pray that God will challenge these young volunteers and they would go all-out for Him. May has been the greatest month we have ever experienced, with over two hundred children coming to the Lord for salvation. Their teachers and parents are bearing testimony to the changes in their little lives. It's great to be in the work!"

Colin Tinsley

"What a wonderful and blessed week it has been! To hear the volume of almost three hundred kids singing and praising the name of Jesus is a mighty experience. We prayed for showers of blessing and God saw fit to pour them upon us. To see a large number of children calling upon Christ melts the heart of the believer. Even now as I write this message, I am filling up with the thought of the droves of children hearing about the Lord. Praise God from whom all blessings flow. God has been so good and moved in a mighty way. To Him be all the glory!"

A church leader from Kilkeel

"Colin, thank you so much for all that you have done this week with our children in Kilkeel. My little daughter Julia told me on Wednesday that she had asked our Lord into her life on Monday evening at the barn. A Christian at seven years old! May God guide her through her life and always be in her heart!"

A joyful parent from Kilkeel

"Please pass my thanks on to all the team. My little granddaughter Lucy, aged five put her trust and faith in the Lord. May He continue to bless your work for Him."

A grandmother from Kilkeel

"Thank-you for a wonderful week! My three children never missed a night. I thank God for your witness and teaching. My daughter Ellie came home and told us she got saved on Wednesday evening. I will be praying for you all as you continue to spread the Good News of salvation. 'My word shall not return unto me void.' God bless."

An appreciative mother from Kilkeel

"Don't know if you remember me or not, but you came to Denamona Primary School in Fintona and you're the reason I am a Christian today. Thanks and remember me when you come back to our school on Monday."

A pupil from Denamona

CHAPTER SIXTEEN

My Local Village

A S I SHARED earlier, Joanna and I have settled in the village of Kinallen, five miles south of Dromore in County Down. A couple of years after establishing Hope for Youth Ministries and conducting Bible Clubs all over Northern Ireland, we felt we ought to organise one in our own locality. Initially, we booked a small hall in the neighbouring village of Dromara, but when we realised how many children attended the local primary schools, we reckoned it wouldn't be big enough so we found a larger one. When the mission began, we were relieved that we had chosen the larger hall as children from Kinallen, Dromara and Dromore all landed in. We were delighted at the response in our own 'Jerusalem'. The next year we booked the local primary school in Kinallen and the principal gave me a set of keys on the Monday and told me to drop them in the following week. The school is only a stone's throw away from our house, so after the Bible Club each night we often invited the volunteers round for a cup of tea and fellowship. These are precious times as we enjoyed each other's company and prayed for the work.

One morning the next week, I called into the school to return the keys and pay them for the use of their facilities. I was taken aback when they told me it was completely free because they appreciated what I did for the children! We have returned to the school every year since and Kinallen is now one of the biggest missions we do each year, often drawing in two hundred children every night. We have had the joy and privilege of seeing dozens of children profess faith in God from our own neighbourhood and that is extra special.

For the majority of the evening missions we conduct each year, we use three or four minibuses to take local children to and from the venue. Dozens of drivers and helpers volunteer to look after the logistics of this part of the mission and thankfully, many churches and friends from all over the country lend us their buses which saves the ministry thousands of pounds.

On the whole, the children's parents are very supportive and genuinely appreciate what we do for their children. One evening, as I stood in the school carpark trying to get children onto their designated bus, a man slipped an envelope into my hand. I was so focused on the children's safety as cars moved back and forwards, I didn't even get a proper glance at the man. After everyone had gone home and I had locked up the school, I took the envelope out of my pocket and opened it to find a large sum of money inside. At the time, we really needed it and again the Lord honoured us for being faithful to Him and met our needs through the gifts of His people. Such provision enables us to keep going full steam ahead, without having to ask for any form of payment or having to cut back on the work due to lack of finance. Every donation, regardless of the value really encourages us and gives us reason to rejoice at how the Lord continually looks after us. On occasions we do have collections for a particular aspect of the work and teams frequently organise fundraisers when going on mission trips to Poland and other countries. This is to help bring children from poor backgrounds to camp who otherwise could not afford it.

Not far from Kinallen is the old market town of Dromore. After praying for an opening in the town for a few years, a new principal was appointed in the primary school, and not long after taking up her post, I contacted her and asked if we could do an after-school Bible Club for a week. This turned out to be one of the greatest after-school clubs we have ever had. From the moment we set foot in the building, there was a buzz of excitement amongst the children and we could feel they were ready to hear about Jesus. They loved the singing and sat completely still during the Bible lesson, taking in every word. Before long, one after another, children started coming to the Lord with the help of volunteers to counsel them. On Thursday afternoon we had a testimony time, where children were given an opportunity to tell their friends about their faith. The principal was almost in tears as she sat in amongst us. When the Bible Club was over, she wrote us a beautiful letter thanking us for coming.

Heading west from Dromore towards Lurgan is another little village called Maralin. Back in 2010, my good friends Kyle and Elaine Graham had the vision to organise a week-long evening Bible Club in the village primary school. This has become an annual event in our calendar and in the run up to the club each year, we meet in their home to pray that God will bless the faithful preaching of His Word. Just like in Kinallen, the school principal could not have been more obliging or helpful towards us. For the Maralin Bible Club, we run four buses to cover the Moira, Dollingstown and Donacloney areas and most nights, the school assembly hall is packed to capacity.

On the Saturday morning after this mission in 2017, I got a call from Kyle as he was returning one of the buses to its owner. He told me how after the Friday meeting, all the volunteers came round to his house for fellowship after a blessed week. As they were all eating a Chinese takeaway downstairs, his five-year-old son, Matthew, was praying to Jesus in his bedroom upstairs. He told the Lord he really wanted to become a Christian and asked Him to take away all his sin and help him live as a Christian. So, even after the mission finished, another child got saved! Kyle and Elaine were over the moon and it gave everyone another reason to rejoice! Dozens of children have trusted in Christ at this mission in Maralin over the years.

Below are some of my memoirs regarding these local Bible Clubs:

"The attendance at our local Bible Club in Kinallen has increased to almost two hundred children. Ten children have now trusted in the Lord plus four others in one of the schools today. One parent told her child they couldn't go tonight because the mother had another meeting. The child told her mum, 'How would you like it if Granny said that you couldn't go to a meeting and hear about God?!' An incredible week and the best is yet to come!"

"This week has been one of our most fruitful so far reaching children with the gospel. Dromore has been on my heart for many years and we have witnessed more children putting their trust in the Lord Jesus here than at any other club we have conducted thus far! The testimony time was just amazing and teachers have reported that the Bible Club is all that the children have been talking about in school. Parents get challenged regarding their position with God through the testimony of their children. It's just brilliant! The kids want the Bible Club to stay for another week!"

"Like last year, Maralin Primary School seems to be the busiest Bible Club so far, with four buses ferrying children to and from the meetings. Thirty volunteers assist in reaching over two hundred children. This week children have professed faith every night with many of the volunteers helping the children. There is such a stillness and the presence of God is so real in the meetings."

"Tonight, we witnessed one of the most amazing nights ever in the final mission of this week near Moira. Before the meeting, a young boy wanted to get saved. As I led him to the Lord another three girls came over and said they too wanted to get saved. The presence of the Lord came down as children got the opportunity to testify unto the Lord. It lasted for almost half an hour as one after another, children got up to speak. We discovered children had got saved every night this week at home that we weren't even aware of. Also tonight, during the meeting, another boy called upon the Lord. We had no time for the story, quiz or even a song to finish. Another seventeen children have called upon the Lord this week – these are very special days of the Lord raising up an army of little children. Recently we have witnessed school principals and parents in tears at children professing Christ as Lord! I love this work so much and count it such an honour to be used of God to reach these kids for Christ. Moving next week to Augher, Portadown and finishing off in Banbridge Baptist. Pray for all these small children!"

CHAPTER SEVENTEEN

The Meaning of Camp

AS A YOUNG boy, the highlight of my year was the annual Boys' Brigade camping weekend. It was held at Tollymore Forest Park, near Newcastle in County Down. I loved every minute of it and even back then, I thought it would be wonderful to arrange such camps for children when I was older. Joanna also, as a young girl went camping with her family and loved the outdoors. Praise God that for over ten years now, this dream has become a living reality.

The first camp I organised was during my year of deputation with the church mission board. It was a weekend for young people in Tollymore and I advertised it in church newsletters and amongst friends. It turned out to be a really successful camp – completely different to anything the teens had ever experienced before since it was real camping in proper army tents. As I didn't own any equipment, I borrowed what I could from BB companies and hired the rest. We had blessed meetings and great times of fellowship; especially singing around the campfire and listening to the young people share how God was working in their lives.

The next two years, we expanded the camp ministry and ran a weeklong children's camp after the teens' weekend. The children and leaders loved it, so we were confident it would continue for many years. I thought it would be prudent to buy tents rather than hiring them each year, so I bought lots of cheap Indian-style tepee tents that were light to transport and spacious for the kids to sleep in. We always had great weather so I reckoned they were just perfect.

On the morning camp was due to commence, a team of volunteers erected the tents before the young people arrived that afternoon. It was a hot summer's day and there was no indication that the weather would change anytime soon. When one of the volunteers told me a storm was forecast that Saturday night, I didn't take him seriously as he was always a real joker! The teens arrived and played games until it was time for our evening meeting round the campfire. Then after supper, everyone retired to their tents, while a few leaders stayed up, as they always do, until the last camper was sleeping. About midnight, Joanna and I went to our tent and soon fell asleep.

In the middle of the night, I was awakened by the sound of rain hitting the tent and by the wind, which had become quite boisterous. I got up and checked the campsite but the tents were all fine and a few leaders were still about so I went back to sleep. The next thing I remember was my niece, Cherie, popping her head into our tent and screaming that her tent was blowing away! The winds had reached gale-force and the first thing that came into my mind was my responsibility for the safety of all the young people. It was like having a nightmare, but I knew it was real as the rain pelted down on our tent and the wind swayed it violently to and fro. I was nearly knocked over when I stood up to pull my jeans on. When I looked outside, the teepees were flapping about like kites, even though they were all still firmly anchored to the ground. The big meeting tent was also blowing about and one side had already lifted and wrecked the kitchen!

Our first priority was the safety of the teenagers, so we woke them up and marched them up through the forest to another campsite where we found sturdy army tents firmly fastened to the ground. Strangely, we didn't have to explain ourselves or ask for shelter because there wasn't anyone around. We left the campers in the safe care of a few leaders and the rest of us scampered back to try to save the big tent from floating off into the forest. We lined all the cars up adjacent to the tent and tied the canvas to them. It was a long night, but thankfully everyone was safe and the big tent didn't blow away. The next morning, the sun shone brightly against a clear blue sky and only a gentle breeze was noticeable in the campsite. If anyone had just arrived that morning, they would never have believed that a fierce storm had ripped through the campsite hours earlier. We praised the Lord and thanked Him for protecting us all. We later discovered that the tents on the other campsite were a permanent fixture and that particular night was the only time they were not hired that entire summer!

The remainder of camp went really well, but when we got home we spent a lot of time pondering if we should organise any more camps under canvas. Although God worked mightily in the lives of many children and teenagers, we had a huge responsibility for their safety. We reckoned that those who had attended that year would be too afraid to return or their parents would not permit them to come. After putting the camp on the back burner for some months, one day we got a letter from a camper in which she shared her experience of the storm. She told us that even though she was scared, she prayed God would keep everyone safe and it really encouraged her faith to see her prayer answered. At the end of the letter, she asked that we put her name on the list for camp the following summer. We took this as a sign to continue the camp ministry but realised we needed to make some changes to guarantee the safety and wellbeing of the campers, regardless of the weather. The only solution we came up with was to purchase proper army tents, similar to the ones we took shelter in at the other campsite. I sourced some at an army surplus store in England and went over and purchased sixteen of them.

After trying a few different camp combinations, we have now settled on two separate week-long children's camps with a youth weekend in between. At the three camps, everyone remains in the beautiful surroundings of the forest park the entire time. It is a massive logistical operation in comparison to hiring a residential camp centre, but nothing beats the excitement and sense of adventure living in tents. In recent years, we have catered for over four hundred campers and leaders and it's truly amazing how folks from all over the country offer their time and talents to make camp happen. The day before camp, twenty to thirty friends come along to put up the large tent and erect the smaller tents, set up the kitchen, lay out the chairs, etc. Then when camp is over, we have to take it all down again. We have running water and an electrical generator for the big tent and have the use of permanent toilets and shower blocks a short distance away. Joanna plans all the meals and we keep all the food in big fridges and freezers we purchased second-hand. A favourite visitor to camp is our Golden Retriever dog, Tas. He has attended every camp we have ever done at Tollymore and the kids love his company. Although due to old age, he has now retired from camping in Tollymore.

Whilst the camps are an intense time of fun and adventure especially with the slippery slope and swimming in the river, the primary purpose of camp is to teach children the Word of God. A secondary benefit is that the children have an opportunity to look upon committed Christian leaders as role-models, twenty-four hours a day. Obviously, everyone has their faults, but we do our best to live transparent lives before them. Our desire is that they go home knowing that Christian adults can have great times of fun together without drinking alcohol or using foul language, etc.

When the weather permits, we go deep into the forest for our morning meetings. In those beautiful surroundings, the children sing out lively choruses that uplift the name of Jesus. Then, we have sword drills and scavenger hunts before settling down to focus on the Word of God. After the lesson, we have a quiz with exciting challenges and sing a few more choruses before closing the meeting in prayer. On our way back to the campsite, everyone gathers branches and sticks to burn in the campfire later that night.

God has really blessed our camps at Tollymore and we've witnessed souls coming to Christ at every camp. In the summer of 2017, we had an amazing breakthrough when God came down in a remarkable way and twenty-nine children were counselled and won for Christ. We do not take this for granted but return each year with an expectancy for the Lord to save souls. After all, His Word does state: *"the Lord is not slack concerning his promise, as some men count slackness; but is longsuffering to us-ward, not willing that any should perish, but that all should come to repentance"* *(2 Peter 3:9).*

On the final night of camp, we always have a testimony time where children are given the opportunity to tell everyone when they became a Christian and how it has changed them. Often it lasts for over an hour and dozens of children boldly tell what Jesus has done in their lives. It is a very touching time of deep consecration and reflection in the heart of every believer. God uses it to challenge the hearts of those children who still do not know Him. It's what we call, 'the meaning of camp'.

In addition to the weather occasionally giving us problems at camp, sometimes children get homesick whilst there are others who are just disruptive. One year, we had a girl who was particularly troublesome and it seemed she took delight in agitating the other children. Numerous times, her group leader and I spoke to her about her attitude and behaviour, but it didn't seem to have any lasting effect on her. Then one afternoon in the middle of the week, she came over and asked if she could speak with me. I was expecting another complaint about something but she started to tell me her story of how she realised her life was a mess. She poured out her heart and admitted that everywhere she went she got into trouble and deep down she didn't want to be that sort of person. She asked if I could pray for her and lead her in a prayer to become a Christian. As I listened to this troublesome kid pray, I couldn't contain my tears as she came to Jesus right in front of me. She sobbed her way to Jesus, asking Him to forgive her past and to help her live a life pleasing to Him in the future. The immediate transformation in the life and behaviour of this child was incredible and really made an impact on all the other children and leaders! This is just one of many unique stories I could share about children who have found the Lord at Tollymore Bible camps.

Of all the teams and camps we lead around the world, Tollymore is definitely our favourite. The fellowship with other leaders and witnessing them being blessed and built up in their faith as they minister to local children warms our hearts. Most years at Tollymore, we have a number of volunteers who go through the waters of baptism in the Shimna river that flows through the Forest Park. It's a real joy to facilitate this as well as being a great witness to all the children.

The week after our camps finished at Tollymore in 2017, we returned to the field to reflect and give thanks to the Lord. For some it's just a field but for others it's where they found Jesus. The Spirit of God was present and worked in lives that summer in ways we had never witnessed before.

As camp only accounts for two weeks of the school summer holidays, a few years ago we felt exercised to look for other ways to reach children when they are off school. Then one day, the owner of a caravan park contacted me and asked if we had ever conducted our Bible Clubs in caravan parks. I admitted to her that I'd never thought about it, but it sounded an excellent idea. When I came off the phone I couldn't believe that I had never considered that before, so I contacted the owners of a dozen caravan parks in Newcastle, Cranfield, Portrush and Portstewart. All of them gave me permission to hold Bible Clubs on their sites over the Easter and summer holiday periods.

When we arrived at the first caravan park in Cranfield, a little girl was already sitting waiting for us. I noticed she was really enthusiastic during the singing and throughout the lesson she listened impeccably. Afterwards, as I was packing up she came over and asked me if I would help her become a Christian. She seemed to understand the way of salvation quite well but had never made a decision to trust the Lord to save her. I gladly answered her questions and then led her to Christ that very moment. Whenever we asked her where she was from, she told us she lived at the park and we later learned it was her mum who initially contacted me about doing Bible Clubs in caravan parks – isn't that amazing?

Another fond memory was meeting two little friends who were with their families at a caravan park in Newcastle. Both of them got saved on the same evening at the Bible Club. Then nine months later, I was in their school and they came running over and asked, "Colin, do you remember us?" With a puzzled expression on my face, I asked them for a hint and explained that I meet thousands of children every year. They said, "We're the two girls who hid your water pistol at the caravan park in Newcastle! Remember you helped us to become Christians?" Then it dawned on me who they were and it really cheered my heart seeing them so full of life and rejoicing in the Lord.

Another vivid memory I have is of a young lad called James who came to a Bible Club at a caravan park in Portrush. After the meeting, he reminded me we had visited his school in County Cavan a few months earlier. He said he wanted to get saved after that club but didn't know what to do. So right there, we opened the Bible and showed him what steps he needed to take to become a Christian. It thrilled our hearts to realise that God had orchestrated this reunion so he could finally get saved.

Due to the nature of the caravan park ministry, some of the Bible Clubs are small, while others are huge. If it isn't raining, we hold it beside the play area so that we draw as many children in as possible. However, if it rains, most of the parks have a function room which they let us use. Many Christian parents appreciate their children being taught the ways of the Lord while they're on holiday, whilst other parents are just glad to get some time to themselves and send their children along!

In August 2017, one week we conducted nine Bible Clubs, which is the most we have ever done. That equated to nine meetings every day or forty-five over the course of the week! Although the number is not so important, we believe this is an excellent way to reach hundreds of children with the gospel. Without the help of a willing band of volunteers, this ministry couldn't happen, so we're thankful that each year the Lord stirs up a faithful group of volunteers who sacrifice their holidays to serve Him. These days, many young adults spend most of their holidays working to finance their studies or motoring expenses, so we know they make a big sacrifice to volunteer. However, the Lord is no man's debtor and all of them return home full of the joy of the Lord.

Below are short testimonies from camps in Tollymore:

"Tollymore Forest Park was brilliant! The camp was wonderful thanks to all of the helpers. The water fights and slippery slope were unreal! I loved every single moment and you can be sure to see me next year. This camp has helped me grow as a Christian."

A camper

"Would just like to congratulate you on the work you do. Niall became a Christian after your summer camp in Tollymore and has very much stuck to his promise and is indeed leading a better life. Thank you and see you next year."

A mother

Below are some testimonies from the caravan parks:

"We have just completed Easter Bible Clubs in the caravan parks at Cranfield, Newcastle and the North Coast. Over five hundred kids were reached and

almost twenty of them trusted in the Lord! Totally amazing times – I just love it! Parents have come forward and told us how they appreciate the impact the Bible Clubs are having in their children's lives. Stepping things up now coming into May and June, with an average of four or five missions every week. Next week in Maghaberry, Antrim and my original home village of Dundrod."

Colin Tinsley

"My two children, Liana and Tyler are attending Hilltop Holiday Bible Club. They also went to the one at Ballykeel Primary School and really love them. They have returned home both days so excited and are looking forward to the rest of the week. Thanks to all the team for sharing with our kids!"

A mother of children at a caravan park

CHAPTER EIGHTEEN

Back to Poland We Go

"HEY, COLIN! WOULD Joanna and you like to come on a mission trip to Poland with us?" This request came from a group of students who attended the Christian Union at the University of Ulster campus in Coleraine. They were planning to conduct a Christian camp in Warsaw for orphans and children who came from poor and disadvantaged homes. They had been in contact with a Christian man called Henryk, who ran a foodbank ministry based at the Warsaw Baptist Bible Seminary. The strategy of his ministry was to deliver food to poor families who were on the social security register; then once he earned their trust, he invited their children to a Christian camp. While at the camps, many of the children trusted in the Lord, so that gave Henryk an opening to speak to their parents about their need of salvation as well.

This opportunity was presented to us just a few months after we started Hope for Youth Ministries. Working in Poland was part of our vision, but I didn't envisage the door opening so soon. Unfortunately, the dates of the camp didn't suit Joanna as she was involved in an art exhibition. I, on the other hand, was free so I was delighted to accept their invitation and signed up for the team. A few of them had been out with Henryk before and knew the setup, but it was a big step into the unknown for me. On previous trips, the foreign teams were only responsible for organising an activity programme for the children and the Christian Polish leaders taught the children about the Bible in their dorms at night. However, at the first team meeting, Henryk said he felt the time was right for the Northern Irish team to conduct a meeting each morning and evening as well, so the children would get lots of Bible teaching. He asked if anyone on the team could teach a Bible lesson and everyone looked at each other hoping someone else would respond! After a moment, I broke the silence and said, "I can!" Most of the students looked at me in surprise as if to say, "Can you really?" – not aware that I had recently started a full-time children's ministry.

We had a fabulous time at camp getting to know the kids through the workshops and games, with the aid of interpreters. However, the real highlight for me was having the opportunity to present the gospel to them, just like I did in missions at home. Henryk was delighted with how our team was able to complement the ministry of the Polish Christian leaders and during the week he asked me to pray about returning to Poland. He said he had contact with hundreds of children and was willing to organise lots of camps, but he needed someone like me to bring my Bible and preach to them. Many of these children were from different areas, so the camps had huge potential to reach thousands of Polish people who had never heard the gospel message before.

Even before Henryk spoke to me about returning someday, in the quieter moments of camp I spent a lot of time in prayer asking the Lord if He was identifying Henryk as a potential mission partner in Poland. I left Poland without making any commitments to Henryk, but I was certain the Lord was opening the door of opportunity for us. When I got home and told Joanna all about camp and how Henryk kept in contact with the children and their families afterwards, she was thrilled. After some discussion, we planned a winter camp the following February in the mountainous town of Wisla, near the Czech border. This was Hope for Youth Ministries' first international mission trip and what a fantastic week it was, with God blessing it in so many ways.

We followed the template that the university team had used – Henryk took care of all the logistics, children and interpreters, whilst our team of seven organised games, crafts, workshops and a spiritual programme. Despite the language barrier, we got on well with the kids who proved to be great fun. We also met some lovely Polish Christians who looked after the children at the camp whilst our team ran the programme. Joanna had the important job of being our translator for the week. Every morning and evening, we spent over an hour teaching the children just as I did in the kids' missions in Northern Ireland. I taught the Bible lesson and other team members shared their testimonies, favourite verses and object lessons. At the start of the week, I laid a foundation by teaching them about God's nature through the story of creation. Then I spoke on 'the fall' and explained how each one of us is born a sinner. With that understanding, they grasped why Jesus is so important and the necessity of the cross. Towards the end of the week, the lessons were mainly from the New Testament, focusing on characters like the rich young ruler (how we need to make a decision) and Zacchaeus (how becoming a Christian should change our behaviour).

We also taught the children some of the choruses we sing in English and Joanna explained to them in her mother tongue what the words meant. Many of the Polish leaders could speak some English and encouraged us by sharing how much of the lessons the children remembered during the dorm discussions each night. Most encouraging of all though, was that a number of children put their faith in the Lord Jesus that week, which gave everyone a reason to rejoice. Since then, nearly every time we go to Poland we witness a number of children calling upon the Lord to save them. The ministry there has become attached to our hearts and we feel a great sense of fulfilment returning to build on the foundations that previous teams have laid.

During the week of camp, everyone on the team has an opportunity to use their gifts and perhaps discover new ones that they weren't even aware they had! In addition to the meetings each morning and evening, we have workshops in the afternoon where the volunteers bond with the children through activities like games, sports, baking and crafts to name a few.

The teams also have blessed times of fellowship and great banter on these trips. In fact, when sharing their testimonies, many of the team members tell how a mission trip to Poland gave them a renewed vision of how to serve God purposefully after returning home. Some of them are now working with Christian organisations such as CEF, The Faith Mission or have gone to Bible College and are serving as ministers, pastors or doing some other form of full-time Christian work.

We cherish dozens of special memories from camps in Poland, but I would like to share two that really stand out for me. At one particular camp, there was a little girl who was very defiant and disruptive. She seemed to delight in disrespecting her leaders and generally causing everyone endless grief. We later learned that she was from an orphanage and didn't have any parents. At times she would even scream and fight with other children, but on the Thursday night while Henryk was closing the meeting something special happened. This little girl suddenly got up from her seat and walked straight to the front and whispered something to Henryk and he gave her the microphone.

We didn't know what to expect and were completely amazed when she started to sing with a beautiful, angelic voice. Even though we couldn't understand a word she was singing, we watched her start to cry as she sang and soon there was hardly a dry eye in the place. This little girl had just given her heart to the Lord and was singing a song about having a friend called Jesus and Him being her King. During the meeting, the Spirit of God had moved and ministered to her heart. Many other children came forward to be counselled and Joanna and the other Polish leaders spent several hours showing them how they could put their trust in the Lord. That evening, our team of volunteers split into small groups and prayed specifically for those little children as they started walking with God. Such times when we experience the tangible presence of God are very special.

Another sweet testimony is a lovely little girl who sought out Joanna every day to speak to her in Polish. Then one afternoon, towards the end of the week, she came over to me and pointed to the sky and then to her heart. She was indicating to me she had invited Jesus into her heart – such a precious moment!

As well as girls getting saved, we have witnessed the conversion of many young Polish boys. Many of them arrive at camp as tough little men, some ready to fight with their very shadows, but as the week progresses they are softened and transformed by the power of the gospel. It can only be the Lord's doing when we see how much some of them change – no one is too hard for the Lord!

For a normal camp, we aim to recruit between sixteen and twenty volunteers. This gives a good balance so everyone gets plenty of opportunities to be involved, but not be so overwhelmed with duties that they don't have time to enjoy it. Often the way flights are scheduled, our teams arrive a day before camp starts or depart a day after it finishes. This gives us an opportunity to help Henryk with his food distribution ministry or to distribute thousands of John's Gospels on the streets of Warsaw and in the big residential tower blocks in the city. While in Poland, we have met other pastors such as Pawel and Janek, who have asked for our assistance to lead camps in their churches in other parts of Poland. Although evangelical Christians in Poland are few in number, they have big hearts and are labouring fervently for the Lord. Please remember these believers in your prayers.

In January 2017, we marked our fortieth camp in the country by having a special weekend celebration at the Warsaw Baptist Seminary. We brought fifty-five volunteers, including my elderly parents, to thank God for all He has done through the camps. Many of the volunteers had served years earlier and whilst we were all blessed serving the children, for many of us it was a personal time of reflection and thanksgiving.

Even though our objective in heading out to Poland is to bless the children, we always return home blessed beyond measure ourselves. The children may not speak fluent English but we are immensely challenged as we minister to them and witness their response to the love of God.

As mentioned earlier, at each camp the gospel message is taught systematically and after preaching on the cross, the children are taught the importance of counting the cost of becoming a Christian and how there should be a change in their behaviour. At some point towards the end of the week, often there is a spiritual breakthrough and many children respond to the Word of God. I have witnessed teenagers and adults from all walks of life weeping at these meetings. For the first time in years, or even in their lives, they have sensed the presence of God in a special way. When the Holy Spirit enters a meeting, it is one of the most incredible and remarkable experiences ever. No one wants to leave and teams often sit long into the early hours weeping and praying over souls and giving thanks to the Lord for having mercy on the children. We pray that through these efforts the children will continue to follow the Lord and become great ambassadors for Christ in Poland. We are already seeing signs of this as some of the present-day leaders were children who got saved during our first few camps. These young Polish Christians are mature in their faith and have powerful burdens to see God transform little lives, just like He changed theirs. God has a job, plan and purpose for every one of his children.

It really thrills my heart when I reflect on how we have been able to return to Joanna's home country to serve the Lord together. We believe it was His perfect will for us to do so and we have visited Poland more times than any other foreign country. Joanna could never have envisaged impacting so many of her own people with the gospel, especially children with their whole lives ahead of them. She hopes this can continue and we trust God will open more doors of opportunity in the future for us to return to this beautiful land. On average, we organise three or four camps in Poland every year at different campsites all over the country. In order to make it possible for children to attend the camp who otherwise couldn't afford it, we raise thousands of pounds to pay for the Polish children to come.

In recent years, the ministry has expanded with the caravan parks and other overseas trips so we're not able to take as many teams to Poland as we used to. That presented an opportunity for former volunteers to create a ministry specifically for Poland called 'The Joy Foundation'. They do a lot of amazing work all year round – in particular, monthly discipleship weekends for teenagers as well as gathering up clothing and toys, etc. for Henryk to distribute to families in need. It is a joy to see others catching the vision and putting their shoulder to the wheel. During the summer of 2017, a mother of one of the volunteers came to visit her at camp. The volunteer trusted in the Lord as a young girl at the very first camp we led in Poland ten years earlier. As the mother sat in the meeting, she came under conviction of sin and got saved that night. Can you imagine the excitement that brought to the daughter to see her mum trust in the Lord as she had done?

Here are some of the thoughts of some of the volunteers who have been to Poland:-

"'God, You're good to me, opened my eyes and let me see! Heard me knock and opened up the door!' ... The words of this chorus sum up my time in Poland. God moved and answered prayer and we had the privilege of seeing thirty-three children come to the Lord! Hallelujah, what a Saviour! He blessed my own heart while being there and I had the privilege of sharing this camp with the best team I have experienced. The seed is planted, but greater things are yet to come."

A volunteer in Poland

"Colin, I just want to let you and Joanna know the impact your ministry is continuing to have on Luke. Tonight at a party he spent all his time talking with a girl who was struggling and feeling lost in her faith. He was able to encourage her and this would not have happened before he was under your influence. We are continuously grateful to you both for the positive impact you have made in his life."

A proud mother of one of the volunteers

"I can definitely say that Poland has been a major mountain-top experience in my spiritual walk, pushing me to become more Christ-like and to rely on God in all I do."

A team member

"Before going to Poland this year, I didn't know what to expect or what I might learn. After the experience I feel I am much more grounded in my faith and I have taken so much from this trip that I want to implement into my own life back home."

Andrew

"It's so hard to put into words just how much I love going to Poland and how the fellowship and devotions with the team helps me grow closer to God. Honestly I wouldn't be where I am today in my faith if it wasn't for these teams."

Caroline

"I can't even begin to tell you how your work has changed my life over this last year. You have been a great encouragement and I've also gained many new friends through the work."

Luke

"Thank you for all that you do and how inspiring you are. I feel very encouraged and challenged by this week."

Emma

"I have been mightily blessed once again in Poland with you both. I've been reminded of the power and importance of prayer and have an increased desire to serve God. Thank you for this opportunity."

Hannah

"This trip has been unreal. What a blessing it was to be part of this team. I'm going away from this trip really challenged within myself and when I go home I want to live life closer to God."

Cheryl

"Thank you so much for this incredible opportunity to serve our amazing God on this team. I had mixed emotions about coming on a team where I didn't know anyone but everyone made me very welcome. This team has been an absolute blessing and I feel I've grown so much in my faith this week."

Ruth

CHAPTER NINETEEN

A Preacher Without a Voice

A T THE TURN of 2011, the ministry was busier than ever before and requests were coming in from all directions to do Bible Clubs, missions and camps over the next twelve months. Before the end of January, we had committed to over fifty of these bookings and I was really looking forward to an intense year of ministry.

With such a busy schedule, the two things I needed more than anything was my wife and good health. Firstly, Joanna is the perfect helpmate for me in every imaginable way. She has an amazing passion for the work and does every little thing she can to keep me on the frontlines with as few distractions as possible. In addition to looking after our home and the administration of the ministry, Joanna makes sure I am well-fed, well-loved and well-looked-after! She also is the first to notice if my focus ever starts to wane and gently rebukes me; yet she is also the first to encourage me whenever I need a lift. Secondly, I needed good health, as without it I would struggle to fulfil the bookings we had committed to. Money can buy many things, but neither love nor health.

Six weeks into 2011, we set off to Poland for two consecutive week-long winter camps. Unfortunately, Joanna had a bout of flu, so she rested at her family's house in Krakow the first week so she wouldn't give it to other team members or campers! Despite the outside temperature being minus twenty Celsius, inside things had got off to a blistering start at camp. The little children continually ran about wanting to be chased or playing 'hide-and-seek' so I was completely in my element reliving my childhood! The spiritual programme was also going well and the children were very attentive in the meetings and engaged well with the team in the Bible discussion workshops.

However, a few days into the second camp I noticed my voice weakening. Day by day it was losing volume and power – something I can never remember happening to me before. I assumed it was a consequence of breathing in cold air when we were outside during the afternoons, but two days later I was completely mute. Thankfully, we had an experienced team and others were able to fill the slots that I was scheduled to speak in. The team saw the funny side, as I was normally the loudest one barking out instructions, but had now been reduced to using hand signals! It was all in good humour and the same ones who joked were the ones who prayed most sincerely that God would heal me.

When I woke the next morning, the first thing I did was to test my voice, but there wasn't even a faint squeak. Four days later, when the camp ended it still hadn't returned and I was starting to panic! The best way I can describe trying to speak was like revving a car engine trying to move it forward, but not having it in gear. No matter how hard I strained my vocal chords or forced air out of my lungs, I was completely mute.

When we returned home to Northern Ireland, I rested a few days but there was still no improvement in my condition and I started to be concerned that my voice was gone forever. I texted many friends and asked for prayer, but after another week there was still no change. For the first few days, Joanna maybe enjoyed a quiet house, but times began to get desperate with me being at home all day and not able to make a noise. Whenever the phone rang and I answered it, the person would ask for me and kept saying, "Hello, hello, hello?" until they hung up after muttering something to themselves. I was there the whole time, but I was so silent, the caller assumed the line was dead.

Thankfully, volunteers stood in and fulfilled the Bible Club bookings we had, while I made appointments with doctors and ENT (ear, nose and throat) consultants. Various tests were carried out and I was diagnosed as having Bronchitis, Laryngitis and Tonsillitis all at the same time! The doctors said there was nothing they could do for me and time would be the only healer. We were in a real dilemma as we had dozens of Bible Clubs booked in the schools and we didn't want to let them down. I texted lots of Christian friends who had volunteered with us over the years and asked if they could stand in for me. We quickly got a rota put together and I still went along and operated the computer. Despite the short notice, everyone who came forward coped admirably and Joanna was able to do slots that no one else was able to do. This continued for two full months as my throat condition didn't improve. Amazingly, we didn't have to cancel a single engagement and many children sought the Lord.

As I lay in bed each night, many times I was tempted to believe that the Lord was finished with me and deep down I felt scared, isolated and lonely. Many mornings and evenings, I walked up and down the country roads near our home talking to God silently. No doctor could help me speak and none of the

My Caddy van

First ministry van

Joanna's draft designs for the new van's graphics

Early Youth Weekends & Children's Missions

CHILDRENS HOLIDAY BIBLE CLUB
MON 24th JULY - FRI 28th JULY - 6.30pm to 8.00pm

CHILDREN'S BIBLE WEEK
7-9 pm
1st Week in AUGUST
1st 5th & 7th

Children's Missions 2007-2017

Antrim 2007

Maghaberry 2009

Ross' Farm

Lisburn 2008

Antrim 2007

Ballyroney Farm 2011

Randalstown

Markethill

Lisburn 2012

Children's Missions

Belfast

Cookstown

MARALIN VILLAGE PRIMARY SCHOOL
With Colin Tinsley Youth Ministries
FUN March 7pm-8pm Maralin Primary School
SINGING ACTIVITIES
SHEETS BIBLE STORIES
PRIZES QUIZZES
ALL BOYS & GIRLS WELCOME!
"JESUS SAID COME UNTO ME..." MARK 10:14

Dunene 2013

Belfast

Ballynahinch 2013

The book Hall garden

Joanna praying with a child in Maralin

Maralin Mission

Queen's Jubilee fun-day in Wallace Park, Lisburn

Kinallen

Dromore

Kilkeel

Cheryl counselling children

Volunteers 2013

Acts 16:31
...Believe on the Lord Jesus Christ, ...thou shalt be saved..

Romans 10:13
For whosoever shall call on the name of the Lord shall be saved.

Teaching the Bible verses

Our own village Kinallen, 2015

Singing in Kinallen

Counselling children

Bible story

Child's note in their Stepping Stones book

Notes for me :
The day I became a Christian
26th March Wednesday
2014

Cavan 2015

Belfast school with 530 kids

Cookstown

'I may never march with the infantry' song!

1 Samuel 3v19
Samuel grew, and the
LORD was with him

Maghaberry

Ballymena

Londonderry 2016

Buses for collecting the children

Londonderry 2016

Ballymena Tent Mission 2016

Paul & Cheryl, our regular volunteers

Portadown

Ballymena

Portadown

Rathfriland 2016

Rathfriland

Praying at
the Bible
Club

Lisburn

POND PARK
PRIMARY SCHOOL

A generation of new volunteers

Preparations

In our own village

Bus stop in Kinallen

Volunteers big & small!

Preparing bus stops & big signs 2016

Fourth steel container arrives for storage of ministry materials.

Van ready for a week of Bible Clubs

Sorting out the worksheets

My Polish in-laws visiting the containers

Newsletters & Tollymore Camp forms ready for posting!

Tollymore Camps 2002-2017

Our first camp kitchen!

Joanna's little helpers 2007

First Tollymore Camp 2002

Children's Camp 2006

Tollymore 2007

Youth Camp 2006

YE MUST BE BORN AGAIN

Tollymore Camp 2006

Ready for a water fight!

Leaders 2006

Testimony times in the forest

TOLLYMORE CAMP
with Colin Tinsley

Slippery slope

Children's Camp 2007

Leaders 2008

Leaders 2007

Youth Camp 2008

Children's Camp 2009

Volunteers 2010

Youth Camp 2009

Camp meeting in the forest

The oldest camper Alex overtakes Colin on the slippery slope!

Youth Camp 2012

Children's Camp 2011

Pastor Pawel from Poland

Four Polish teens from the orphanage invited to Tollymore!

Olympic Children's Camp 2012

Children's Camp 2013

Youth Camp 2013

Introducing the leaders 2014

Rise & shine!

Helping to empty the bins!

Boys from the Polish orphanage

Singing in the forest

Tollymore Camp
10ᵗʰ Anniversary

Joanna, Marion & Cheryl preparing food
before the camp

Slippery slope

Edwin & John cutting wood for the fire

Joanna's famous Spaghetti
Bolognese sauce

Putting up the big
marquee

Time for FUN

Chinese buffet

Youth Camp 2016

Children's Camp 2015

TOLLYMORE CAMP
COLIN TINSLEY
HOPE FOR YOUTH MINISTRIES

Children & Youth Camps
2017

Baptism in the Shimna River

Caravan Parks 2012-2017

Cranfield

Volunteers 2015

Volunteers 2013

Portstewart Strand

Portrush

Volunteers 2016

Portrush

Cranfield

Poland 2007-2017

Team 2008

Team 2007

Joanna translating

Camp Arka 2008

Volunteers 2009

Volunteers 2009

Camp Narewka 2009

Camp Ostroda 2009

Preaching

Poland

After Joanna led a Polish child to the Lord

Green School 2011

Soup kitchen

Camp Wisla 2011

An orphanage 2009

Food delivery to needy families

Camp Ostroda 2009

Camp devotions 2010

Young believers at our first Polish camp

Open air 2011

Team 2011

Preparing for food delivery 2011

Krakow 2012 - with our nieces and nephew

With Reach team

POLAND 2009

Warsaw 2011

Devotions & prayer time

Bible story time

Helping deliver food

Quiz

Team devotions

Warsaw 2012

Early morning prayer time

The night when many children got saved

Zakopane 2013

Teddy bears crocheted by people from NI

Team October 2012

Team devotions 2013

Krakow 2013

Romance developing with Richard & Cherith!

Team led by Paul & Cheryl McIntyre, when I was in hospital 2015

Visiting children in their villages

Ostroda Camp 2014

Life lesson

Object lesson

Preparing food parcels

Samaritan's Purse project

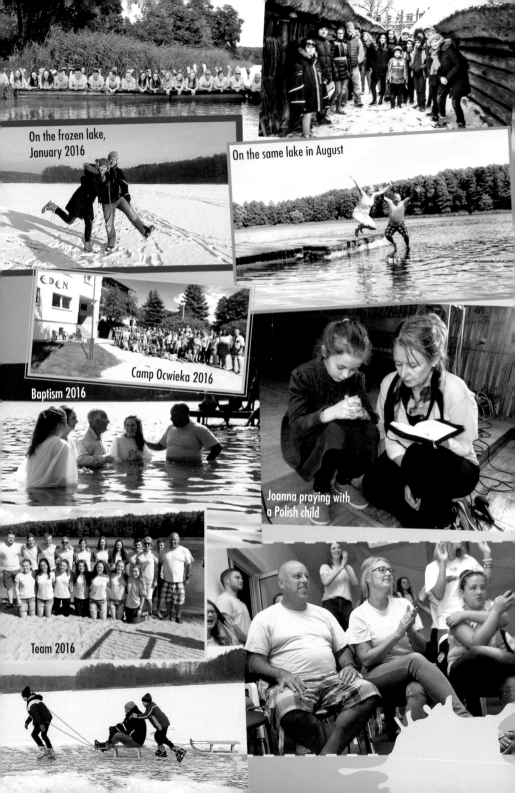

On the frozen lake, January 2016

On the same lake in August

Camp Ocwieka 2016

Baptism 2016

Joanna praying with a Polish child

Team 2016

The biggest team ever!

Celebrating our 40th trip to Poland, January 2017

Supper with children in the orphanage

Camp Elblag 2016

Counselling a camper

My parents & brother James at our 40th trip to Poland

My friend Jonny Ormerod preaching

Some schedules for Bible Clubs & Missions over the years

2010

	Date	Event	Time	Place
1	1-5 March	Children's Mission	7:00pm	Limavady
2	8-12 March	School Bible Club	11:45am	Gilford
3	22-26 March	School Bible Club	11:00am	Bellaghy
4	22-26 March	School Bible Club	2:00pm	Toome
5	7-9 April	Children's Mission	7:00pm	Moira
6	19-23 April	School Bible Club	3:00pm	Belfast
7	26-30 April	School Bible Club	12:15pm	Rasharkin
8	26-30 April	School Bible Club	3:00pm	Cullybacky
9	26-30 April	Children's Mission	7:00pm	Finvoy
10	3-7 May	Children's Mission	7:00pm	Dromara
11	10-14 May	School Bible Club	11:00am	Ballymoney
12	10-14 May	School Bible Club	1:00pm	Ballymoney
13	10-14 May	School Bible Club	2:00pm	Ballymoney
14	10-14 May	Children's Mission	7:00pm	Ahoghill
15	17-21 May	School Bible Club	1:00pm	Coagh
16	17-21 May	Children's Mission	6:30pm	Larne
17	24-28 May	School Bible Club	2:00pm	Belfast
18	24-28 May	Children's Mission	6:30pm	Maghaberry
19	31 May-4 June	School Bible Club	3:00pm	Lisburn
20	31 May-4 June	Children's Mission	6:30pm	Maghaberry
21	7-11 June	School Bible Club	11:00am	Pomeroy
22	7-11 June	School Bible Club	1:30pm	Donaghy
23	7-11 June	School Bible Club	3:00pm	Cookstown
24	7-11 June	Holiday Bible Club	6:30pm	Bessbrooke
25	14-18 June	School Bible Club	11:00am	Fintona
26	14-18 June	School Bible Club	1:45pm	Kilskerry
27	21-25 June	School Bible Club	1:00pm	Donaghmore
28	21-25 June	School Bible Club	3:00pm	Dungannon
29	21-25 June	Holiday Bible Club	6:30pm	Saintfield
30	28-30 June	School Bible Club	11:00am	Augher
31	28-30 June	School Bible Club	9:45am	Clougher
32	28 June-2 July	Children's Mission	6:00pm	Ballygawley
33	5-9 July	Holiday Bible Club	6:30pm	Fivemiletown
34	15-18 July	Youth Camp	6:30pm	Tollymore Forest
35	19-24 July	Children's Camp	2:00pm	Tollymore Forest
36	26-30 July	Holiday Bible Club	10:30am	Rathfriland
37	2-6 August	Holiday Bible Club	2:00pm	Antrim
38	2-6 August	Holiday Bible Club	6:30pm	Toomebridge
39	9-13 August	Holiday Bible Club	6:30pm	Banbridge
40	16-20 August	Holiday Bible Club	6:30pm	Randalstown
41	23 August-4 September	Mission trip		Poland
42	6-10 September	Children's Mission	6:30pm	Cloughmills
43	30 September-3 October	Mission trip		Poland
44	11-15 October	Children's Mission	6:45pm	Limavady

Diary of Missions, Bible Clubs & Camps 2008

Meeting	Area	Venue	Date
1. Holiday Bible Club	Toombridge	School	30th March-3rd Ap
2. Holiday Bible Club	Belfast	School	27th April-1st May
3. Holiday Bible Club	Portglenone	School	4th-8th May
4. Children's Mission	Ahoghill	Hall	4th-8th May
5. Holiday Bible Club	Ballymena	School	11th-15th May
6. Holiday Bible Club	Coagh	School	18th-22nd May
7. Holiday Bible Club	Lisburn	School	25th- 29th May
8. Children's Mission	Maghaberry	Tent	25th- 29th May
9. Holiday Bible Club	Lisburn	School	1st-5th June
10. Children's Mission	Maghaberry	Tent	1st-5th June
11. Holiday Bible Club	Lisburn	School	8th-12th June
12. Youth Camp	Castlewellan	Youth Centre	12th-14th June
13. Holiday Bible Club	Garryduff	School	15th-19th June
14. Holiday Bible Club	Ballymoney	School	15th-19th June
15. Holiday Bible Club	Coleraine	School	15th-19th June
16. Holiday Bible Club	Fintona	School	22nd-26th June
17. Holiday Bible Club	Clogher	School	22nd-26th June
18. Holiday Bible Club	Seskinore	School	22nd-26th June
19. Holiday Bible Club	ulcavy	Tent	29th June-2nd July
	oland	Camp	2nd-11th July
	llymore Forest	Tents	20th-24th July
	llymore Forest	Tents	24th-26th July
	thfriland	Hall	27th-31st July
	awfordsburn	Youth Centre	31st July-2nd Augu
	ntrim	Garden	3rd-7th August
	okstown	Church	10th-14th August
	ndalstown	Tent	17th-21st August
	land	Camp	24th Aug- 7th Sep
	leraine	Church	14th-18th Septem

amily Fun Day
Easter Saturday 11th April 200

HOPE FOR Youth MINISTRIES

Colin Tinsley

www.hopeforyouthministries.org

Bible Clubs & Missions 2011

	DATE	AREA
1	15-22 February	Poland
2	22 February-1st March	Poland
3	7-11 March	Rasharkin
4	7-11 March	Portglenone
5	21-25 March	Kinallen
6	28 March-1 April	Ahoghill
7	28 March-1 April	Duneane
8	4-8 April	Garvagh
9	4-8 April	Cullybackey
10	4-8 April	Kilrea
11	11-15 April	Donacloney
12	11-15 April	Magheralin
13	28 April-2 May	Poland
14	9-13 May	Augher
15	9-13 May	Augher
16	11-13 May	Balmoral Show
17	16-20 May	Belfast
18	16-20 May	Belfast
19	16-20 May	Belfast
20	16-20 May	Ahoghill
21	23-27 May	Cookstown
22	23-27 May	Cookstown
23	23-27 May	Larne
24	30 May-3 June	Bessbrook
25	30 May-3 June	Newry
26	30 May-3 June	Camlough
27	6-10 June	Lisburn
28	6-10 June	Moneyslane
29	13-17 June	Ballymoney
30	13-17 June	Ballymoney
31	13-17 June	Ballymoney
32	13-17 June	Finvoy
33	20-24 June	Donaghmore
34	20-24 June	Dungannon
35	20-24 June	Saintfield
36	27-30 June	Clogher
37	27-30 June	Fintona
38	27-30 June	Kilskeery
39	27-30 June	Moneymore
40	4-8 July	Kesh
41	14-17 July	Tollymore
42	18-23 July	Tollymore
43	25-29 July	Banbridge
44	1-5 August	Carrickfergus
45	1-5 August	Antrim
46	1-5 August	Duneane
47	15-19 August	Tullyvallen
48	15-19 August	Randalstown
49	22 August-4 September	Poland
50	29 September-2 October	Poland
51	10-14 October	Limavady
52	15-22 October	Isle of Man

Bible Clubs & Missions 2013

	DATE	TIME	EVENT	AREA
1	28 Jan- 1 Feb	2:45-3:45pm	Bible Club	
2	4-8 February	9:45-10:45am	Bible Club	
3	4-8 February	3-4pm	Bible Club	
4	10-17 February	1 week	Mission Trip	
5	17-24 February	1 week	Mission Trip	
6	25 Feb- 1 mar	2-3pm	Bible Club	
7	1-3 March	Weekend	Youth Weekend	
8	4-8 March	1-2pm	Bible Club	
9	4-8 March	3-4pm	Bible Club	
10	4-8 March	7-8pm	Children's Mission	M
11	11-15 March	9:30-10:30am	Bible Club	M
12	11-15 March	1:50-2:50pm	Bible Club	K
13	11-15 March	6:30-7:30pm	Children's Mission	L
14	18-22 March	9:30-10:30am	Bible Club	N
15	18-22 March	1-2pm	Bible Club	N
16	18-22 March	2-3pm	Bible Club	N
17	18-22 March	6:30-7:30pm	Bible Club	N
18	25-28 March	9:15-10:15am	Bible Club	Ballygowan
19	25-28 March	11-12pm	Bible Club	Ballygowan
20	25-28 March	2-3pm	Bible Club	Newtownards
21	25-28 March	7-8pm	Bible Club	Galgorm
22	1-5 April	10:30-11:30am	Bible Club	Dromore
23	8-12 April	1-2pm	Bible Club	Belfast
24	8-12 April	7-8pm	Children's Mission	Carrickfergus
25	15-19 April	9:30-10:30am	Bible Club	Carrickfergus
26	15-19 April	11-12pm	Bible Club	Carrickfergus
27	15-19 April	2-3pm	Bible Club	Carrickfergus
28	15-19 April	7-8pm	Bible Club	Kinallen
29	22-26 April	10:45-11:45am	Bible Club	Hamiltsonbawn
30	22-26 April	1-2pm	Bible Club	Mountnorris
31	22-26 April	7-8pm	Children's Mission	Markethill
32	29 April-3 May	9:45-10:45am	Bible Club	Antrim
33	29 April-3 May	11-12pm	Bible Club	Ahoghill
34	29 April-3 May	3-4pm	Bible Club	Antrim
35	29 April-3 May	7-8pm	Bible Club	Ballynahinch
36	6-10 May	9:30-10:30am	Bible Club	Ballymena
37	6-10 May	11-12pm	Bible Club	Ballymena
38	6-10 May	2-3pm	Bible Club	Ballymena
39	6-10 May	3-4pm	Bible Club	Ballymena
40	6-10 May	7-8pm	Children's Mission	Magaberry
41	13-17 May	9-10am	Bible Club	Moorefields
42	13-17 May	11-12pm	Bible Club	Larne
43	13-17 May	3-4pm	Bible Club	Larne
44	13-17 May	7-8pm	Children's Mission	Ballymena
45	20-24 May	12-1pm	Bible Club	Belfast
46	20-24 May	1-2pm	Bible Club	Belfast
47	20-24 May	3-4pm	Bible Club	Belfast
48	20-24 May	7-8pm	Bible Club	Belfast
49	27-30 May	11-12pm	Bible Club	Donaghy
50	27-30 May	1-2pm	Bible Club	Armagh
51	27-30 May	3-4pm	Bible Club	Armagh
52	27-30 May	7-8pm	Bible Club	Richhill
53	3-7 June	10-11am	Bible Club	Pomeroy
54	3-7 June	12:30-1:30pm	Bible Club	Cookstown
55	3-7 June	2-3pm	Bible Club	Cookstown
56	3-7 June	3-4pm	Bible Club	Cookstown
57	3-7 June	7-8pm	Bible Club	Magherafelt
58	10-14 June	11-12pm	Bible Club	Lisburn

	DATE	TIME	EVENT	AREA
			Bible Club	Lisburn
			Bible Club	Lisburn
			Children's Mission	Moira
			Bible Club	Portadown
			Bible Club	Portadown
			Bible Club	Portadown
			Bible Club	Portadown
			Bible Club	Portadown
			Bible Club	Magherafelt
			Bible Club	Magherafelt
			Bible Club	Magherafelt
			Children's Mission	Cookstown
			Mission Trip	Lithuania
			Children's Camp	Tollymore
			Youth Camp	Tollymore
	July	11-12pm	Caravan Bible Club	Cranfield
75	22-24 July	12:30-1:30pm	Caravan Bible Club	Cranfield
76	22-24 July	2-3pm	Caravan Bible Club	Cranfield
77	22-24 July	3:30-4:30pm	Caravan Bible Club	Cranfield
78	22-24 July	5:30-6:30pm	Caravan Bible Club	Newcastle
79	22-24 July	7-8pm	Caravan Bible Club	Newcastle
80	29 July-2 August	10:30-12:30pm	Bible Club	Cootehill
81	29 July-2 August	3-4pm	Bible Club	Ballybray
82	29 July-2 August	7-8pm	Bible Club	Oram
83	5-9 August	2-4pm	Bible Club	Antrim
84	5-9 August	6:30-8pm	Bible Club	Randalstown
85	12-16 August	11-12pm	Caravan Bible Club	Portstewart
86	12-16 August	12:30-1:30pm	Caravan Bible Club	Portstewart
87	12-16 August	2-3pm	Caravan Bible Club	Portstewart
88	12-16 August	4-5pm	Caravan Bible Club	Portrush
89	12-16 August	5:30-6:30pm	Caravan Bible Club	Portrush
90	12-16 August	7-8pm	Caravan Bible Club	Portrush
91	18 August- 2 Sept		Mission trip	Poland
92	16-20 September	6:30-7:30pm	Children's Mission	Killyleagh
93	23-27 September	6:30-7:30pm	Children's Mission	Killyleagh
94	3-6 October		Mission trip	Poland
95	7-11 October	3-4pm	Bible Fun Week	Limavady
96	7-11 October	6:30-7:30pm	Children's Mission	Limavady
97	12-17 October		Mission trip	China
98	17-26 October		Mission trip	Laos
99	17-26 October		Mission trip	Vietnam
100	26 Oct-5th Nov		Mission trip	Philippines
101	25-29 November	10-11am	Christmas Bible Club	Armagh
102	25-29 November	1-2pm	Christmas Bible Club	Caledon
103	25-29 November	3-4pm	Christmas Bible Club	Aughnacloy
104	2-6 December	10-11am	Christmas Bible Club	Ballymoney
105	2-6 December	1-2pm	Christmas Bible Club	Ballymoney
106	2-6 December	3-4pm	Christmas Bible Club	Ballymoney
107	9-13 December	10-11am	Christmas Bible Club	Armagh
108	9-13 December	1-2pm	Christmas Bible Club	Armagh
109	9-13 December	3-4pm	Christmas Bible Club	Armagh
110	16-18 December	10-11am	Christmas Bible Club	Fintona
111	16-18 December	1-2pm	Christmas Bible Club	Clogher
112	16-18 December	3-4pm	Christmas Bible Club	Augher

www.hopeforyouthministries.org

Check out Colin's NEW Books at the back of this Newsletter

Bible Clubs & Missions 2014

www.hopeforyouthministries.org

	VENUE	DATE	EVENT	TIME
1	Ballymena	6-9 January	School Bible Club	1pm
2	India	10-24 January	Mission Trip	2 Weeks
3	Nepal	25-31 January	Mission Trip	1 Week
4	Stewartstown	10-14 February	School Bible Club	11am
5	Pomeroy	10-14 February	School Bible Club	1pm
6	Dungannon	10-14 February	School Bible Club	2:45pm
7	Poland	16-23 February	Winter Camp	1 Week
8	Poland	23-28 February	Outreach	1 Week
9	Moorfields	10-14 March	School Bible Club	9am
10	Carrickfergus	10-14 March	School Bible Club	11am
11	Larne	10-14 March	School Bible Club	2pm
12	Broughshane	10-14 March	Children's Mission	7pm
13	Ballymena	17-21 March	School Bible Club	9am
14	Ballymena	17-21 March	School Bible Club	10am
15	Rasharkin	17-21 March	School Bible Club	12:30pm
16	Ballymena	17-21 March	School Bible Club	2pm
17	Ballymena	17-21 March	School Bible Club	3pm
18	Newtownards	24-25 March	School Bible Club	11am
19	Newtownards	24-25 March	School Bible Club	12pm
20	Newtownards	24-25 March	School Bible Club	1pm
21	Hamiltonsbawn	26-28 March	School Bible Club	9:30am
22	Caledon	26-28 March	School Bible Club	11am
23	Loughgall	26-28 March	School Bible Club	1pm
24	Donecloney	24-28 March	School Bible Club	3pm
25	Maralin	24-28 March	Childrens Mission	7pm
26	Coleraine	31 March-4 April	School Bible Club	9:30am
27	Coleraine	31 March-4 April	School Bible Club	11am
28	Coleraine	31 March-4 April	School Bible Club	1pm
29	Ballymena	31 March-4 April	School Bible Club	3pm
30	Cullybackey	31 March-4 April	Children's Mission	6:45pm
31	ROI	4-6 April	Youth Camp	Weekend
32	Lisburn	7-11 April	School Bible Club	9am
33	Lisburn	7-11 April	School Bible Club	10:30am
34	Lisburn	7-11 April	School Bible Club	1pm
35	Lisburn	7-11 April	School Bible Club	3pm
36	Kinallen	7-11 April	Children's Mission	7pm
37	Cranfield	16-18 April	Caravan Bible Club	10:30am
38	Cranfield	16-18 April	Caravan Bible Club	12pm
39	Cranfield	16-18 April	Caravan Bible Club	1:30pm
40	Newcastle	16-18 April	Caravan Bible Club	4pm
41	Newcastle	16-18 April	Caravan Bible Club	5:30pm
42	Newcastle	16-18 April	Caravan Bible Club	7pm
43	Portrush	20-22 April	Caravan Bible Club	10:30am
44	Portrush	20-22 April	Caravan Bible Club	12pm
45	Portrush	20-22 April	Caravan Bible Club	1:30pm
46	Portrush	20-22 April	Caravan Bible Club	4pm
47	Portrush	20-22 April	Caravan Bible Club	5:30pm
48	Portrush	20-22 April	Caravan Bible Club	7pm
49	Maghaberry	28 April-2 May	School Bible Club	11am
50	Nutts Corner	28 April-2 May	School Bible Club	1pm
51	Dundrod	28 April-2 May	School Bible Club	2pm
52	Markethill	28 April-2 May	Childrens Mission	7pm
53	Antrim	6-9 May	School Bible Club	9:15am
54	Ballynure	6-9 May	School Bible Club	11am
55	Doagh	6-9 May	School Bible Club	1pm
56	Killbride	6-9 May	School Bible Club	2pm
57	Newry	12-15 May	School Bible Club	11am
58	Newry	12-15 May	School Bible Club	1pm
59	Dromore	12-15 May	School Bible Club	3pm
60	Rathfriland	12-15 May	School Bible Club	6:30pm
61	Cookstown	19-23 May	School Bible Club	9:30am
62	Cookstown	19-23 May	School Bible Club	11am
63	Cookstown	19-23 May	School Bible Club	1pm
64	Cookstown	19-23 May	School Bible Club	2pm
65	Cookstown	19-23 May	School Bible Club	3pm
66	Belfast	19-23 May	School Bible Club	7pm
67	Belfast	26-30 May	School Bible Club	9:30am
68	Belfast	26-30 May	School Bible Club	11am
69	Belfast	26-30 May	School Bible Club	1pm
70	Belfast	26-30 May	School Bible Club	3pm
71	Ballynahinch	26-30 May	School Bible Club	7pm
72	Antrim	2-6 June	School Bible Club	11am
73	Antrim	2-6 June	School Bible Club	1pm
74	Antrim	2-6 June	School Bible Club	3pm
75	Randalstown	2-6 June	School Bible Club	7pm
76	Portadown	9-13 June	School Bible Club	9am
77	Portadown	9-13 June	School Bible Club	10:15am
78	Portadown	9-13 June	School Bible Club	11:30am
79	Portadown	9-13 June	School Bible Club	1:30pm
80	Portadown	9-13 June	School Bible Club	3pm
81	Richhill	9-13 June	School Bible Club	7pm
82	Lurgan	16-20 June	School Bible Club	9:30am
83	Lurgan	16-20 June	School Bible Club	11am
84	Lisburn	16-20 June	School Bible Club	1pm
85	Lisburn	16-20 June	School Bible Club	3pm
86	Lisburn	16-20 June	School Bible Club	7pm
87	Dungannon	23-26 June	School Bible Club	9am
88	Clogher	23-26 June	School Bible Club	10:45am
89	Fintona	23-26 June	School Bible Club	12:30pm
90	Killskerry	23-26 June	School Bible Club	2pm
91	Poland	27 June-6 July	Summer Camp	10 days
92	Tollymore	11-13 July	Youth Camp	Weekend
93	Tollymore	14-18 July	Children's Camp	1 week
94	Canada	19-26 July	Children's Camp	1 week
95	Canada	27 July-1 August	Youth Camp	1 week
96	Canada	4-8 August	Bible Club	1 week
97	Banbridge	15-19 September	Children's Mission	11am
98	Banbridge	15-19 September	School Bible Club	1pm
99	Loughbrickland	15-19 September	School Bible Club	6:30pm
100	Ballygowan	22-26 September	Childrens Mission	11am
101	Newtownards	22-26 September	School Bible Club	1pm
102	Killyleagh	22-26 September	School Bible Club	6:30pm
103	Crossgar	22-26 September	School Bible Club	11am
104	Comber	22-26 September	School Bible Club	1pm
105	Killyleagh	29 Sept-3 October	Childrens Mission	6:30pm
106	Limavady	6-10 October	School Bible Club	11am
107	Limavady	6-10 October	School Bible Club	1pm
108	Limavady	6-10 October	Childrens Mission	6:45pm
109	Philippines	24 Oct-4 Nov	Mission Trip	2 weeks
110	Thialand	10-15 November	Mission Trip	1 week
111	Laos	16-19 November	Mission Trip	1 week
112	Vietnam	20-22 November	Mission Trip	1 week
113	Antrim	24-28 November	Christmas Bible Club	9am
114	Antrim	24-28 November	Christmas Bible Club	11am
115	Antrim	24-28 November	Christmas Bible Club	1pm
116	Antrim	24-28 November	Christmas Bible Club	3pm
117	Armagh	1-5 December	Christmas Bible Club	9am
118	Armagh	1-5 December	Christmas Bible Club	11am
119	Armagh	1-5 December	Christmas Bible Club	1pm
120	Armagh	1-5 December	Christmas Bible Club	3pm
121	Belfast	8-12 December	Christmas Bible Club	9am
122	Belfast	8-12 December	Christmas Bible Club	11am
123	Belfast	8-12 December	Christmas Bible Club	1pm
124	Belfast	8-12 December	Christmas Bible Club	3pm
125	Dungannon	15-19 December	Christmas Bible Club	9am
126	Dungannon	15-19 December	Christmas Bible Club	11am
127	Dungannon	15-19 December	Christmas Bible Club	1pm
128	Dungannon	15-19 December	Christmas Bible Club	3pm

Bible Clubs and Missions 2015

Hope for Youth Ministries

	DATE	AREA	TIME
1	5-9 January	Ballymena	1pm
2	12-16 January	Randalstown	11am
3	12-16 January	Maghera	1pm
4	12-16 January	Castledawson	2pm
5	12-16 January	Castledawson	3pm
6	19-23 January	Belfast	10am
7	19-23 January	Belfast	1pm
8	19-23 January	Belfast	2pm
9	26-30 January	Moorefields	9am
10	26-30 January	Ballynure	10:45am
11	26-30 January	Dough	1pm
12	26-30 January	Kilbride	2pm
13	1-8 February	Poland	Camp
14	23-27 February	Cookstown	9:30am
15	23-27 February	Aughnacloy	11am
16	23-27 February	Pomeroy	1pm
17	23-27 February	Dungannon	3pm
18	2-6 March	Hamiltonsbawn	9:30am
19	2-6 March	Caledon	11am
20	2-6 March	Loughgall	1pm
21	2-6 March	Killylea	2pm
22	2-6 March	Armagh	3pm
23	9-13 March	Ballyclare	9am
24	9-13 March	Ballyclare	10am
25	9-13 March	Ballyclare	11am
26	9-13 March	Newry	2pm
27	16-20 March	Lisburn	9am
28	16-20 March	Lisburn	10:30am
29	16-20 March	Lisburn	12pm
30	16-20 March	Lisburn	1:30pm
31	16-20 March	Maghaberry	3pm
32	16-20 March	Lisburn	7pm
33	23-27 March	Lisburn	9am
34	23-27 March	Lisburn	11am
35	23-27 March	Lisburn	1pm
36	23-27 March	Donecloney	3pm
37	23-27 March	Maralin	7pm
38	2-4 April	Chestnutt CP	11am
39	2-4 April	Cranfield bay CP	12:30pm
40	2-4 April	Shanlieve CP	2pm
41	2-4 April	Newcastle CP	4pm
42	2-4 April	Woodcroft CP	5:30pm
43	2-4 April	Mournview CP	7pm
44	6-8 April	Skerries CP	11am
45	6-8 April	Kellies CP	12:30pm
46	6-8 April	Hilltop CP	2pm
47	6-8 April	Blairs CP	4pm
48	6-8 April	Juniper Hill CP	5:30pm
49	6-8 April	Carrick dhu CP	7pm
50	13-17 April	Lurgan	9am
51	13-17 April	Lurgan	11am
52	13-17 April	Straid	1pm
53	13-17 April	Ballyclare	2pm
54	13-17 April	Ballyclare	3pm
55	20-24 April	Cloughmills	9:30am
56	20-24 April	Dunseverick	11am
57	20-24 April	Bushmills	1pm
58	20-24 April	Ballytober	2pm
59	20-24 April	Ahoghill	7pm
60	24-26 April	Down South	Camp
61	27 April-1 May	Ballymena	9am
62	27 April-1 May	Ballymena	10am
63	27 April-1 May	Ballymena	12:45pm
64	27 April-1 May	Ballymena	2pm
65	27 April-1 May	Ballymena	3pm
66	27 April-1 May	Ballymena	7pm
67	4-8 May	Newtownards	9am
68	4-8 May	Newtownards	11am
69	4-8 May	Newtownards	1pm
70	4-8 May	Newtownards	2pm
71	8-10 May	Ministry Weekend	Weekend
72	11-15 May	Spa	9am
73	11-15 May	Ballynahinch	11am
74	11-15 May	Dromore	3pm
75	11-15 May	Kinallen	7pm
76	18-22 May	Stewartstown	9:30am
77	18-22 May	Coagh	11am
78	18-22 May	Donaghy	1pm
79	18-22 May	Cookstown	2pm
80	18-22 May	Cookstown	3pm
81	18-22 May	Rathfriland	7pm
82	26-29 May	Belfast	9:30am
83	26-29 May		11am
84	26-29 May		
85	26-29 May		
86	26-29 May		
87	1-5 June		
88	1-5 June		
89	1-5 June		
90	1-5 June		
91	1-5 June		
92	8-12 Ju		
93	8-12 J		
94	8-12		
95	8-12		
96	8-12		
97	15-2		
98	15-		
99	15-		
100	15		
101	15		
102	2		
103	2		
104			
105			
106			
107			
108			
109			
110			
111			
112	1-4 July	Newcastle CP	4pm
113	1-4 July	Woodcroft CP	5:30pm
114	1-4 July	Mournview CP	7pm
115	6-10 July	Larne	2pm
116	20-24 July	Tollymore Camp	Camp
117	24-26 July	Tollymore Camp	Camp
118	27-31 July	Tollymore Camp	Camp
119	3-7 August	Dundonald	9am
120	3-7 August	Ballyclare	6:30pm
121	10-14 August	Skerries CP	11am
122	10-14 August	Kellies CP	12:30pm
123		Hilltop CP	2pm
124			

Bible Clubs and Missions for Autumn/Winter 2016

Hope for Youth Ministries

1	12-16th	September	Keady	6:30pm	Childrens Mission
2	19-23	September	Moneyrea	9am	School Bible Club
3	19-23	September	Comber	11am	School Bible Club
4	19-23	September	Killyleagh	6:30pm	Childrens Mission
5	26-30	September	Killyleagh	1pm	School Bible Club
6	26-30	September	Crossgar	3pm	School Bible Club
7	26-30	September	Killyleagh	6:30pm	Childrens Mission
8	3-7th	October	Londonderry	9am	School Bible Club
9	3-7th	October	Londonderry	11am	School Bible Club
10	3-7th	October	Limavady	1pm	School Bible Club
11	3-7th	October	Limavady	3pm	School Bible Club
12	7-9th	October	Portrush	24/7	Youth Weekend
13	18-20	November	Moira	24/7	Youth Weekend
14	21-25	November	Caledon	9:30am	School Bible Club
15	21-25	November	Killylea	11am	School Bible Club
16	21-25	November	Aughnacloy	1pm	School Bible Club
17	21-25	November	Aughnacloy	7pm	Childrens Mission
18	28 Nov-2 Dec	November	Portavogie	9am	School Bible Club
19	28 Nov-2 Dec	November	Portavogie	11am	School Bible Club
20	28 Nov-2 Dec	November	Portavogie	1pm	School Bible Club
21	28 Nov-2 Dec	November	Portavogie	2:15pm	School Bible Club
22	5-9th	December	Fivemiletown	9am	School Bible Club
23	5-9th	December	Lisnaskie	11am	School Bible Club
24	5-9th	December	Tempo	1pm	School Bible Club
25	5-9th	December	Augher	2:15pm	School Bible Club
26	12-16th	December	Upperlands	9:15am	School Bible Club
27	12-16th	December	Ahoghill	10:45am	School Bible Club
28	12-16th	December	Garvagh	1pm	School Bible Club
29	12-16th	December	Portglenone	2pm	School Bible Club
30	19-21st	December	Belfast	9:30am	School Bible Club
31	19-21st	December	Belfast	11am	School Bible Club
32	19-21st	December	Belfast	1pm	School Bible Club
33	19-21st	December	Belfast	2pm	School Bible Club

Please pray for all these gospel meetings as well as many more school assemblies and other such meetings, God bless, Colin and Joanna Tinsley

"Fear the LORD thy God, and serve him." Deut 6:13

Bible Clubs & Missions 2016

www.hopeforyouthministries.org

#	Date	Time	Event	Area
1	4-8 January		School Bible Club	Carrickfergus
2	17-24 January		Winter Camp	Poland
3	24-31 January		Winter Camp	Poland
4	1-5 February	9:15am	School Bible Club	Moorefields
5	1-5 February	11am	School Bible Club	Antrim
6	1-5 February	1pm	School Bible Club	Doagh
7	1-5 February	2pm	School Bible Club	Kells
8	8-12 February	9am	School Bible Club	Dungannon
9	8-12 February	10:45am	School Bible Club	Dungannon
10	8-12 February	1pm	School Bible Club	Loughgall
11	8-12 February	2pm	School Bible Club	Loughgall
12	15-19 February	6:30pm	Children's Mission	Crossgar
13	22-26 February	9:15am	School Bible Club	Carrickfergus
14	22-26 February	1pm	Children's Mission	Carrickfergus
15	22-26 February	6:30pm	School Bible Club	Portadown
16	29 Feb-4 March	9:30am	School Bible Club	Greyabbey
17	29 Feb-4 March	11am	School Bible Club	Millisle
18	29 Feb-4 March	1pm	School Bible Club	Portavogie
19	29 Feb-4 March	2pm	School Bible Club	Kircubbin
20	29 Feb-4 March	3pm	School Bible Club	Kircubbin
21	7-11 March	9am	School Bible Club	Moyallen
22	7-11 March	10am	School Bible Club	Bleary
23	7-11 March	11am	School Bible Club	Gilford
24	7-11 March	1pm	School Bible Club	Portadown
25	7-11 March	3pm	Children's Mission	Donacloney
26	7-11 March	9am	School Bible Club	Maralin
27	14-18 March	10am	School Bible Club	Carrickfergus
28	14-18 March	11am	School Bible Club	Carrickfergus
29	14-18 March	2pm	School Bible Club	Lisburn
30	14-18 March	3pm	School Bible Club	Ballymena
31	14-18 March	9am	School Bible Club	Ballymena
32	21-23 March	10am	School Bible Club	Lisburn
33	21-23 March	11am	School Bible Club	Lisburn
34	21-23 March	1pm	School Bible Club	Lisburn
35	21-23 March	2pm	School Bible Club	Lisburn
36	21-23 March	3pm	School Bible Club	Lisburn
37	24-26 March	12pm	Caravan Bible Club	Cranfield
38	24-26 March	1pm	Caravan Bible Club	Cranfield
39	24-26 March	2pm	Caravan Bible Club	Cranfield
40	24-26 March	4pm	Caravan Bible Club	Newcastle
41	24-26 March	5pm	Caravan Bible Club	Newcastle
42	24-26 March	12pm	Caravan Bible Club	Portrush
43	24-26 March	1pm	Caravan Bible Club	Portrush
44	28-30 March	12pm	Caravan Bible Club	Portrush
45	28-30 March	1pm	Caravan Bible Club	Portrush
46	28-30 March	2pm	Caravan Bible Club	Portrush
47	28-30 March	4pm	Caravan Bible Club	Portrush
48	28-30 March	5pm	School Bible Club	Churchtown
49	28-30 March	6pm	School Bible Club	Kilrass
50	4-8 April	9:45am	School Bible Club	Pomeroy
51	4-8 April	11am		
52	4-8 April	1pm		
53	11-15 April	9am	School Bible Club	Ballymena
54	11-15 April	10am	School Bible Club	Ballymena
55	11-15 April	11am	School Bible Club	Ballymena
56	11-15 April	1pm	School Bible Club	Ballymena
57	11-15 April	2pm	School Bible Club	Ballymena
58	11-15 April	3pm	School Bible Club	Lurgan
59	18-22 April	9am	School Bible Club	Lurgan
60	18-22 April	11am	School Bible Club	Lurgan
61	18-22 April	1pm	School Bible Club	Bessbrook
62	25-29 April	9am	School Bible Club	Newry
63	25-29 April	11am	School Bible Club	Hamiltonsbawn
64	25-29 April	1pm	School Bible Club	Armagh
65	25-29 April	2pm	School Bible Club	Newtownards
66	9-13 May	9:30am	School Bible Club	Newtownards
67	9-13 May	11am	School Bible Club	Dromore
68	9-13 May	3pm	School Bible Club	Kinallen
69	9-13 May	7pm	School Bible Club	Stewartstown
70	16-20 May	9:15am	School Bible Club	Coagh
71	16-20 May	11am	School Bible Club	Donaghy
72	16-20 May	1pm	School Bible Club	Cookstown
73	16-20 May	2pm	School Bible Club	Cookstown
74	16-20 May	7pm	Children's Mission	Magherafelt
75	16-20 May	9am	School Bible Club	Belfast
76	23-27 May	11am	School Bible Club	Belfast
77	23-27 May	1pm	School Bible Club	Belfast
78	23-27 May	3pm	School Bible Club	Belfast
79	23-27 May	9am	School Bible Club	Portadown
80	6-10 June	11am	School Bible Club	Portadown
81	6-10 June	1:30pm	School Bible Club	Portadown
82	6-10 June	3pm	School Bible Club	Ballymena
83	6-10 June	7:8pm	School Bible Club	Lisburn
84	6-10 June	10am	School Bible Club	Lisburn
85	13-17 June	11am	School Bible Club	Lisburn
86	13-17 June	1pm	School Bible Club	Lisburn
87	13-17 June	2pm	School Bible Club	Lisburn
88	13-17 June	3pm	School Bible Club	Kenya
89	13-17 June		Mission Trip	
90	19 June-2 July	7pm	Children's Mission	Armagh
91	4-7 July		Summer Camp	Tollymore
92	18-22 July		Summer Camp	Tollymore
93	22-24 July		Children's Bible Club	Belfast
94	25-29 July	9am	Children's Mission	Lurgan
95	1-5 August	7pm	Summer Bible Club	Portrush
96	8-11 August	10:30am	Caravan Bible Club	Portrush
97	15-19 August	1pm	Caravan Bible Club	Portrush
98	15-19 August	2pm	Caravan Bible Club	Portrush
99	15-19 August	4pm	Caravan Bible Club	Portrush
100	15-19 August	5pm	Children's Mission	Bushmills
101	15-19 August	6:45pm	Summer Camp	Poland
102	15-19 August			
103	22-31 August			

We would really appreciate your prayers as we keep at the work, Colin and Joanna

"Do the work of an evangelist, make full proof of thy ministry." 2 Timothy 4:5

Bible Clubs/Missions 2017

#	DATE	LOCATION	TIME
1	27-29 Jan	Poland	Camp
2	1-5 Feb	Poland	Camp
3	6-10 Feb	Ballytober	9am
4	6-10 Feb	Ballymoney	11am
5	6-10 Feb	Ballymoney	1pm
6	6-10 Feb	Ballymoney	2pm
7	13-17 Feb	Enniskillen	9am
8	13-17 Feb	Enniskillen	11am
9	13-17 Feb	Enniskillen	1pm
10	13-17 Feb	Enniskillen	2pm
11	20-24 Feb	Stewartstown	9:30am
12	20-24 Feb	Coagh	11am
13	20-24 Feb	Churchtown	1pm
14	20-24 Feb	Magherafelt	3pm
15	24-26 Feb	Bushmills	Camp
16	27 Feb-3 Mar	Coleraine	9:30am
17	27 Feb-3 Mar	Coleraine	10:45am
18	27 Feb-3 Mar	Coleraine	1:20pm
19	27 Feb-3 Mar	Coleraine	2:15pm
20	6-10 Mar	Dungannon	9am
21	6-10 Mar	Dungannon	10:45am
22	6-10 Mar	Dungannon	1:15pm
23	6-10 Mar	Dungannon	2:15pm
24	13-17 Mar	Belfast	9am
25	13-17 Mar	Belfast	10am
26	13-17 Mar	Carrickfergus	11:15am
27	13-17 Mar	Carrickfergus	1pm
28	13-17 Mar	Carrickfergus	2pm
29	20-24 Mar	Lurgan	9:30am
30	20-24 Mar	Lurgan	11am
31	20-24 Mar	Lurgan	1pm
32	20-24 Mar	Lurgan	2pm
33	20-24 Mar	Lurgan	3pm
34	27-31 Mar	Poyntzpass	9am
35	27-31 Mar	Newtownhamilton	11am
36	27-31 Mar	Mountnorris	1pm
37	27-31 Mar	Bessbrook	2pm
38	3-7 Apr	Tandragee	9:30am
39	3-7 Apr	Tandragee	10:45am
40	3-7 Apr	Loughgall	1pm
41	3-7 Apr	Moy	2:15pm
42	3-7 Apr	Maralin	7pm
43	12-14 Apr	Cranfield	12pm
44	12-14 Apr	Cranfield	1pm
45	12-14 Apr	Cranfield	2pm
46	12-14 Apr	Cranfield	3pm
47	12-14 Apr	Newcastle	6pm
48	12-14 Apr	Newcastle	7pm
49	17-19 Apr	Portrush	12pm
50	17-19 Apr	Portrush	1pm
51	17-19 Apr	Portrush	2pm
52	17-19 Apr	Portrush	3pm
53	17-19 Apr	Portrush	6pm
54	17-19 Apr	Portrush	7pm
55	24-28 Apr	Dungannon	9:15am
56	24-28 Apr	Dungannon	11am
57	24-28 Apr	Dungannon	1pm
58	24-28 Apr	Dungannon	2pm
59	5-6 May	Gracehall Dinner	
60	8-12 May	Portadown	8:45am
61	8-12 May	Bleary	10am
62	8-12 May	Gilford	11am
63	8-12 May	Portadown	1:30am
64	8-12 May	Portadown	3pm
65	8-12 May	Portadown	7pm
66	15-19 May	Belfast	9:15am
67	15-19 May	Belfast	10:15am
68	15-19 May	Belfast	10:45am
69	15-19 May	Belfast	1pm
70	15-19 May	Belfast	3pm
71	22-26 May	Anahilt	9:45am
72	22-26 May	Lisburn	11am
73	22-26 May	Lisburn	1pm
74	22-26 May	Dromore	3pm
75	22-26 May	Kinallen	7pm
76	31 May-2 June	Carrickfergus	9am
77	31 May-2 June	Carrickfergus	11am
78	31 May-2 June	Carrickfergus	1pm
79	341 May-2 June	Carrickfergus	2pm
80	5-9 June	Banbridge	9:30am
81	5-9 June	Mullaglass	11am
82	5-9 June	Kingsmills	1:30pm
83	5-9 June	Banbridge	3pm
84	5-9 June	Rathfriland	7pm
85	12-16 June	Ballymena	9:45am
86	12-16 June	Ballymena	11am
87	12-16 June	Ballymena	2pm
88	12-16 June	Ballymena	3pm
89	12-16 June	Antrim	7pm
90	19-23 June	Ballymena	9:15am
91	19-23 June	Ballymena	10:50am
92	19-23 June	Ballymena	12:30pm
93	19-23 June	Ballymena	2pm
94	19-23 June	Ballymena	3pm
95	19-23 June	Ballymena	7pm
96	26-30 June	Lack	9am
97	26-30 June	Tempo	10am
98	26-30 June	Kilskerry	11am
99	26-30 June	Fintona	1pm
100	26-30 June	Omagh	2pm
101	3-7 July	Portadown	10am
102	17-21 July	Kids Camp	Camp
103	21-23 July	Youth Camp	Camp
104	24-28 July	Kids Camp	Camp
105	7-11 Aug	Lurgan	6:30pm
106	14-18 Aug	Portrush	10am
107	14-18 Aug	Portrush	11am
108	14-18 Aug	Portrush	12pm
109	14-18 Aug	Portrush	1pm
110	14-18 Aug	Portrush	2pm
111	14-18 Aug	Portrush	3pm
112	14-18 Aug	Portrush	6pm
113	14-18 Aug	Portrush	7pm
114	14-18 Aug	Portrush	8pm
115	21-30 Aug	Poland	Camp

CHILDREN'S EVANGELIST, COLIN TINSLEY

PLEASE PRAY FOR THESE AND MORE BIBLE CLUBS ALREADY PLANNED FOR 2017

"Christ Jesus came into the world to save sinners" 1 Timothy 1:15

Hope for Youth Ministries

medicines I tried from the local chemist's shop made the slightest bit of difference. I was really confused and just couldn't understand why this particular condition had beset me. If it was an injury to any other part of my body, such as a broken arm or leg, I would likely have been able to soldier on. However, without my voice to speak to the children, I felt useless. It was one of the most challenging and frustrating periods of my life and totally beyond my control. In fact, the temptation to think I was finished in the ministry shook me more than not being able to speak again. I desperately needed a touch from the Lord.

Then one morning in May, Joanna brought a cup of tea into my study and as she walked away, subconsciously I whispered, "Thank you". Joanna stopped in her tracks and slowly turned around with tears in her eyes and asked, "What did you just say?" I was so shocked I just nodded my head as if to say nothing. "No," she insisted, "you said something – I heard your voice!" She sat on my knee and put her ear to my mouth. I strained my vocal chords and said "Kocham Cie", which means 'I love you' in Polish. It was just about audible but she heard me clearly and hugged me really tight.

We cried tears of joy and pleaded to God that He would completely restore my voice. With each new day, the volume increased until ten days later, exactly three months after I lost it, my voice returned to its full capacity again. I was so thankful and it reminded me how often we take the simple things in life for granted. It certainly wasn't much fun being a preacher without a voice. Thankfully, I was able to return to the Bible Clubs in the schools and haven't had any issues with my voice since.

Some four years later, on the last Saturday of June 2015, we were making our final preparations to take another team to

Poland for a summer camp. I spent most of the afternoon finalising rotas for workshops and printing off worksheets and so on, until around five o'clock when Joanna called me for tea. When I got up from my desk to walk towards the kitchen, I felt an excruciating pain on the side of my stomach. It reminded me of the severe stitches I used to get when running races at school just after lunchtime. I didn't have any choice but to lie down for a while, hoping it was just a severe cramp that would ease itself.

We had invited our good friends, Paul and Cheryl McIntyre to stay at our house that night, as the team was getting a bus to Dublin airport from Banbridge early the next morning. When they arrived and saw me lying on the couch, they thought I was playing a prank on them! When I stood up on my feet, I almost collapsed in agony as the pain intensified. I knew something serious was wrong with me and I needed to go to hospital immediately. As we drove to the Royal Victoria Hospital in Belfast, I remember telling Paul, "Go faster! Go faster!" but then when he went over a bump, I yelled "Slow down! Slow down!"

After an initial assessment in the Emergency Department, the medical staff led me straight into a cubicle, where they carried out some tests and put me on a drip. The doctor told me there was no chance at all I would be flying to Poland the next morning, so I called Paul and Cheryl in and asked them if they would be willing to lead the team. Joanna wanted to remain at home to look after me, so they rose to the challenge and went back to our house and lifted everything I had printed earlier that afternoon. The next morning as the team were en route to Poland, I was diagnosed with diverticulitis – a condition where small bulges or pockets develop in the intestine and become inflamed. I wasn't able to eat but the feeling of hunger was negligible compared to the acute throbbing pain of the condition I had. On one occasion when the consultant was assessing me, he poked his finger into my side and it was so sore, I jumped and nearly fell out of the bed! The next four days, I lay in constant pain while the doctors monitored me and discussed what the best form of treatment would be. Finally, they told me if I was still in pain the fifth day, they would have to take me to theatre and operate. I dreaded this thought as I had a really busy summer planned with Tollymore, caravan parks and other missions. I didn't even want to consider the thought of missing them, so I lay in bed and prayed fervently for a touch from the Lord.

I woke early on Thursday morning after a peaceful night's sleep and was ecstatic to discover that the pain was gone! To make sure I wasn't dreaming, I climbed out of bed and stretched, then walked around and jumped up and down! I felt great and was able to eat breakfast, which was the first food I had eaten since being admitted to hospital five days earlier. I was presented with the menu for lunch and was so hungry I ordered the chicken and beef dishes! When the doctor arrived on his morning rounds, he found me dressed and sitting in the chair at my laptop working on a new children's book. He looked at me and said, "Are you Mr Tinsley – the man who was in this bed?" I smiled and replied, "Yes, but I am better now – no more pain!" He asked me to stand up and started to examine me. When I saw him prepare to poke me in the spot where it ached a few days earlier, I tensed myself up but thankfully didn't feel the slightest bit of pain. He looked at me and exclaimed, "That is remarkable – someone is looking after you! You can pack your bags and get ready for home."

A couple of days later, Joanna and I drove to Banbridge to greet the Poland team on their return. They couldn't believe how well I looked. A week earlier when they arrived at the bus stop, they were all shocked to hear I wouldn't be going. Then while they were away, they had seen photos that Joanna had posted as a prayer request on Facebook, of me lying in hospital connected to a drip. Praise God that just like when I lost my voice four years earlier, others stepped up to the mark and did a fantastic job fulfilling my duties at camp in Poland. The team returned home with joy in their hearts, with the knowledge that a number of children had put their faith in Jesus. To also see me back on my feet, ready for another week in the schools was the icing on the cake for them! During that week, many of them had texted assuring me of their thoughts and prayers, so to see their jubilation and praise towards God for my recovery was powerful.

When I reflect on those two periods of illness, it reminds me of two important truths: our health can fail without warning at any given moment, and the work is bigger than any one man. That is why I believe it is vitally important to train young people in the work of God and to give them as many opportunities as possible to get experience. Then, if anything happens to a minister, pastor or missionary, the work of God goes on because there are people trained to do it. I am greatly encouraged that during both these periods of illness, the work of God kept going on.

CHAPTER TWENTY

Everything We Need and More

WHEN I LOOK back at how the ministry has developed since launching out in faith just over ten years ago, I am genuinely awestruck at God's constant provision. Just six months after starting the ministry, a recession hit the UK and Joanna's income from selling paintings virtually ceased. And furthermore, we had used most of our savings to publish my first three books!

So right from the beginning, we faced the challenge of proving God could look after us – just like we read how He provided for Abraham, Isaac and Jacob in the Bible. As a young believer, I was always intrigued and challenged when I read accounts of people such as George Müller who lived entirely by faith. For over ten years now, Joanna and I have lived in such a manner without a salary or wage and have relied on the Lord to provide for our daily needs through the kindness of other Christians. I sometimes tell Joanna if we ever don't have enough money to buy food, we will visit our neighbours and pray they will offer us something to eat! She always looks at me a little strange when I suggest that, but thus far we haven't had to, as the Lord has always provided us with daily bread!

There's no doubt that launching out in faith to work full-time in the ministry is a big challenge. There is a natural humanistic fear of not receiving enough money to get by or facing embarrassment if plans don't work out. Thankfully in my situation, the crystal-clear promises I received from God through His Word gave me an assurance and excitement that was stronger that any feelings of fear.

It has been a steep learning curve as right from the beginning, there have been many bills and expenses associated with the ministry and sometimes it seemed like God chose to wait until the last possible moment to meet our need! I now realise that God used those situations to teach us to really trust Him, even when it seemed we were going under. We can honestly testify that He has never once failed us and His provision in small things has helped us plan big in the ministry.

From day one, my parents have been our best supporters and often save their last pennies and sacrifice luxuries in life to support us. The Lord has also burdened other Christians for the ministry and many of them have given generously for many years and we will always be indebted to them.

It never ceases to amaze me how every time we seek to progress an aspect of the ministry, the necessary funds always come in; whether we're publishing a new book, purchasing necessary equipment or planning an overseas mission trip. The only way I can explain it is to humbly say that God is in it and I trust when you read some examples of how He has provided for us, you will be challenged to trust Him more!

One Saturday night shortly after starting out, I was testifying to young people at an event called Dunamis in Craigavon. I shared my vision for the ministry and asked the young people to pray that God would clearly confirm those plans. After the meeting, a man that was on the committee called Robin Harper introduced himself and said if I ever needed anything to let him know and he would try to help. At that time, the only place we had to store our literature and the equipment for Tollymore camp was in our own home. At times, it was nearly impossible to invite visitors around as there were literally dozens of boxes sitting all over the place! We had been praying that God would provide us with a safe location to store it all, so I asked Robin if he knew of anyone who had a field near Kinallen where I could put a storage container. Robin gave me his address and told me to call round some day the following week. To my amazement, he lived less than a mile from my house and when I reached the top of his lane, there was a large yard that he used for his furniture business. He pointed over to the corner and asked me if the container would fit there. It was the perfect location as it would be secure and was incredibly convenient for me. Within a week or two, we had a container delivered and a friend who was an electrician kitted it out with lighting and background heating so the books wouldn't get damp in winter. It was amazing to get our home back again, and over the years as the ministry has grown, we have added three more containers adjacent to it.

Another vital tool for the ministry is the van I use to carry necessary equipment and literature around the country on a daily basis. In the early days when I was only doing assemblies I was able to use my car, but once the Bible Clubs started I was sometimes in five different schools, reaching up to a thousand children each day. This required five thousand tracts and worksheets each week and an additional hundred books for prizes, so I brought the matter of buying a van before the Lord. On New Year's Eve of all nights, I was at a friend's house and he asked me to step outside a moment and gaze across the yard. He asked, "Would that red Volkswagen Caddy minivan parked over there be any use to you Colin?" It was exactly what I was after, so I asked how much he was looking for it. He told me to accept it as a gift since it would be used for the Lord's work!

Each year I cover over thirty thousand miles driving around the various schools, so a lot of diesel and regular maintenance is required for the van. On one occasion when I was visiting schools in the Cullybackey area, I pulled into a service station to fill the van up with diesel. As I was filling up, I began chatting with another man who was refuelling his car beside me. When I told him about the work I was doing, he said he would pay for my fuel! I was really touched by such a kind gesture from a complete stranger. On other occasions when I have been in an area, people have told me to fill my tank at certain petrol stations and to charge it to their account. It's their way of being part of the ministry and it really encourages me knowing that others are with me in the work.

Sadly, one afternoon three years later, that wee van stuttered to a halt on the hard shoulder of the M1 motorway. I called my brother, Edwin, who is a mechanic and from what I described, he reckoned it had seized and wasn't worth repairing. It had over two hundred thousand miles on the clock and had served me well. Once I got it recovered from the motorway, my thoughts turned to how I would get a replacement van as we hadn't any money saved up for one. I sent a text to a few friends and posted a status on Facebook about the need for a new van. To my amazement, within two weeks folks had pledged enough money to enable me to buy a newer model with only fifty-three thousand miles on the clock.

Just like our campervan in Australia, the first thing I did was put the ministry's logo and Scripture verses on it. One of them is *"I will go in the strength of the Lord" (Psalm 71:16)*. I also put 'Souls not sales' on the back of it as the van would be used to equip children with the free and life-saving message of the gospel. When I went to collect the van from the sign writer, it looked brand new with bright decals and I was thrilled when he told me I didn't owe him a penny!

After buying the van, additional gifts arrived, so I used them to purchase a twin-axle box trailer to transport the large signs we use to advertise evening Bible Clubs, as well as other bulky equipment needed for special events.

Then in 2017, as we celebrated ten years of ministry with a weekend of thanksgiving and celebration, donations were given towards another new van as the current one had almost two hundred thousand miles on it. We were astounded to receive enough money over the weekend to buy a brand new one! Our hearts were touched again as the Lord provided by touching the hearts of believers to help us. We didn't sell the old van but gave it to our volunteers, Paul and Cheryl McIntyre who assist us so much in the ministry.

By 2014, the work had got very intense with over one hundred Bible Clubs a year, excluding the overseas mission trips. Many volunteers offered their time freely and it was invaluable having folk to review the worksheets and counsel children during the meeting. Understandably though, most of the volunteers could only join me a day or two each month as they had their own job to go to during school hours. Joanna was very willing to assist when required, but such was the administration work to schedule the Bible Clubs, order literature and organise camps, she really needed time to focus on that.

Just when we were contemplating putting a limit on the number of bookings we accepted, a group of men from a fellowship met me and asked how they could support the advancement of the ministry on a monthly basis for a year. They specified that they didn't want to support vehicles or buildings so immediately I thought about Cheryl, a young woman who had been volunteering with us for some years. She worked full-time in a shop but joined me in the schools every Friday on her day off. I suggested to the men I could ask her if she would be willing to work with the ministry part-time and the support from the group could cover the wages she lost from her secular employment. The men were delighted with the proposal and when I put the proposition to Cheryl, she was ecstatic and accepted the offer immediately.

Cheryl has proved to be an immense help as she got more opportunities to use her gifts speaking at the Bible Clubs and assisting Joanna with the administration work. She has had the joy of leading hundreds of children to the Lord. Her husband, Paul is also very talented and comes along to many of the Bible Clubs in the evening after he finishes work. At the end of the twelve months, there were sufficient funds in the ministry to continue supporting Cheryl and it's testimony that God knows our needs.

One of the largest daily operating expenses the ministry has is the cost of the literature we give out to children. It is vital to help them learn more about God and to get Scripture into their homes. To date, we have printed over a million tracts and thousands of books. The most used one is called Stepping Stones, which I described earlier. It costs thousands of pounds to print them, but the more we give out, the more funds the Lord sends to replenish them! Many times whenever Joanna and I talk and pray about God's wondrous provision, we often end up in tears as we reflect on the goodness and faithfulness of God!

Northern Ireland is an incredible country with many wonderful Christian people who have a great desire to invest their money in advancing the Lord's work. I believe when we are involved in a God-led work, the promise will always prevail that *"God shall supply all your need according to his riches in glory by Christ Jesus" (Philippians 4:19).*

Sometimes when I'm picking stuff up from the containers, I get overwhelmed by the Lord's ceaseless provision when I look at all the books and leaflets that go through our hands. It makes me reflect on how powerful God is and how He works circumstances out to accomplish His purposes. Little did I realise that being married to an artist would make a perfect helpmate! Whilst I can write the books, tracts and newsletters, I need someone to do the graphics and layout. No-one understands the work better than Joanna, so her artistic talent is priceless for this purpose.

Finally, as a couple we also endeavour to support and bless others financially, as we know what receiving little gifts mean to us. Most summers, we pay for a few new campers to come to Tollymore who otherwise could not afford it. On other occasions, when we take teams to Poland and the team fails to meet their fundraising target, we make up the balance to ensure no children miss out. Many of them are orphans or come from extremely poor families and would otherwise miss out and possibly never hear the wonderful life-changing message of the gospel. The Lord gives us much, so naturally, we want to give as much back as we can.

We may not fully understand or be able to describe how God's provision works, but then some things are best believed without explanation. God has never once failed us or left us feeling that we lack anything. No matter how great or small the need is, He meets it every time, on time!

CHAPTER TWENTY-ONE

Enlarging my Coast

WHEN WE PLAN our Bible Clubs at the start of each year, we pencil in weeks of rest that we protect at all costs. As the intensity of the ministry has increased over the last few years I realise, now more than ever before, how necessary it is to set time aside for refreshment. In full-time ministry, when you enjoy God's work so much, it is tempting to push your body beyond its limits. I once heard a wise preacher say, "If the devil can't stop you, he will push you on until you burn out."

Also, children are very good at sensing if someone speaking to them is just going through the motions; so it's important for me to look after my well-being if I want to keep them engaged as I teach the Bible.

As I shared earlier, Joanna and I have a great passion for travelling and experiencing different cultures across the world. On holiday as well as travelling off the beaten track and exploring our surroundings, we also spend a lot of time chilling out, which gives me an opportunity to write new tracts and books for the children. It's only in such calm environments with no distractions that I have the time, inspiration and patience to write.

In our minds, each place we visit is a spiritual milestone – where we have lots of time to reflect on God's goodness during the previous year and seek His guidance for the one ahead.

I would like to share some of these experiences with you, but I'll go right back to my first time travelling outside Northern Ireland when I was nineteen years old:

U.S.A.

I mentioned earlier how I had volunteered at my local YMCA branch in Lisburn. It had links with Christian camp centres in America and I was offered a place on a summer internship programme at a horse-riding camp in Ohio. The campsite was in the middle of a large forest with a crystal-clear lake. Each morning, I was responsible for saddling up the horses and then teaching the children how to ride. In the afternoons, we did water sports in the lake and played team games on the grounds. After tea, there was a gospel meeting and I was given many opportunities to teach Bible stories and share my faith with the campers.

On one particular day after we finished a session with the children, I had a really frightening experience! Most days, we exercised the horses by taking them for a gallop through the forest on the way back to the barn. As on many other occasions, I rode bareback (without a saddle), but that particular day something spooked my horse and it took off at full speed through the woods. I couldn't stop it and genuinely feared for my life. I knew I only had enough energy to hang on for a short time so I had no choice but to look for a suitable place to jump off before I fell off! Thankfully we came to a flat grassy area, so I took my opportunity and leapt off the horse and crashed to the ground. I was pretty shaken up after the ordeal, but thankfully I was physically unharmed and the horse eventually made its way back to the barn. Apart from that incident, I enjoyed my time there so much I returned the following summer to repeat it all over again.

On both occasions after the nine weeks of camp were over, my two friends, Gary and Ian, flew out and joined me to go on road-trips. The first year, we travelled north and crossed the Canadian border and spent a few days in Toronto, then drove down the east coast through New York and finished up in Florida. The second year, we headed west through Texas and took in most of the southern states the whole way across to California. During the two trips, we ventured into forty different states and shared some incredible experiences together. When I reflect back on those summers, I can clearly see how God used those camps in America to teach me how to lead a camp in preparation for Tollymore ten years later.

Switzerland

In 2000, after I completed Bible College, Joanna and I spent three months at the CEF (Child Evangelism Fellowship) European headquarters in Kilchzimmer, Switzerland. Since we hadn't seen Joanna's family for a long time, we decided that instead of flying to Switzerland, we would take the car and drive there via Poland. After spending a week with Joanna's family in Krakow, we headed south-west and crossed the River Rhine on the German-Swiss border near Basel. Then, we had a steady climb through the dense forests of the Swiss Jura Mountains until we reached Kilchzimmer. At nearly one thousand metres above sea-level, the views were outstanding and the air was incredibly pure. It may have been a time of refreshment to our bodies but it was definitely an intense workout for our minds! Each morning, we attended lectures and then completed practical assessments in the afternoons. The social highlight of each day was the volleyball match which everyone participated in just before teatime. After tea, everyone separated for personal study to work on assignments and complete background reading to complement the lectures. Then, before retiring to bed, we got together for a quick cuppa. During one of the weeks, we had a great experience visiting an American army base to conduct a Bible Club there for the soldiers' kids, and put into practice everything we'd been taught.

We had many team devotions which focused on the importance of reaching children with the gospel but one tragic incident changed my outlook on life and the importance of children's evangelism forever. There was a family from Belgium on the course and one evening, just a few hours after we had all been playing together, their young son collapsed suddenly and died. It shook the entire group and was a stark reminder of how fleeting life is and how important it is to reach children early in life.

Jamaica

Shortly after returning from the CEF course in Switzerland, we were deployed to Jamaica for a one-year placement to pastor a church in Little London, Westmoreland. I thoroughly enjoyed this year as it was my first opportunity to engage in full-time ministry. I preached in the church most Sundays, and nearly every morning we did an assembly in a public school. One of our closest friends in Jamaica was a young man called Bryan Morris. He helped us settle quickly and kept us out of danger's way during our stay there. Sadly in June 2012, we were devastated to hear he was murdered at work while carrying out his duties as a security guard. Bryan was a living example of pure and simple Christianity. He was blessed with remarkable gifts and could sing and preach powerfully to children and adults alike. It is a solemn reminder that any of us could have our lives taken away from us at any moment.

Australia

As I mentioned earlier in this book, a year after returning from Jamaica, a vacancy came up to pastor a church in Australia and we were asked if we would be interested in going for two years. We were delighted to accept the offer and were grateful that the church mission board trusted us with such a responsibility many miles from home.

The church was in the town of Lock, one hundred miles north of Port Lincoln on the south coast of Australia. During our placement there, I preached about six times each week and helped with a church-plant sixty miles away. After completing our two-year pastorate in the church, we spent a third year driving around Australia in a campervan. We drove to Perth, then up to Darwin, across to Cairns and down the east coast. Whilst on tour, we spoke in over a hundred schools and gave out thousands of gospel tracts. We spent our last few months 'Down Under' assisting a church in Tasmania, an island three hundred miles south of Australia.

Vanuatu

During our time in Australia, I read a book about John Paton, a missionary from Scotland who travelled to The New Hebrides Islands, north-east of Australia. Prior to his visit, the people there knew little of the Christian faith, but after much perseverance and determination, John led many of them to faith in Christ. We visited one of the islands called Vanuatu and gave out lots of tracts and small Bibles and spoke in ten different schools. On Sunday mornings most of the Sunday schools commenced at 7 a.m., so it was beautiful wakening up to the sound of children singing in the distance.

...One man can influence a home, village or country for good or evil. John Paton certainly left his mark on this land for good, and for God!

Poland

After getting married, we made an effort to go to Poland at least once each year to visit Joanna's family. It was great to renew friendship and for Joanna to spend time with her friends and family. However, it was often quite a frustrating time for me as none of them could speak English and I couldn't speak Polish – one can only sit and smile at their mother-in-law for so long! One day, I had a brainwave to buy a laptop and start writing books for the ministry. Every time since, I have brought it with me and am perfectly content typing in the background, while Joanna chats away in Polish without feeling I'm bored!

Soon we started taking teams to Poland to spread the gospel message through Christian camps. The teams are responsible for raising money through fundraising activities to pay for underprivileged Polish children to attend these camps. There are many folks who are not able to go to Poland for a week, but they support the work financially and without their generosity, the camps couldn't take place. At the time of writing, we have taken over forty teams to Poland and in the process, have booked over a thousand flights for team members. Although we always set out to be a blessing, many of the volunteers return home abundantly blessed in their own souls and have since gone on in leaps and bounds in their Christian faith.

Many of the Polish children and young people who get saved at camps find it very tough when they return to their families and schools. Every year, we hear different stories about the challenges they face living as a believer there and our hearts go out to them.

Despite the persecution and mockery they face, we are really encouraged to see them remain faithful and bold for the Lord and continue to live out their faith and shine for Jesus.

A less pleasant experience that will forever be etched in my mind was an infamous late-night trip to the shop for sweets! One night while the children were all asleep, the team wanted some snacks from the shop. However, the caretaker had locked the door at the main entrance and the only way out was through the back door beside his room. We didn't want to waken him so we decided to climb out a window. Since it was completely dark, I volunteered to go first to make sure it was okay. As I climbed out the window and turned around to lower myself to the ground, my wedding ring caught on the metal edge of the window ledge. As I dropped to the ground, the force pulled my ring into my finger and I yelled with pain. It was so sore I almost fainted and since it was dark, I couldn't even see if the finger was still attached to my hand. When we got a torch, I was relieved to see it still there but it was bleeding heavily. Joanna insisted I went to hospital so we drove two hours in the middle of the night to the nearest emergency department.

When we arrived and Joanna explained to the doctor that I was climbing out of a window to go to a shop, I believe he thought I was a thief! He directed me to a bed in a cubicle and muttered something before walking off. Under the bright lights of the hospital, I could see that my finger was completely black and covered in blood. When the doctor returned a few minutes later, he had a massive pair of bolt cutters! *My finger is gone* I assumed. Just then my phone beeped and I looked at it assuming it was some of the team back at camp looking an update. However, it was my friend, Paul McCammon texting from Northern Ireland, totally unaware of the situation. His text was simply a verse from the Bible: *"Behold, I have graven thee upon the palms of my hands; thy walls are continually before me" (Isaiah 49:16).*

The verse refers to the palms of the Lord Jesus, but once I read it, I was overcome by an incredible sense of peace and an assurance that I would be keeping my finger even though it had looked pretty certain I was going to lose it, such was the severity of the wound. The doctor instructed me to hold out my finger and look away while keeping my hand totally still. As I did so, the bolt cutters came down and pressed hard against my finger. Then he set down the bolt cutters and before I worked up the courage to look round again, he presented the broken ring in front of me. He then stitched my finger up and put a big bandage on it. When he was finished, he told me if I had waited until the morning I would definitely have lost my finger.

To this day, I still have a scar to remind me how treating my friends to sweets nearly cost me a finger! Often in Bible Clubs, I use my fingers and thumbs to teach the children the Ten Commandments. I smile and thank God every time I do this, wondering how I would manage to do it if I had only nine fingers! A couple of days later, Joanna took my broken ring to a jewellery shop in Krakow and got it mended so I could put it back on my finger when it healed. It reminds me of God's promise *"My times are in thy hand" (Psalm 31:5).*

Egypt

In November 2007, we went on holiday to the Sinai Peninsula in north-east Egypt, which is an area full of biblical history. Joseph was taken there as a slave and then four hundred years later, Moses freed the Israelites from slavery and led them out of Egypt, across the Red Sea and through the wilderness for forty years en route to the Promised Land.

One morning we set out early to climb Mount Sinai, where God gave Moses the Ten Commandments. Watching the sunrise that morning is probably one of the most beautiful sights my eyes have ever beheld. It was remarkable to consider that Moses had spent forty days in God's presence on that very ground, while the mountain was enveloped in smoke because God's presence had descended. Even though it was three and a half thousand years later, as I rested in those peaceful surroundings and read the middle chapters of Exodus, the story was very real in that location. Just to sit in the presence of God and meditate on His Word was very moving and inspirational.

Morocco

A few years after getting married, Joanna and I had a holiday inter-railing around southern Europe. Joanna really wanted to visit Morocco in Africa, which was a short boat trip from southern Spain. At the port in Spain, we were told that British citizens would be given a tourist visa on arrival. I assumed since Joanna was my wife she would get one too, but whenever we reached the Moroccan embassy, she was refused entry because she was travelling on a Polish passport.

I pleaded with the immigration officer at the desk to give her a visa for one week but he point-blank refused. He told me I had to go to either London or Warsaw to get a visa. We were at a complete stalemate and Joanna was tired and teary. Suddenly out of the corner of my eye, I saw what looked to be an important man in a suit entering an office. I took my chance and made a beeline for the door to speak to him. The officer at the desk shouted at me to come back, but I knocked the door and walked in. The executive smiled at me and pointed at the window. I was wearing a t-shirt, shorts and a baseball cap and I think he reckoned I was the window cleaner! The other man burst in and started shouting something in Arabic but the executive in the suit calmed his employee down and asked me who I was and what my job was. I told him I worked in Marks & Spencer. "Marks & Spencer!" he shouted with glee and jumped to his feet. "Mr Marks & Spencer, I am so glad to meet you!" he continued. He pointed to his shirt, tie and suit and said "All from your shop."

To this day, I am convinced he thought I was the owner of the multinational enterprise! "How can I help you, sir?" he politely asked. I explained that I wanted to take my wife to Morocco for one week and all I needed was a visa and a stamp on her passport. "Of course I can do that for you, sir!" he replied as he opened his drawer and took out a stamper. He handed me back Joanna's passport and wished me a wonderful time in his country. I smiled and asked him if he would take Joanna's passport to her and personally invite her to Morocco, which he did!

South Africa

In 2008, we spent seven weeks in Johannesburg, the largest city in South Africa. Our host was a missionary friend called Paul Craig, who pastored a church there. I preached a couple of Sundays for him and we helped him lead the church family camp. Joanna had an enjoyable time assisting the art teacher at the school run by the church.

Swaziland

Although we didn't know anything about Swaziland nor anyone living there, since it was only two hundred miles from

Johannesburg, we reckoned it would be great to visit some schools there and preach the Word of God. When we got there, we simply pulled up outside any schools we could find and ventured in and enquired if they would like two white people from Northern Ireland to tell their children about Jesus.

Most of the schools welcomed us with outstretched arms and in one school the headmistress was so delighted to see us, she led us straight to the staffroom and started an impromptu prayer meeting with other teachers. When I listened to those teachers intercede for the children in their care, it melted my heart. We were humbled to be in their presence and nearly felt inadequate to speak to the children with such devout teachers in the room. In another school after we had finished speaking to the children, the principal addressed the students and encouraged them to come to Christ without delay.

Mauritius
This tropical island, famous for its palm trees, lagoons and coral reefs was also near Johannesburg, so we made the most of the opportunity and spent a week there relaxing and writing books. One thing I love about writing books is that it forces me to slow down and really understand what the Bible is saying.

Mexico
In January 2010, after an intense autumn and winter in the work, we found an amazing place in Mexico where we holidayed for a fortnight. It was there that I started writing my first children's devotional book – 'Walking with God' – where I took a fresh look at characters in the Old Testament and applied their wisdom to Twenty-First-Century living.

Isle of Man

Most people go to the Isle of Man to watch the famous Manx TT motorbike races but in April 2011, Roy and Sharon Wilson invited us to join their outreach team on the island. During that week we conducted four Bible Clubs, took assemblies in ten different schools and gave out over two thousand Bibles and books on creation. In one school, we had the joy of witnessing several children putting their trust in the Lord.

Israel

In the spring of 2012, we took a team of eight people to do outreach in Israel, the land of the Bible. We stayed in CEF accommodation in Nazareth as a couple of tradespeople had joined our team to carry out essential maintenance work on the building. The rest of us assisted them each morning, then in the afternoons, we headed out to the schools to present the gospel message alongside the local CEF workers. Some of the schools had an evangelical ethos while others were Arab, Druze or Roman Catholic; but all of them welcomed us with open arms.

After an intense week of work, we packed away the tools and spent a week touring around many of the locations we read about in the Bible. It was quite emotional at times and it certainly added an extra dimension to the Bible stories that many of us were familiar with. We visited the Wailing Wall in Jerusalem and then had a communion service in the Garden of Gethsemane. Afterwards, we trod the sad steps Jesus likely took to Golgotha, where He bore each of our sins on the cross. Then we journeyed to the site believed to be the Garden Tomb, where Jesus rose from the grave – for me this was the highlight of the trip!

On our last day, we had a relaxing afternoon at the Dead Sea, which is actually the lowest point on earth, at over four hundred metres below sea level. We had the opportunity to cover our bodies in the rich mineral mud that supposedly reinvigorates your skin! After lying in the sun for the mud to cake (and apparently take years off our appearance), we waded out into the buoyant waters of the Dead Sea. I had previously seen photos of people floating on their backs reading newspapers, but to do it myself was exhilarating.

Gambia

In January 2013, we spent a fortnight holidaying in this gem of a country, sandwiched between Senegal and Guinea-Bissau, on the west coast of Africa. At the time, I desperately needed to write some new literature, as we needed fresh material to offer children when we returned to their school for maybe the fourth or fifth year. With all-day sunshine and a fresh Atlantic breeze keeping us cool, we were able to sit outside from sunrise at five o'clock until sunset, searching the Scriptures and jotting down thoughts that came into our minds. On this trip, I also wrote most of my young people's devotional book I entitled, 'Impact'.

Every day, we noticed a local man walking by with his horse. He looked quite lonely so we always said 'hello' and struck up a friendship with him. We spoke with him for five or ten minutes every time he passed and we always tried to bring the conversation around to talking about the Lord. We don't know if he ever got saved but it reminded us of the importance of taking every opportunity to witness for Christ.

CHAPTER TWENTY-TWO

That All the Earth may Know

IN THE LAST few years, we have taken mission teams to even more countries to share the Good News of Jesus Christ. Oswald J Smith once said:

"No one has the right to hear the gospel twice, while there remains someone who has not heard it once."

Those are strong words, but the Lord Jesus gave His disciples the great commission: *"Go ye into all the world, and preach the gospel to every creature" (Mark 16:15)*. This is the primary reason that we try to visit as many countries as possible to do outreach and tell the locals about Jesus. Secondly, it gives team members an opportunity to step out of their comfort zones and progress further in their Christian walk. I will share some experiences from the countries we have ministered in:

Lithuania

This country shares its border with Poland and is the southernmost of the three Baltic States that gained their independence from the former Soviet Union in 1991. We have been to Lithuania twice to assist local CEF workers with summer camps. One of the helpers, a young woman called Diana, spent a summer in Northern Ireland helping us with Tollymore camp, the caravan park ministry and other types of outreach. The purpose was to give her experience and a vision for her work back home. Since then, she has completed a training course with CEF and is now serving the Lord amongst the children in Lithuania.

India

In January 2014, the Ross family from Randalstown invited us on a trip to India to support the work of a pastor in a local Baptist church. During the daytime, we had an intense programme of Bible Clubs for the children, various youth activities and door-to-door outreach. Then in the evenings, the entire village came along and sat down in the middle of the road for an open-air meeting. When a car or bus arrived, they all got up and let it pass, then sat down again. Some of the villages made us think of how life was two thousand years ago with women carrying clay water pots on their heads as they returned from drawing water at the well. We had the joy of leading several girls from the church orphanage to the Lord. Shortly after we returned home, we received a letter from the pastor telling us they were going on well with the Lord and one of them had already been baptised.

Nepal

After ministering in India, we travelled northwards to Nepal and visited my friend, a pastor called Amos. He invited me to preach in his church on the Sunday, then we spent the rest of the week visiting local schools. Each day, we packed gospel literature into his Land Rover and set out on the dangerous mountain roads to preach the Word of God to the children. In every school, we gave each child a copy of the Scriptures in their own language.

In one school, a lovely little girl about nine years old came over and told us she was the only Christian in her class and was delighted we had come to tell her friends about Jesus. We gave her the biggest hug ever!

Canada

In 2014, the Faith Mission invited us to lead a summer camp near Vancouver on the west of Canada. We had an amazing time with the team conducting two camps and a summer Bible Club in a big barn. In the evenings, we played exciting missionary-themed games to give children an insight into the life of a missionary. After camp, we journeyed through the Canadian Rockies and had a whistle-stop tour of Vancouver. Rather than flying straight home, we took a detour via Alaska. On this journey we bumped into friends we met whilst in Tasmania many years before.

Republic of Ireland

Over the years, we have spoken at approximately twenty schools in the Republic of Ireland when various churches and evangelical groups have invited us to conduct Bible Clubs for children. Some of these were held in Gaelic clubs and many Roman Catholic children attended. We have also taken teams south of the border to do outreach and tract distribution – it's truly a vast mission field on our doorstep!

China

With a population of over 1.3 billion, China has more citizens than any other country in the world. In fact, twice as many people live in China than on the entire continent of Europe!

AsiaLink, the Christian mission agency that seeks to connect with the unreached people of Asia, estimates that there are eighty million evangelical Christians in the land of China. The communist government permits state-run churches, but the majority of believers attend unofficial house-churches. Often, the entire congregation of a house-church have to share a single Bible. This obviously restricts the growth of individual believers who have a real thirst for the Word of God. For several years we have volunteered on teams, coordinated by my friend Stephen, to bring Bibles into China for these Christian brothers and sisters. Most of the trips were for two weeks, we collected Bibles in Hong Kong and then carried them across the land border into China.

On most occasions, we got through immigration successfully but sometimes we were stopped and had most of our Bibles confiscated. When that happens, we go on into China without them and then a few hours later, we pay a small administration fee to get them back when we return to Hong Kong. People of all ages and from all walks of life take part in this great work. The fellowship with the full-time workers is amazing and we feel we are part of a massive operation. Everyone feels a great sense of satisfaction, knowing that every single copy we get across the border will be read intensively. We pray that in coming years, these labours will help thousands of Chinese believers mature and make a significant impact for God in their country.

Hong Kong

Hong Kong is one of the few countries in Asia where people are free to worship God and read the Bible. For this reason, it is regularly used as a base for taking Bibles into neighbouring China. On one trip I had two large suitcases, which we nicknamed 'beasts' – because they were so big and cumbersome! We used public transport, so getting them on and off the Metro without them falling apart or getting stuck was a real challenge!

When the 'beasts' were packed with Bibles, pulling them was a struggle and I sweated profusely on my journey to the border. We tried to look relaxed going through immigration and security, and it felt incredible every time I got through unhindered. It is vital to get the Word of God to our brothers and sisters in Christ who live in these persecuted lands.

Cambodia

Like Hong Kong, Cambodia is one of the few Asian nations where Christians are allowed to live without harassment from the authorities. It has a recent sad history because of the genocide carried out by the Communist Khmer Rouge party between 1975 and 1979. It is estimated that the evil regime killed over a fifth of the Cambodian population.

On two occasions, we have visited this remarkable country and the first time, when we ministered in Christian schools, we were welcomed with open arms. When we returned home, we sent Bibles and Christian literature out to them; such was their desire for the Word of God. On our second visit to this land, we took time to relax after ministering in a neighbouring country and it was during those weeks I wrote the majority of this book!

Vietnam

In contrast to neighbouring Cambodia, Christians in Vietnam are severely persecuted by the authorities and sometimes even by their own families. I have heard many terrible stories of pastors being put into prison for doing evangelism in this land. Like China, there is a real shortage of Bibles and if locals are caught bringing them in from outside, they face severe punishment. However, if Westerners are stopped, the worst punishment we can expect is to have our Bibles confiscated and our visas cancelled. Thankfully, this has never happened to anyone on any of our trips and we have been successful at delivering our parcels to a third-party to protect the identity of local believers.

For security reasons, we rarely get to meet and encourage local believers, but their predicament is understandable. Often the way flights are scheduled, we have a few days to rest and visit places like the Vietnam War Museum where you can get up close to old planes, helicopters and jeeps that were captured from the Americans during the twenty-year conflict. In the cities, the streets are packed with all kinds of street-traders trying to make a living with literally thousands of mopeds zooming around everywhere. Despite its troublesome past and the opposition from the government, it is very encouraging to hear that the church in Vietnam continues to grow rapidly.

Laos

This hidden jewel of a country between Thailand and Vietnam is probably my favourite of all the Asian countries I have visited. We have been there five times to deliver Bibles to persecuted believers and this trip is the most adventurous of all, as it involves travelling by bus, boat and Tuk-Tuk (3-wheeled motorbike taxi). We dress like backpackers and carry as many Bibles as our rucksacks can hold!

On a couple of occasions, we have been privileged to visit an underground church. One time, a sixteen-year-old girl translated the service for us and at the end of the meeting we discovered that she had only got saved the previous Sunday. She told us whenever she returned home and told her parents, they told her to renounce her new faith in Christ or pack her bags and go. Inquisitively, we asked her what she was going to do – without flinching, she pointed over to the side of the building and told us the bags sitting by the wall were all of her possessions. She had decided to follow Jesus and was not going to turn back, no matter what the cost. Remarkably, the majority of the believers in the church had similar stories to tell. The coordinator informed us that the growing Christian population requires twelve thousand Bibles each year, but only one thousand are brought in. That is the main reason I keep going back, as I feel a deep sense of obligation to satisfy the hunger that these true brothers and sisters have for the Word of God.

On another trip, we were at a different church and the pastor was speaking about persecution. He encouraged everyone to live for Jesus every day despite the fact that soldiers could come at any time and arrest them. As he was labouring this point, the plastic chair that I was sitting on cracked and smashed into pieces and I tumbled to the ground. The noise scared everyone, especially after what the pastor had just said! I was very embarrassed and apologised but everyone saw the funny side. When the service was over, the ladies in the church prepared a traditional Lao meal for us. We followed the custom of the locals and sat on a mat in a circle with our legs crossed. The meal consisted of spicy soup with rice noodles for a starter, then coconut curry served on banana leaves. It was delicious!

In 2015, after the team departed, we remained for a holiday and it was during this time I wrote my second children's devotional book entitled 'Running for God'. This one was based on the New Testament and focused on the life of Jesus and prominent men like the Apostle Paul.

Philippines

Noel Stevenson, otherwise known as 'Uncle Noel', left Belfast in 2003 to pioneer a work amongst poor children in the Philippines. Since it is so far away from Northern Ireland, Noel rarely sees any folk from home; so on a few occasions when we have been travelling in Asia, we made a point of going over to visit him.

For twenty-five years, he worked full-time as a children's worker in Belfast during the height of 'The Troubles' and during those years, I witnessed his consistent love for God and his desire to see young people get saved. Since moving to the Philippines, Noel has built a church and school in a poor area of the capital city, Manila. Hundreds of children attend the school and as a result of his ministry, many of them have come to faith in Christ. We have taken teams out to do camps with Noel on three occasions and it's always a blessing to see children who have very little materially, so happy and content. What impacts us most though is the Filipino believers' love for the Lord and their zeal to serve Him – it is really contagious and we always return home inspired! When we are out there, Noel also asks me to preach in his church, so I'm only too glad to give him a well-deserved week off.

After one of the camps was over, Joanna and I took a short flight to Palawan Island for a week's holiday before returning home. We had envisaged a peaceful week doing activities like snorkelling amongst the coral and sea turtles or trekking into the jungle to see the parrots, cockatoos and other tropical birds. The holiday got off to a perfect start when we were dropped off at our accommodation – a little bamboo hut on the beach. We did pass comment that it was very quiet and there weren't many people about, but we just assumed that was because it was the off-peak season.

Unbeknown to us a hurricane was on its way! We later realised that the resort was quiet because everyone else had heard the village was in line for a direct hit by the storm and most of them had left. That first night, we went to bed as normal but around 2 a.m., I was awakened by the wind. I peeked out the door but since there was only moonlight, all I could see were massive waves.

I went back to bed and tried to go to sleep but I was genuinely scared and an hour or so later, flashes of lightning lit up the sky. With the boisterous winds battering our door and spray from the waves blitzing our roof, I reckoned it was too late to make a run for it. As we had only arrived a few hours earlier, we hadn't explored the area and I didn't have any idea where to go for refuge. The whole time, Joanna lay fast asleep like a baby but I realised I was responsible for her safety. All I could do was pray intensely that the Lord would keep us safe in the storm and while doing so, I meditated on His promises for protection.

Whenever we got up in the morning and looked outside, we almost cried with disbelief. We realised the Lord had protected us from one of the greatest storms the Philippines had ever faced. It was Super Typhoon Yolanda on 8th November 2013, one of the most intense tropical cyclones on record with wind speeds exceeding 200mph! Tragically, over six thousand people died and thirty thousand were injured. As we walked around and surveyed the carnage, it felt surreal how our surroundings had changed from the beach paradise we had arrived to less than twenty-four hours earlier. Beautiful boats were scattered across the beach as if it was a junkyard and many homes were flattened. We found a local Baptist church and helped them administer aid and food to the locals alongside believers from other churches whose buildings had been destroyed or badly damaged.

The telephone networks were down for three full days so we had no way to assure our families and friends back home we were safe. As soon as the internet service was restored, we were able to make contact and asked them to put out an appeal to help those most in need. Within a few days, kind-hearted people in Northern Ireland raised thousands of pounds, which we were able to give directly to the church folk so they could provide food aid and help believers get their homes and churches repaired.

Our holiday plans had been turned upside down, but it meant little when we witnessed the devastation that the storm left behind. We tried our best to help in some small way by bringing comfort to those worst affected and this gave us a lot more satisfaction than a relaxing week in the sun.

Kenya

On two occasions, we have been involved with mission work in Kenya. The first time was in 2002, when we laboured with a local church in the western part of the country doing outreach in schools and distributing gospel tracts. Then in 2016, some fourteen years later, we returned with a team to conduct children's meetings in over twenty primary and secondary schools. Our local contact was a pastor friend named Titus, whom I studied with at Bible College.

The national language of Kenya is Swahili and everyone also speaks their own tribal language. However, the schools teach English as they see it as the key to prosperity, so we were able to communicate easily. The country does have a nominally Christian culture, with public prayers still offered in schools and many vehicles displaying stickers with Christian slogans on them. Sadly though, little of it is rooted in a personal relationship with Jesus Christ but rather a desire for divine protection or good fortune. There is also much confusion amongst the people with false cult groups and the emergence of the erroneous health and wealth gospel, which promises people material prosperity if they seek God. Many false teachers from the West have brought a man-centred gospel that lowers God to a genie-type figure to cater for man's every material whim. Then whenever people don't become financially prosperous, they ditch God and resist any future attempts to evangelise them. Therefore, we always emphasised to the children that money doesn't bring happiness – only a personal relationship with Jesus Christ can make us truly satisfied in life. In one school there were over three thousand children, so we split our team into five groups and held simultaneous meetings with the different age groups.

In the afternoons, we took to the streets and gave out over twenty thousand gospel tracts. There is a great hunger and respect for the Word of God and many drivers stopped in the middle of the road to get a piece of literature. On a few occasions, we were mobbed by school children as they walked home in large groups. If we had been giving out money, I don't believe it would have been more frenetic!

After five days in the city, we headed eastwards to a mission station in the Mwingi district. We only had a few days to see the work and encourage the permanent missionaries. Although the work has only been going twenty years, they have a fantastic complex that is continually administrating care for nearly two hundred orphan children. There is also a baby clinic on the main site and a few satellite clinics in the wider community that do a great work, providing proper medical care to mothers and their babies. Everything they do focuses on evangelism and many of the children in the complex have put their faith in Christ and have a thorough understanding of Scripture. They have a church on the site and when we joined their service on the Sunday, the singing and Scripture recitation by the children lifted our hearts. In recent years, a resource centre has been built to equip and train local pastors and offer quality teaching materials. We spent an afternoon visiting local homes in small groups and even challenged the local workers at the mission station to a volleyball match. Northern Ireland won the final game by a single point! Our team was really challenged and encouraged by the work at the mission station – in fact, one of them formed a team within his own church and ten of them headed out in the summer of 2017 to do some building work!

Before heading home, we spent two days on safari in the Meru National Park. It was a relaxing end to an extraordinary trip where we basked in awe at God's wondrous creation. We got close to zebras, elephants, giraffes, hippos and many other types of wildlife and it was a gentle reminder of God's faithfulness as these species exist without any input from man.

A special part of this trip was the devotion times. In Nairobi, we read through the book of Revelation together; then the team leader at the mission compound opened the Scriptures and shared his heart on the challenges and blessings of living in the bush.

CHAPTER TWENTY-THREE

Eating and Praying

ONE THING I always savour when we are overseas on holiday or doing mission trips, is whetting my taste buds with the local cuisine.

Starting with Poland, Joanna's native country, the beetroot soup is a firm favourite of mine, as are the herrings, stuffed cabbage, bigos stew and dumplings. At weddings and on Christmas Eve, Polish people have a traditional twelve-course meal! It goes on for hours as the food just keeps on coming, one course after another! I love weddings in Poland for this reason.

In Jamaica, the jerk chicken with its tangy flavours stood out for me. Street traders cooked it by the roadside as their Bob Marley music boomed out in the background! The favourite food of young people at the church we served in was ackee and saltfish, which also happens to be the national dish of Jamaica. Then there was the leafy callaloo, fried bananas, coconuts and the fresh mangos which grew on the tree outside our kitchen window. On Christmas day that year, Joanna and I barbequed some turkey breasts on the beach for our dinner. However, the local speciality on Christmas day is curried goat – and instead of greeting each other and saying, "Enjoy the turkey!" they say, "Have a nice curried goat!"

When we lived in Australia a couple of years later, we were surprised to discover that kangaroo meat is as common as beef or pork in some areas. We didn't have to wait long to taste it, as a farmer from the church had packed our freezer with kangaroo steaks and sausages. With its perfect climate, it is normal to go to the beach all year round and cook breakfast on the 'barby'. Outdoor cooking is very common in Australia and most of the parks have gas and charcoal barbeques for public use, as well as 'billy-cans' to boil water for a cup of tea.

However, whenever we visited Asia, the exotic nature of the local cuisine reached an entirely new level. In Cambodia, we were served ants that were still alive and in Laos, we sampled barbequed grasshoppers, which tasted like grilled chicken. While travelling in China, we tried frogs' legs and on one occasion in Vietnam, we were served lotus flowers as a side.

In India, as I expected, the curries were delicious, but when we attempted to copy the locals and eat with our bare hands, we ended up with food all over our faces like a bunch of toddlers!

In Israel, hummus and falafel was my favourite dish, then in Spain when we stayed with missionaries, each morning for breakfast I cut a few slices off the smoked pig's legs that hung in the kitchen!

If you haven't already guessed, eating is one of my favourite 'things-to-do'. In fact, Joanna often jokes that I only have one meal a day – that begins with breakfast and finishes at bedtime! When I think back to my childhood, my brothers and I all had appetites like horses and it amazes me to this day how Mum was able to provide for us all. Since we didn't have a television at home or mobile phones to play with, we were continually active so none of us were ever overweight as children.

However, as I got older, like most adults, I became less active and my metabolism slowed down. At the same time, I got married and had a great wife cooking delicious meals for me – so my physical appearance began to change! It became a real challenge to burn off excess energy and before long flab started to appear.

Over the years, I have often made pledges to myself to consume less junk food and eat healthier to lose weight. Regrettably, those good intentions often fell by the wayside when friends called round and suggested ordering a pizza or Chinese takeaway. Far too often, I wake up in the morning feeling really sluggish because I ate a big feed the night before. Then when I look in the mirror and stand on the scales, I get very frustrated with what I see and often wish I could look just like I did in my teens.

However, with my experience working amongst teenagers, saved and unsaved alike, it alarms and saddens me how many of them are dissatisfied or even hate how they look. Whenever I lead youth camps and organise discussion groups at special meetings, we often discuss such issues. I've realised that many Christian young people who love the Lord wholeheartedly are almost depressed because of how they perceive their appearance. No matter what way we look, the devil always tempts us to believe it would be better if we looked different. In Africa I have seen dark-skinned people dust baby powder onto their skin to make them look whiter, yet at home people apply fake tan and use sunbeds to make them look more brown!

It's important to realise that no matter how we feel or look, the Bible tells us that *"God created man in his own image" (Genesis 1:27)*. Rather than agree with the lies of the devil, we should meditate on the words of the Psalmist: *"I will praise thee; for I am fearfully and wonderfully made: marvellous are thy works; and that my soul knoweth right well" (Psalm 139:14)*.

Obviously, we can abuse our bodies by eating either too little or too much. The Bible commands us to let our moderation be known unto all men and also, we should not let anything (including food) have mastery over us.

In recent years, Joanna and I have tried to discipline ourselves to various diet plans to look after our bodies and general health. However, when we are doing missions far from home, we often have to eat out or in peoples' homes and we break our strict regimes and then feel discouraged in ourselves. We have learned instead of feeling down and disheartened about it, we should talk to the Lord and simply ask Him to take away the craving for food and to help us in this area. After all, He exclaimed: *"Behold, I am the Lord, the God of all flesh: is there any thing too hard for me?"* *(Jeremiah 32:27)*.

It is important to realise that, just like gaining victory over any other temptation to sin, we must do our part too and not keep our kitchen cupboards full of junk food.

As well as paying attention to what food we put into our bodies, it is important to guard what images enter our eyes and what words are heard by our ears. Most of us have smartphones, television and the internet in our homes, which all have the potential to corrupt our minds. It is a constant battle to remain pure so we must learn the habit of switching TV channels or closing pop-up windows online immediately.

As I mentioned in an earlier chapter, it is important that we take an adequate amount of rest and look after our bodies but we need to ensure we don't become lazy and indulge in an excessive amount of entertainment. When I get to heaven, I won't mind if my body has been worn out from serving the Lord – all I want to hear is the Lord Jesus saying: *"Well done, thou good and faithful servant"* *(Matthew 25:21)*.

The Bible also warns us to let *"no man take thy crown"* (*Revelation 3:11*). This is a crown that God has assigned for each Christian if they follow Him and carry out His will for their life. Whenever I stand before the Lord to give an account of my service here on earth, I want to be sure that I have carried out His will so I will definitely receive my crown. The verse implies that God's purposes won't be hindered if we neglect our calling. Rather, God will raise up someone else to do it and they will get the reward and crown that God had ordained for us. How terrible would it be to miss out on the 'well-done' commendation of God?

Just as each of us has a responsibility for looking after our physical and mental health, Christians must also maintain a healthy spiritual life. This involves disciplining ourselves to prioritise the most important things in life – particularly our personal time with God. One of my earliest childhood memories is my parents instilling the great importance of daily Bible reading into our young lives. Just as our routine before going to bed included eating supper and brushing our teeth, we also settled down for ten minutes to hear a Bible story and pray. This habit remained with me throughout my rebellious teenage years and most nights I read my Bible and a devotional book in bed, even though it didn't make much of an impact in my life.

However, after getting saved a great desire rose up within me to feast on the Word of God and the Bible really came alive to me. It was like a great jigsaw of many pieces, which gradually began to come together in my mind. The Bible itself explains why as an unsaved person (natural man) I didn't feel it was a life-changing book: *"But the natural man receiveth not the things of the Spirit of God: for they are foolishness unto him: neither can he know them, because they are spiritually discerned" (1 Corinthians 2:14).*

As a new-born Christian, my prayer-life also transformed from running over repetitive, trivial prayers to praying unique and spontaneous ones with real intent and an expectancy that God would answer. Things in life that I previously took for granted became things to offer prayers of thankfulness for. At times when I needed wisdom and guidance to make good decisions, I brought the matter before the Lord and often He gave me clear answers through His precious Word.

I would be lying if I gave the impression that I have maintained such a desire for having a quiet-time with God each day. Sometimes we automatically assume if someone serves the Lord in a full-time capacity, then they pray a lot more than other Christians. This should be the case as those are the ones who ought to be setting an example, but if I am honest, prayer is one of my biggest struggles. I always have been quite a restless person but in recent years the incredible advancements in technology have distracted me even more.

Some evenings after a busy day of Bible Clubs, I have planted myself down on the sofa with a cup of tea and flick on the TV to watch the news. On too many occasions, I have ended up watching long films and when they are over, I am already half asleep before I even make it to bed. Then on other nights when I did get to bed early, instead of reading my Bible and talking to God in prayer, I checked social media sites like Facebook on my phone. A few years ago, it was a brief, two-minute browse through my newsfeed but now with hundreds of friends connected to me, it is easy to sit for an hour scrolling through their posts and watching funny videos. However, as soon as I put my phone down, I was overcome with tiredness and lifting my Bible was a real struggle.

In similar fashion, in the mornings when I woke up I instinctively lifted my phone to see what time it was. Often, in addition to checking the time I looked at my emails, the news headlines and weather forecast. Before I caught myself on, I realised it was time to get up and I had missed another opportunity to spend time with the Lord. It became increasingly difficult to keep reading and praying and I hated what I was doing so much. Those mornings I even felt groggy and unclean, just like if I'd skipped breakfast or hadn't brushed my teeth before leaving the house.

Unfortunately, the great distraction followed me wherever I went. Between Bible Clubs or when stopped for lunch, I saw notifications on my phone and was compelled to see who had 'liked' or commented on my posts. It maybe took only a few seconds but deep down I knew it was competing with God for my attention. When anything or anyone steals our 'God moments', we are playing the fool and are losing out. I realised I had to overcome the distraction or it would overcome me.

For many of us, managing our time to ensure that we give God His rightful place in our lives is a daily battle. One of my favourite verses is, *"I can do all things through Christ which strengtheneth me"* *(Philippians 4:13)*. This promise assures me, that with the Lord's help, I can give Him the time He deserves. It wasn't a matter of just praying the prayer and expecting my desires to change – I also needed to become more disciplined and control my phone before it controlled me. When I felt the urge to click on social media apps, I would pray to the Lord and ask Him to strengthen my resolve.

Practically, I have helped myself by putting my phone onto silent and leaving it in the kitchen each night. I am then able to have my quiet-time with God and lie down to meditate on what I read without distractions. It also ensures I get a sufficient amount of sleep, which is vital as I need to be fully focused and alert at the Bible Clubs and missions. When I wake in the mornings, I am able to give the Lord my first moments by reading my Bible and praying to Him with a clear mind. If anyone has messaged me during the night, I read their messages as I eat my breakfast.

Another mistake I stumbled into was using the Bible app on my phone instead of my paper Bible for my quiet-times. It seemed very handy but often, while I was reading Scripture on it, texts and other notifications popped up. Even if I ignored them and continued to read, subconsciously I wondered who they were from and if it was something urgent. For this reason, I believe there is no real substitute for the paper Word of God if I am serious about fighting distraction. The reality of the situation is that there is no turning back from social media. It is here to stay and will likely become even more prevalent in the future so we must take steps to manage it.

On a general note, statistics such as those gathered by the Evangelical Alliance state that only thirty-five percent of church-going Christians say they read the Bible every day. Sadly, many Christians rely on their pastor each Sunday to feed them spiritually for the entire week. Regardless of our calling in life, daily nourishment for our soul is just as essential as food is for our physical bodies. Now, more than ever before, Christians need to be strong to resist daily temptations that can destroy lives, testimonies, marriages, churches and families. The Apostle Paul advised, *"Put ye on the Lord Jesus Christ, and make not provision for the flesh, to fulfil the lusts thereof" (Romans 13:14).* Time in the Word of God is the best way to avoid distractions that could lead us astray.

Thankfully, there are many days when I do rise up early and spend quality time with the Lord. It is always time well invested because I start the day refreshed and full of joy meditating on what I have in Christ Jesus. It also stops me getting frustrated at myself if things don't work out as planned later on, as I know the Lord wasn't caught by surprise and there is likely a reason even if it's mysterious to me.

Samuel Chadwick, a famous English preacher and writer once stated:

> *"The one concern of the devil is to keep the saints from praying. He fears nothing from prayer-less studies, prayer-less work, prayer-less religion. He laughs at our toil, mocks at our wisdom, but trembles when we pray."*

In the area of evangelism, Sidlow Baxter claimed:

> *"Men may spurn our appeals, reject our message, oppose our arguments, despise our persons, but they are helpless against our prayers."*

I have learned over the years that the Lord wants us to talk to Him, so we will grow to become more like Him each day and glorify Him through our lives. Sometimes though, the honest prayer we need to pray is: *Lord, I admit that I don't have a desire to spend much time with You – but I want to, so please give me a yearning for Your presence!*

CHAPTER TWENTY-FOUR

I'm Not Surprised

JUST BEFORE I come to the end of this book, let me share
with you something I recurrently experience in the ministry
that is difficult to describe or explain. It happens frequently, yet I
can never predict when or under what circumstances it will occur.
What I am alluding to is the moment that a child becomes a
Christian at a Bible Club.

Whenever I am leading the singing, reciting the memory verse
or teaching the lesson, my focus is often drawn towards one
particular child – even though there may be over a hundred in
attendance. I don't actively search for it, but at particular
moments, whatever way that child is listening, behaving or
singing causes something to register with me briefly.

Frequently whenever we identify a child who has written 'Last
night I became a Christian' or 'I would like to become a Christian'
on their worksheets, it is the very child that my attention was
drawn to the previous evening. Then at other times, when a
particular child comes to my attention and I get one of the
volunteers to speak to them, often they tell us that they too
became a Christian that week. Even though I don't know any of
them, when the Lord does a new work in the heart and life of a
child, He regularly gives me discernment to seek them out.

Obviously, this doesn't always happen but when it does, it gives us an opportunity to offer them my Stepping Stones discipleship book, along with a Bible if they don't already have one.

Allow me to share a few of these incidents that come to mind: During a Bible Club in Lisburn, I was teaching the children a memory verse. While all the other children were reciting the verse, one little girl made her way up to the front and told me she had learnt six other verses in Sunday school. She proceeded to recite all six of them while I kept the other children repeating the memory verse as I felt bad having to stop her! I mistakenly assumed since she was so well versed that she was saved, but when I was packing up at the end, she came over to me and asked if I could help her become a Christian.

On another occasion in Banbridge, while I was telling the story, my mind became focused on one little girl in the middle of the group of about two hundred children. She listened intently but afterwards walked out with the rest of the children so I never really thought any more about it. The following day, someone wrote on their worksheet that last night they had become a Christian. Whenever I found out who it was, it was that little girl who my attention had been drawn to in the middle of the group! I was delighted to hear we had directed her to the Lord.

Often school is a busy and stressful place for teachers and pupils alike, so when the Bible Club comes along there is always a wonderful buzz of excitement in the air. The children absolutely love it and as the week goes on, we build up a great rapport with them. From the youngest to the oldest, they all interact and it becomes an enjoyable time of learning about God and how He wants to be real in their lives. This is of course when the Holy Spirit comes in and reveals God to them in a way that many of them have never imagined before.

Due to the nature of the work, especially within the schools, it is important to have such discernment. Without exaggeration, hundreds of times our volunteers have led children to the Lord as all the other children and teachers present are completely oblivious to what's going on. It's just amazing to witness a child coming to faith in Jesus Christ and then quietly slipping back into the group.

Sometimes we meet such children years later, either back at their schools or somewhere else and they remind us when and where they got saved.

For example, one Easter we went along to the CEF conference in Portrush and an eighteen-year-old lad introduced himself to me. I admitted I hadn't any notion who he was, but he proceeded to tell me how I helped him become a Christian nearly ten years ago in his primary school and he was still going on well as a Christian and continually growing in his faith.

It is really remarkable how the Lord is pleased to use and bless the school Bible Clubs. I often wonder is He so gracious because many of the children we encounter never attend church or Sunday school and have no other way to hear about Jesus? Thousands of boys and girls hear the wonderful stories and truths of the Bible for the first time in school Bible Clubs – I count it a real privilege teaching them and it's obvious that they love learning about God.

One day whenever we were doing a Bible Club in a caravan park, a child came running over midway through the meeting and sat down amongst the other children. I remember noticing this girl listening intently to the story, though when the club was over she ran off along with all the other children. However, the next day whenever we arrived she was already there waiting for us with her worksheet. On it, she had written 'Last night I became a Christian in my caravan!' We continue to see these children year after year and they never forget the night they got saved. Again, this shows how the Lord works in children's hearts long after they hear us preaching His Word. In God's perfect timing, a child will come to faith in Christ and that is why it should really be no big surprise whenever a child tells us they have just got saved. Whenever God puts a particular child on my heart and indicates to me they are going to get saved, it is almost as if the Lord is whispering, "They are one of My children and now is the time for them to be born into My family."

Whenever I feel the leading, moving and prompting of the Holy Spirit during a Bible Club, it is a most beautiful but very humbling feeling. I never know when it is going to happen and certainly cannot make it happen – I guess in many ways it is like the wind, which comes and goes as it pleases. The message and format of the Bible Clubs are all similar – the children are taught the same stories and learn the same verses, yet it just seems to be on a certain day, at a particular school, tent or farm, God decides to move. Sensing the moving of the Holy Spirit in a meeting is one of the most overwhelming and awe-inspiring feelings to experience. His presence is so real, yet everything else is completely normal. Many times we return to a place, with the same kids and nothing out of the ordinary appears to happen. However, when it does it is amazing to witness God working in the hearts and lives of children, leading them to repentance.

Another thing I have observed is that even when there seem to be great distractions or hindrances around, nothing can stop God working and moving in whatever way He pleases. He works quietly but powerfully in the heart of a child, yet the children all around them are completely unaware of it. Sometimes at a Bible Club, five or six children indicate that they want to become Christians, either by telling myself or one of the volunteers, or else by writing it on their worksheet. During the singing, these children are taken to the back of the hall and are counselled by volunteers. Whenever a child indicates that they want help to get saved, that is fundamentally the most important part of that meeting. We have an awesome responsibility to help such children find their way to Christ if they so desire to. It is the most wonderful feeling in the world pointing a child to the Saviour. From a personal point of view, what touches me most is that God has allowed me to witness Him working in the lives of so many children and He is pleased to use me as His human instrument to bring the gospel to them. Whenever I consider the opportunities the world offers and the riches that come with it, I still would never swap it for being a soul-winner for Christ. I long to get to heaven one day and as other Christians come 'home' one by one, I look forward to hearing how they met Jesus and I wonder how many of them will say it was because the Bible Club visited their school.

No matter how many Bible Clubs we do, it is always exciting starting a new one! Mondays are always a bit daunting because I am new to the children and they are new to me. I am always conscious that I need to be fresh, relevant and real to the children and certainly not appear tired or boring before them. Sometimes in a new school, the concept of a Bible Club – singing songs and listening to Bible stories – is completely new to them all. Often the devil will tempt me with all kinds of thoughts trying to make me doubt the importance of the work. But as the week goes on, the barriers are broken down and the children smile and sing their hearts out, while I get into top gear and preach as best as I know how. Yet most importantly, amidst all the interaction and activity, God gently works in the hearts of the children. Sometimes I sow, other times I reap, but it's always the Lord who gives the increase.

One time when we were doing a Bible Club in Lisburn Leisureplex, a Chinese family attended. The little girl wasn't able to attend on the Friday night because she had to go to gymnastics with her mum, but her brother who was there brought her worksheet from the night before. At the bottom, she had written 'I want to become a Christian!' When we read that and realised she wasn't there I felt a little bit dismayed and wondered what to do. However, while we were packing up, the little girl came running over to me with her mum wanting to get saved. She ran all the way from gymnastics and hoped to catch us before we left. It was a very special moment as her mum translated from English to Chinese and the little girl accepted Jesus as her Saviour. I have so many stories like this to tell – it would take dozens of pages as many children come to my mind. I like to pray for them, that they will walk closely with the Lord and grow to love Him more every day.

CHAPTER TWENTY-FIVE

No Ordinary Journey

I AM THOROUGHLY amazed at the journey God has brought me on since the day I got saved as a young lad of seventeen. Never in my wildest dreams could I have imagined travelling to so many countries, writing over thirty books and conducting hundreds of missions and Bible Clubs – all to tell children about Jesus.

In the Bible, King Solomon claimed, *"He that winneth souls is wise" (Proverbs 11:30).* As a child, I used to sit in meetings as men preached the gospel message and pleaded with people to get saved. Whenever someone responded and asked for counsel, I often wondered what an honour and privilege being a soul-winner must be. In recent years, the Lord has graciously given me my heart's desire and I have had hundreds of opportunities to lead children to the Lord.

Over the years we have witnessed children coming to the Lord in schools, caravan parks, churches, housing estates, buses, barns and so on. However, lots more children quietly seek God on their own during the clubs or at home that we are completely unaware of. Every child has their own salvation story. Even if some of them forget the exact date, they all remember the joyful moment when they repented of their sin and invited Jesus into their life.

One thing that gives me a great sense of fulfilment is when we return to schools and children seek us out after the meeting to remind us that they got saved the previous year and it was the best decision they ever made. Whenever a child says, "Thank you for coming to my school and helping me to find Jesus!" it gives me more joy than any earthly treasure could provide. As well as being truly humbled, I often ponder: *What if I had never answered the call of God but had settled for a comfortable career in Marks & Spencer?*

Many nights when I return home from a busy day ministering in four, five or even six different schools, I love to go for a walk in the fresh air with our dog, Tas. Often my mind is still buzzing with the excitement of the children I met earlier in the day and if some of them responded to the gospel, my heart is overflowing with joy. After walking a few hundred metres along the country road at the end of our development, there are no streetlights and my eyes adjust to the darkness. There is a gate to a particular field where I normally stop and take a moment to gaze up into the sky. As the world goes to sleep for another night, I admire the handiwork of my Creator, God and take a moment to thank Him for blessing another day's ministry. I often find myself smiling and laughing while I pray as I recall the little faces of children and their hilarious reactions and comments. I tell God how I adore Him and love what He has called me to do.

I have learned that money can never buy the will of God for my life. Only total obedience and full surrender to Christ and His way gives genuine satisfaction, fulfilment and contentment. I can honestly say I believe I am right in the centre of God's will for my life at this moment and feel I am living the dream. I could say I have a dream job but since I don't have regular hours or a set salary, it feels more like a full-time hobby. Yet God wonderfully provides and cares for us more than I could ever describe!

One important thing I have learned about the Lord's work is that He doesn't need or ask for servants who have great intellect, gifts or talents. As I have said before, if He did then I would be unqualified for the job. Rather we read: *"God hath chosen the foolish things of the world to confound the wise; and God hath chosen the weak things of the world to confound the things which are mighty" (1 Corinthians 1:27).* I count it a real honour and privilege to be the human instrument that God uses to accomplish His purposes and lead people to Christ.

How true is this statement of C.H. Spurgeon?

"To be a soul winner is the happiest thing in the world. And every soul you bring to Jesus Christ, you seem to get a new heaven here upon earth."

It brings incredible joy to my soul every time I lead a child to the Lord. Let me share with you some conversions that are particularly memorable:

Billy

Gary, a stonemason from Rathfriland, has been the driving force behind a number of children's missions in the town over recent years. One night after the meeting was over, Gary and his wife, Victoria, were leaving children home in the minibus. Meanwhile, their son, Billy, remained in the hall with the other volunteers and a few other children whose parents hadn't yet collected them. I was counselling another child who had remained behind, then Billy came over and tapped me on the shoulder and told me he also wanted to get saved. After I finished dealing with the other child, I had the great honour of leading little Billy to the Lord. Billy had been brought up in a home where he had been taught the Scriptures daily but just needed to take the step of faith and invite Jesus into his young life. I will always remember his parents' reaction when Billy told them when they returned from their bus run. They got down on their knees and hugged Billy with tears in their eyes, rejoicing that the Lord had given them household salvation.

Anya

My friend, Robin, volunteered to be a bus driver when we were doing the Bible Clubs in the caravan parks on the North Coast one summer. His little daughter, Anya, was with him but one afternoon she thought it would be a novelty to travel to the next Bible Club in the van with me, while Robin followed in the minibus. She jumped in all excited and when we got talking, I asked her how long ago it was since she got saved. To my surprise, she told me she wasn't yet a Christian but had wanted to get saved for a long time. I asked her what was stopping her and she said she wasn't sure what to do. As we drove along, I explained the gospel message very simply to her and when we arrived at the next Bible Club, Cheryl had the joy of leading her to the Lord. When Robin got the minibus parked up, little Anya ran over to him and gave him the best news he could ever have wished to hear. It was amazing to witness his reaction as she told him how she had just asked the Lord Jesus into her heart. To see a grown man shed tears of joy when his daughter tells him she has just trusted in the Lord is a very beautiful thing to behold.

Although I travel around the country telling thousands of children about their need of salvation, I often find it difficult telling those dearest to me that they also need to get saved. It really disturbs me to think that I could be eternally separated from my blood relatives if some of them never get saved. Praise God, in recent years I have had the joy of witnessing many of them come to faith.

My brother

At the time I was pastoring the church in Australia, the Lord gave me a peculiar burden to pray for my eldest brother, Trevor. I remember calling him on the phone one day and after catching up I told him quite bluntly that he needed to get saved! From that moment, the tone of our conversation changed and I could tell I'd struck a raw nerve and shortly after he wished me goodbye! However, the Lord used that little word to convict him and six weeks later, he rang me back to tell me he had got saved.

My nephews and nieces

My eldest niece, Cherie, attended the very first Bible camp we organised in Tollymore. One night during devotions in her tent, she realised her need of a Saviour and her leader led her to the Lord. Many years later, her younger sister, Leah, also put her trust in the Lord at Tollymore and has since accompanied us on trips to Poland twice.

My twin brother Edwin's three boys – Luke, Ben and Ross – also attended Tollymore camp. After one of the evening meetings, Luke appeared at my side and boldly said, "Uncle Colin, I want to become a Christian, will you help me?" Together we went to his dad's caravan in the field and in the midst of all the buzz going on at camp, I had the joy of pointing young Luke to the Lord. Then a couple of years later, we were doing a lunchtime Bible Club in the boys' school in Lisburn. One day while Cheryl was telling the story, Ben came over to me and said he wanted to get saved. We shuffled over to the side to talk it through. After Ben bowed his head to pray and ask the Lord Jesus into his heart, he glanced over to Luke, who gave him the thumbs-up, as if to say "Well done Ben!"

My eldest brother, Trevor, and his wife, Lorraine, have three children – Sarah, Andrew and Reuben. After a Bible Club we were conducting in a school in Maghaberry, Lorraine phoned me and said Sarah had something to tell me. "Hi Sarah, what is it?" I asked her. With the most cheerful voice in the world, Sarah told me she had just asked the Lord Jesus into her heart. Tears flowed down my cheeks on the other end of the phone as the news sank into my heart!

In recent years, some of my nephews and nieces who are now young adults, regularly help me with the Bible Clubs. Cherie and her husband, Jordan, have also been to Poland on numerous occasions. James and Anna, (children of my brother James and his wife Margaret) are currently chomping at the bit to get involved in the ministry once they are older. It greatly encourages me to see their desire to serve the Lord. At the other end of the spectrum, my brother, James, went to Poland for his first mission trip in January 2017, along with my elderly parents.

When I pray for my six brothers and their families, it still brings a sense of sadness to my mind, as I realise Joanna and I have not been able to have children to take my family name into the next generation. However, we must accept this is God's will for our lives and the Bible offers great comfort with verses like, *"As for God, his way is perfect" (Psalm 18:30)*. Since I don't have the responsibility to care for children of my own at home, I have the flexibility of being away from home a lot and as a result, have been able to share the gospel with thousands of other children each year.

If we had known years ago how the Lord had planned to use us, perhaps it would have made all those miscarriages Joanna experienced slightly easier to bear. I honestly wouldn't have life any other way and both of us genuinely thank God for His wisdom and for giving us the grace we needed to accept our circumstances.

They say it takes a unique type of woman to be a pastor's wife. After our time pastoring churches in Jamaica and Australia, I completely agree with such a statement as Joanna had to be all things to all people! However, it takes another set of competencies and character traits to be a supportive wife of someone who is engaged in the ministry as intensively as I am. God couldn't have brought a more-suited woman into my life than Joanna, and over the years she has proved herself to be a precious, beautiful and amazing wife.

She pours all her energy into the ministry and works tirelessly at home sorting mail, taking calls, planning my schedule, designing and ordering literature, preparing PowerPoints, editing ministry videos and organising all our overseas trips. Her administrative expertise allows me to get out on the road with a clear head to focus on preaching, knowing that everything else is in her capable hands. Nothing is ever a problem for her and if I call on her for any reason to speak at the front in Bible Clubs, she is very capable of that too. Just like my mother, Joanna knows all my needs and often goes out of her way to treat me with small things of life, like a cheese platter on a Friday night after a busy week! The nature of our ministry requires a lot of personal sacrifice and there are times when we can go for months without sharing our evening meal together on weekdays.

As I have shared in earlier parts of this book, being in the ministry full-time is far from simple and straightforward. There have been many hurdles and obstacles along the way and if I'd any other master apart from the Lord, I would have quit many times. However, when I consider how Jesus persisted and completed the work His Father gave Him to do, I know that quitting is not an option.

I have learned that going through with God costs a great deal more than I initially expected. I have lost friends, supporters and the approval of some churches, but having the certainty that I'm at the centre of God's will is worth a lot more. My ambition, God-willing, is to complete one thousand missions and Bible Clubs and take fifty teams out to Poland. We make plans using the wisdom God has given us, but also remain open to God's leading each day. As we get older, we'll be relying on God to keep us strong, healthy and sharp as we serve Him.

Many years ago a trusted friend wrote me a letter and encouraged me never to change the way I am. That advice has stuck with me and over the years, on many occasions people have tried to force me to change in different ways. However, deep inside I have tried to resist this and remain the person who God made me to be. It has been no ordinary journey but following the Lord has been an absolute thrill and joy. Please pray that the best is yet to come and that God alone will receive the glory for everything we accomplish in His great name!

"Having therefore obtained help of God, I continue unto this day, witnessing both to small and great" (Acts 26:22).

The following appendices tell what the children, the volunteers and I have written about the ministry and its impact upon their lives.

What the Children Say

EACH DAY AS the children leave the Bible Clubs, we give them a worksheet to colour in, which also has a memory verse on it and box for them to ask any questions they might have. The following day, we collect them from the children as they arrive and one of the volunteers flicks through them to pick out meaningful questions the children have written down. We always try to leave time to answer the questions publically so the other children benefit as well. Answering just one of these questions may remove an obstacle that is stopping a child from becoming a Christian.

The most frequent question asked is, "How do you become a Christian?" This gives us a wonderful opportunity to tell all the children and teachers in the hall what Paul told the Philippian jailer when he asked the same. The answer is simply, *"Believe on the Lord Jesus Christ, and thou shalt be saved" (Acts 16:31).*

We explain that believing isn't just a mental acceptance that Jesus existed (like the devil does), but rather it is believing in faith that Jesus is who He said He is and trusting in Him alone for our salvation. Then we emphasise how important it is to believe Jesus' words and teaching – which is to turn away from sin and ask for His help to live a transformed life like Zacchaeus. (Luke 19:1-10)

We are completely dependent on God every day as we endeavour to help children understand the way of salvation. God promises, *"If any of you lack wisdom, let him ask of God, ...and it shall be given him" (James 1:5).*

Over the years, Joanna has filled big scrapbooks with a collection of questions that children have asked us. Some of them are listed below to give you an insight into the mind of a primary school child! Take time to read through them and ask yourself what you would answer on the spot in front of a hundred children!

General questions to Colin:

- What age were you when you first went to church?
- Did you go to Bible Club as a child?
- When did you get saved?
- Who was the first person you told when you became a Christian?
- What is your favourite thing about being a Christian?
- What is your favourite verse in the Bible?
- Do you have fun as a Christian?
- Do you enjoy learning about God?
- Are you happy with the way God has made you?
- What is your favourite Bible story?
- When do you read the Bible and if you forget do you do double the next day?
- Have you ever been tempted to do something bad?
- Do you go to church every Sunday?
- Have you ever had a problem and prayed to God about it and He has helped you?
- Did God tell you to tell children about God?
- Do you like teaching children about the Bible?
- Is it hard doing your job?
- Do you like going to school every day?
- If you go to schools every day, when do you go to work?
- What do you do when you're not at Bible fun week?
- How do you have time for God when you have a busy schedule?
- How do you write all these books?

Questions about the Bible:

- Who wrote the Bible?
- What does the word 'Bible' mean?
- How do you know that God and the Bible are real?
- Why did God give us the Bible?
- Is the Bible the best book that has ever been written?
- Why is the Bible important?
- Why did prophets write the Bible?
- If I was to start reading the Bible where would I start?
- How often should we read the Bible?
- Do I have to read the whole Bible as a Christian?
- How do we know when God is speaking to us through the Bible?

Questions about God:

- How was God created?
- How do we know that God and heaven are real?
- What age is God?
- What does God look like?
- Why does God have no sin?
- How does God know we have sin?
- How can God be everywhere?
- How did God get His powers?
- Does God know everyone on earth by name?
- Has anyone ever seen God?
- When did God think of making the world?
- Are God and the Lord Jesus the same person?
- Why does God still love us when we sin?
- Why can God not stop people being cruel to animals and each other?
- If the Bible says God loves everyone does God love the devil even though he is bad?

- I have sinned a lot – will God still love me?
- Does God laugh when someone does something funny?
- How can Jesus be the son of God?
- Why does God not die?
- Does God still speak to people out loud?
- Why do some people say God isn't real when He is?
- How do I listen for God's voice?
- How do we know God is with us when we don't see Him?
- How can God help me to make good decisions?
- Does God sleep?
- What sin does God hate the most?
- Who is more important: God or Jesus?
- How do we know God answers prayer?
- How can God see me and other people in a different country at the same time?

Questions about the devil:

- Where did the devil come from?
- How did the devil get into the Garden of Eden?
- How did the devil get his name?
- Where does the devil live?
- Who created hell?
- Why was the devil an angel?
- Why did the devil want to be more powerful than God?
- What does the devil do each day?
- Does the devil curse?
- Can the devil ever defeat God?
- How can we defeat the devil?

Questions about Genesis:

- How old is the world?
- Is the big bang true?

- How big is God?
- When did God make the world?
- Where is the Garden of Eden?
- What happened to the Garden of Eden?
- Why did God create those animals that hurt us?
- Did God make dinosaurs and how did Adam and Eve survive with them around?
- Why did God make us?
- Why did God rest on the seventh day?
- Did God know that Adam and Eve would sin?
- Why did God allow them to sin?
- If Adam and Eve had two sons where did the rest of the world come from?
- When the earth was formed how did Chinese, black and white people get here?
- Did Adam and Eve go to heaven?

Questions about the Lord Jesus Christ:

- Did Jesus live before or after the flood?
- How many years ago was Jesus born?
- Who gave Jesus his name?
- Did Jesus have a surname?
- Was Joseph Jesus' Dad as well as God?
- Why was Jesus born in a stable?
- Did Jesus have any brothers or sisters?
- Did Jesus have a best friend?
- Why did Jesus never sin?
- How did Jesus heal people?
- Can Jesus still do miracles?
- Why did the people worship Jesus and then shout "crucify Him"?
- Why did the soldiers put Jesus on the cross?

Devotional books

All these books are available in Christian book shops and online at **www.hopeforyouthministries.org**

In the book shop

COLIN TINSLEY

IMPACT

ADULT DEVOTIONAL BOOK

The **IMPACT** devotional offers the reader daily encouragement and gives them a challenge to make their lives count for God. There are 365 short devotional thoughts on how God impacted the lives of Bible characters and how these principles can be applied to the lives of Christians today. Life is a journey and we must not waste a single day – this book will inspire you to make an impact for God.

(384 pages, full colour, double page spread from inside below)

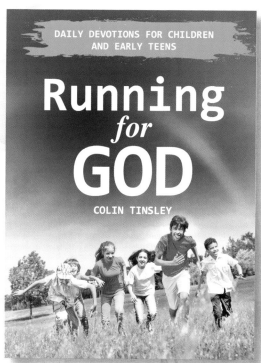

DAILY DEVOTIONS FOR CHILDREN AND EARLY TEENS

Running *for* GOD

COLIN TINSLEY

RUNNING FOR GOD was written as a devotional book for children and young people. The life of the Lord Jesus Christ is covered in detail - from His birth, right through His ministry to His crucifixion and resurrection. With every miracle and parable recorded in the four gospels, there is a lesson and application for the reader. Following on from the ministry of Christ, the reader is taken on a journey following the footsteps of the Apostle Paul. This makes a great devotional for those wishing to run for God.

(384 pages, full colour, double page spread from inside below)

In **WALKING WITH GOD** many great truths of the Bible are explained in simple, easy-to-understand language. This daily devotional was written especially for children and young people, with the objective of giving them a deeper understanding of the Bible and helping them identify with many of the wonderful characters in it. It begins at Creation and focuses on eleven major Bible characters including Abraham, Moses, Joshua, Elijah and Esther.

(384 pages, full colour, double page spread from inside below)

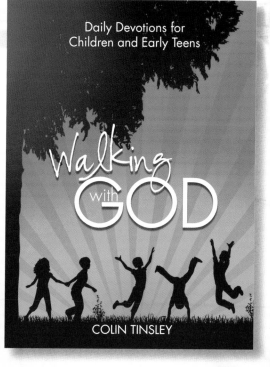

Daily Devotions for Children and Early Teens

Walking *with* GOD

COLIN TINSLEY

Teaching books

STEPPING STONES is a book designed to help new believers get started on their Christian walk. Most people come to faith in Christ when they are children, so this book covers areas such as being the only Christian at home, taking a stand at school, peer-pressure and many other relevant topics.

(128 pages, full colour, double page spread from inside below)

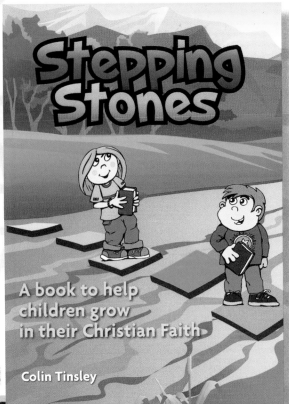

A book to help children grow in their Christian Faith

Colin Tinsley

In 2016 **STEPPING STONES** was translated into Polish and already hundreds of children have benefited from it. In recent days, there have been a number of requests to translate it into Russian which, God-willing, would be an exciting prospect.

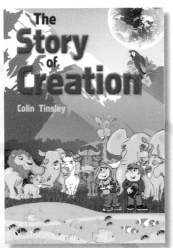

THE STORY OF CREATION explains why creation is one of the most interesting and fascinating subjects we can talk about. All around us we see the perfect handiwork of God - flowers, wildlife and ourselves! This book presents the Genesis account, from the beginning of the world until God destroyed it with a flood, then started to repopulate the earth through Noah's family. (48 pages, full colour)

BOOKS OF THE BIBLE gives the reader an insight to each of the 66 books of the Bible followed by a puzzle or challenge after each one. The brief overviews are less than 300 words long and will whet the reader's appetite to read the book in full. There are also various puzzles and challenges in each one. (140 pages, full colour)

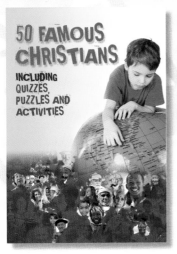

50 FAMOUS CHRISTIANS tells individual stories of 50 well-known missionaries such as Hudson Taylor, CT Studd and Amy Carmichael. Most stories include their conversions and how they lived for God during their lifetime. After each one there are puzzles about and quotations from the missionary which will be challenging for the reader. (104 pages, full colour)

THE STORY OF MARTIN LUTHER is one of the most significant in the world. Five hundred years ago after Martin nailed his 95 Theses to the door of the Castle Church in Wittenberg, Germany, the Protestant Reformation began, which spread across Germany, Europe and throughout the world. (16 pages, full colour)

Puzzle books

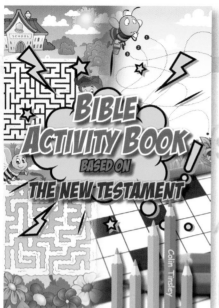

In the **BIBLE ACTIVITY BOOK** there are many fun-filled activities based on wonderful stories contained in the New Testament. The reader will be challenged with various activities such as crosswords, word searches, dot-to-dot, mazes, anagrams and spot the differences. (96 pages, B&W)

In the **BIBLE PUZZLE BOOK** there are many fun-filled activities based on wonderful stories contained in the Old Testament. The reader will be challenged with various puzzles such as crosswords, word searches, dot-to-dot, mazes, anagrams and spot the differences. (96 pages, B&W)

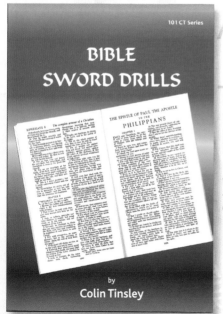

BIBLE SWORD DRILLS are an entertaining way of encouraging and training children to look up scriptural passages in the Bible. The drill commences with everyone's Bible closed and a particular verse is announced. Then after a signal, the participants scurry to find the verse and the winner is the first one to find it. This book has 101 topics including colours, cars, birds, horses, and cooking. (112 pages B&W)

In **BIBLE CROSSWORD FUN** and **BIBLE WORD SEARCH FUN** many of the words are found in the prophetic books of the Bible. Many enjoyable hours can be spent filling in the squares to complete the crossword and searching the grids to find hidden words. The reader will be amazed at some of the words contained within the Scriptures. Some of these words seem old, but many are still used today in our daily conversations. (112 pages, B&W)

In **BIBLE WORD SEARCHES** there are many topics covered including horses, people, places, school, sport, cakes, cattle, creation, kitchens, metals, miracles and music. Furthermore, each word search contains a hidden message! There are over 1,000 words to find, which are all mentioned in the Bible. (112 pages, B&W)

Doing **BIBLE CROSSWORDS** can be a wonderful pastime and an entertaining way to keep one's mind sharp! This book is ideal for all ages and covers a diverse range of topics such as sport, worship, colours, jewellery and marriage. With over 1,000 words to find, that are drawn from all 66 books of the Bible, the reader will soon discover the beauty and relevance of words found in the Scriptures. (112 pages, B&W)

Colouring books

These **COLOURING BOOKS** are for younger children. Each book has pictures relevant to the title as well as a Scripture verse to colour in.
(16 pages, B&W)

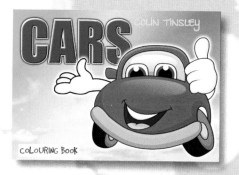

Tracts

Thousands of these children's **TRACTS** have been printed and are used every week in the Bible Clubs. Each tract contains a short story on the theme of the cover, with a gospel application.
(4 pages, full colour)

Dear Colin

How do you ask Jesus in your heart?

Do you have any questions or...

Dear Colin...
I love Bible club because it teaches us about god and Jesus and you teach us to never turn against him

Elena watson P.4.

Dear Colin...
Thank you for coming to my school. you tell the BEST stories, From the Best book, in the BEST way.
Yours Sincerely, Andrea
Do you have any questions, or would like to leave us a message? We would love to hear from you.

Dear Colin...
I think your holiday Bible Club is good
It puts me in a really great mood!
I like to play your games and sing,
It is just an enjoyable thing!
Do you have any questions, or would like to leave us a message? We would love to hear from you.

Dear Colin...
I became a christian last when I was 8, after you came to our school.

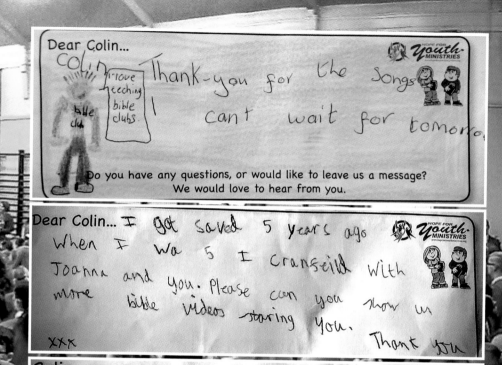
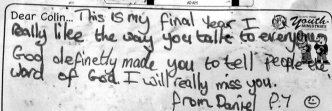

My name is Rachel Cooper and I am 11 years old.

KING SAUL

"The battle is the Lord's"

1st Samuel 17 verse 47

Return your completed sheet to enter the competition to win a prize!

Dear Colin

I AM SAVED!!!!

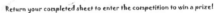

Return your completed sheet to enter the competition to win a prize!

Use the secret code to complete the Bible verse.

Who is on the Lord's side?

Exodus 32 verse 26

Who is king of your life? JESUS!

Dear Colin
I have really enjoyed the first day of bible fun week I can't wait till tomorrow. I have learned so much already. I remember last year with you I became a Christian and since then I have followed the people ... in my faith.

Do you have any questions, or would you like to leave us a message?
We would love to hear from you.

Return your completed sheet to enter the competition to win a prize!

Help Elijah to find the path to the Angel & food

Dear Colin   I Love Bible Club!

I got saved when I was 5!   GOD IS LOVE   Thank-you

How many people have you told about Jesus?

Do you have any questions, or would you like to leave us a message?
We would love to hear from you

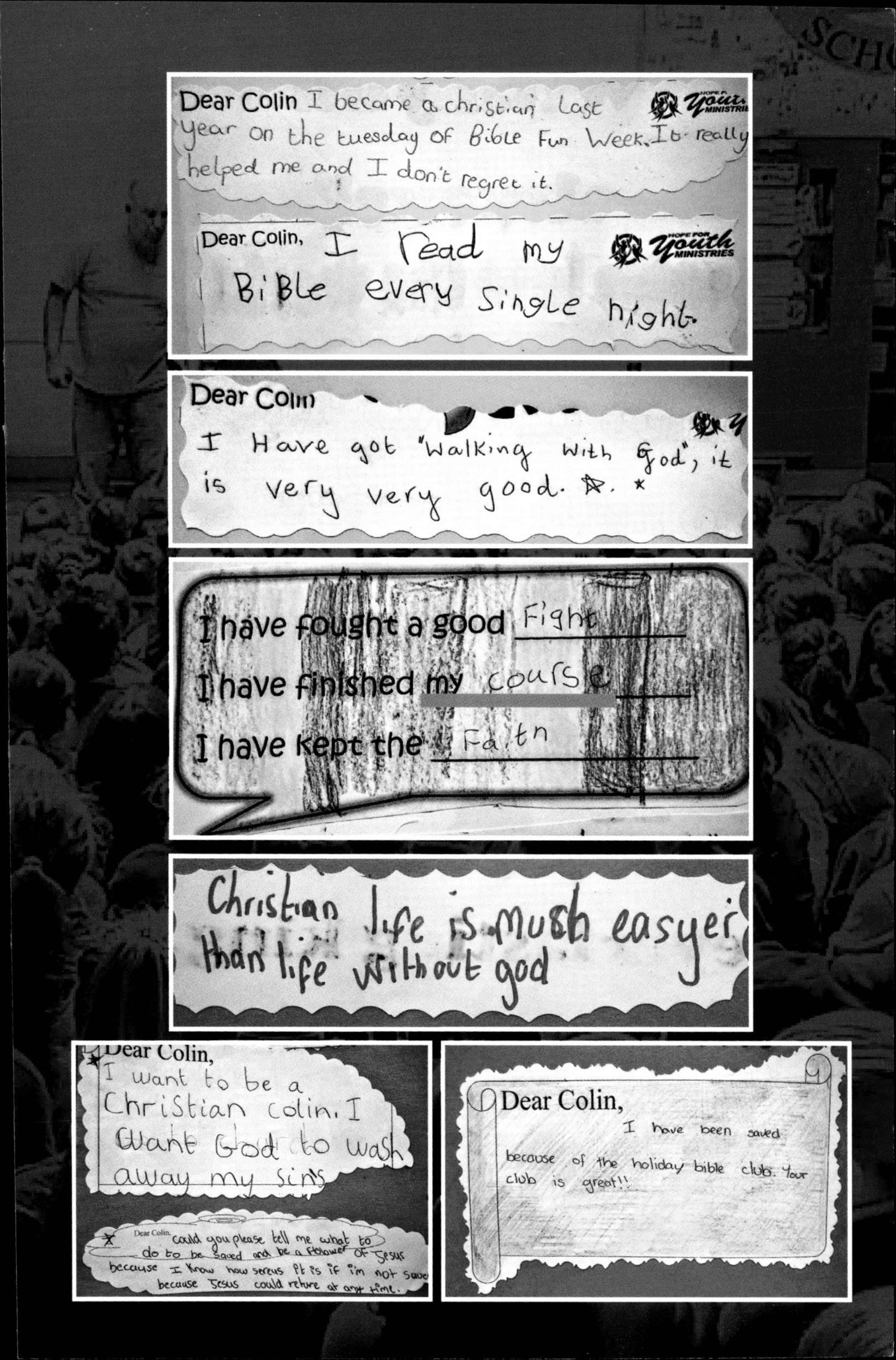

Dear Colin I became a christian last year on the tuesday of Bible Fun Week. It really helped me and I don't regret it.

Dear Colin, I read my Bible every single night.

Dear Colin

I Have got "Walking With God", it is very very good. *

I have fought a good Fight

I have finished my course

I have kept the Faith

Christian life is much easyer than life without god

Dear Colin,
I want to be a Christian colin. I want God to wash away my sins

Dear Colin, could you please tell me what to do to be saved and be a follower of Jesus because I know how serius it is if i'm not saved because Jesus could retire at any time.

Dear Colin,
I have been saved because of the holiday bible club. Your club is great!!

Dear Colin,
I LOVE Bible Fun Week and became a Christian at it last year. I love going to Church and helping in Creche

Do you have a question you would like to ask us? Or even if you want to say hello, or tell us what you enjoy about the Bible Fun Week or tell us you are a Christian, then, we would love to hear from you.

Dear Colin, How do you ask the Lord Jesus into your heart Ella.

I woud like to know how to ask Jesus into my life.

I Woud like to be a christian

Dear Colin, Tell me how to become a christian in your most simplist words.

Dear Colin, How do you get your sin taken away.

How Do I Become a Better Christian

you have a question you

I would lik to be a christcan

"Look unto me, and be ye saved, all the ends of the earth." Isaiah 45:22

Dear Colin, I was Seven when I became a chrisban and I became a chrisban at bright hour when you were bhere. What age were you when you became a chrisban?

Do you have any questions, or would you like to leave us a message?
We would love to hear from you.

Dear Colin Thanks for all you have done and I hope God will be with you through out your life. I hope God will support you forever on your journey through life.

From Alyssa

Do you have any questions, or would you like to leave us a message?
We would love to hear from you.

Dear Colin,
This was... the best summer of my life. I made new friends, learnt new stuff about God and I got a wee bit wet.
P.S. Slippery slope was Amazing.
Colin is Awesome.

Do you have any questions, or would you like to leave us a message?
We would love to hear from you.

from Emma

Dear Colin, Today I became a Christian

Dear Colin, I turn a christian last year and I enjoy ever last bit. ♥ ☺ ☺ ☺ ☺ ☺

Dear Colin, I want you to help me to love God and would you speak to me and let me know how to come a christian

Dear Colin, I got saved last night, and it makes me feel more confident, Praise the Lord!! From Chloe

I would like to be saved.

Dear Colin, Thanks for bringing Roy and Sharon along to bring us those bibles. The bible is my fave book because it helped me become a christian by telling me what Jesus did for me. He died to take away my sin because he loves me.

Dear Colin, I turned a christen last year at Bible Fun Week xxoo ☺ ☺ ☺ ☺ It's amazing!!!!!

Name Hope H   Age 11

BIBLE FUN WEEK

Acts 6:1-8

Stephen is stoned to death   The spread of Christianity

n, I would like to be a christian

Dear Colin

You are so good at teaching us lots of interesting facts and storys in the Bible. I hope to leave the Bible Fun Week as a christian that really trusts in the Lord Jesus Christ.

HOPE FOR *Youth* MINISTRIES

Dear Colin You and your wife's bible club is one of the best I've been to. I am so glad that I am a christian its the best thing ever. I asked my Mum to help me get saved one night thats how I got saved.

HOPE FOR *Youth* MINISTRIES

Dear Colin Thank you Cheryl for helping me become a christan.

HOPE FOR *Youth* MINISTRIES

Dear Colin I would just like to say

Have faith in GOD

Jesus is the Son of God

Thank you for helping me to become a Christan

HOPE FOR *Youth* MINISTRIES

Dear Colin

I really like bible Fun Week, I wish it was on for two weeks instead of one.

Do you have any questions, or would you like to leave us a message? We would love to hear from you.

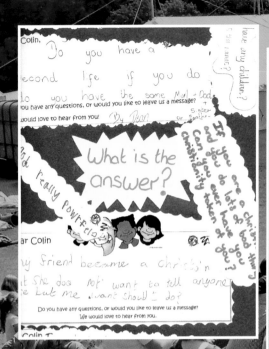

Colin,
Do you have a second life if you do do you have the same Mum + Dad?

Do you have any questions, or would you like to leave us a message?
We would love to hear from you! By Ryan

have any children?

Sister or Brother?

If you are a christian and you do lots of bad things, can you ever have your christianity taken off you?

... really powerful?

What is the answer?

Dear Colin,
My friend became a christian but she does not want to tell anyone else but me. What should I do?

Do you have any questions, or would you like to leave us a message?
We would love to hear from you.

Colin T

BIBLE VERSES CHILDREN MEMORIZE :)

And she shall bring forth a son, and thou shalt call his name JESUS: for he shall save his people from their sins.
Matthew 1:21

Whosoever shall call upon the name of the Lord shall be saved." Romans 10:13

WHAT THE KIDS ENJOY MOST!

Dear Colin,
I love going to the Bible fun week! I never knew learning about the bible could be such fun!

Dear Colin,
I enjoyed the story. I like listening to a bible story.

Dear Colin,
I like everything about the Bible Fun Week especially the stories and the singing.

Dear Colin,
This is my first time at Bible fun week or any childrens meetings and I love it. Mum is going to take me to more
Do you have a question you would like to ask us? Or even if you want to say hello, or tell us what you enjoy about the Bible Fun Week or tell us you are a Christian, then, we would love to hear from you.
meetings over the summer- yipee!

Dear Colin,
I ♥ Bible fun Week!

Dear Colin,
I like the parachute game. I like to be on the airplane...

Dear Colin,
The Bible fun week is fabulous & Brilliant.

CHILDRENS QUESTIONS ?

Dear Colin, How was God made

is everone a christian

When and how does God talk to us

Will everyone go to heaven

If you go to church do you become a christian?

I love your bible classes and I think you are doing a great job teaching children Gods word. & I do sometimes really bad will I still be a christian?

why waters come out of Jesus?
thank you

Dear Colin, How does the devil make us do the wrong things

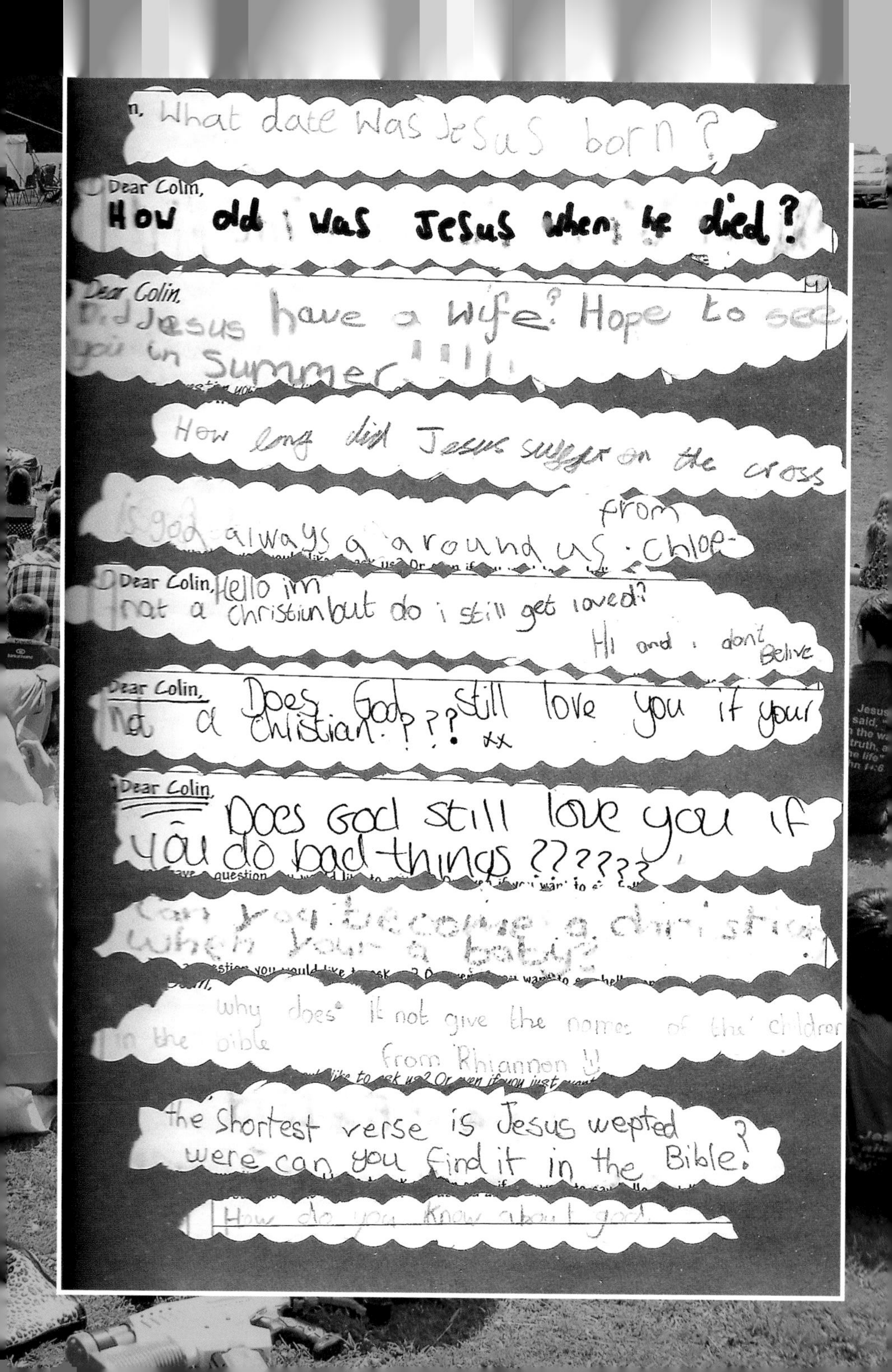

n, What date was Jesus born?

Dear Colin,
How old was Jesus when he died?

Dear Colin,
Did Jesus have a wife? Hope to see
you in summer!!!!

How long did Jesus suffer on the cross
from
Is god always a around us. Chloe-

Dear Colin, Hello im
not a christian but do i still get loved?

Hi and i don't
Belive

Dear Colin,
Not a Does God ?? still love you if your
christian?? xx

Dear Colin,
Does god still love you if
you do bad things ??????

Can you become a christian
when your a baby?

why does it not give the names of the children
in the bible
from Rhiannon U

the shortest verse is Jesus wepted
were can you find it in the Bible?

How do you know about god

My name is Alice B_____ and I am 11 years old.

The Juniper Tree

"I will go in the strength of the Lord GOD"

Psalm 71 verse 16

My name is lucy N_____ and I am 10 years old.

Running from a king

" If God be for us who can be against us?"

Romans 8 verse 31

ELIJAH DEFEATS THE PROPHETS OF BAAL

1 KINGS 18:17-40

God is my salvation; I will trust, and not be afraid. Isaiah 12:2

.r e_ Chloe_____ Age_ P7

BIBLE FUN WEEK
1st Samuel 17:1-52

David fights Goliath   God was with David

"Look unto me, and be ye saved, all the ends of the earth." Isaiah 45:22

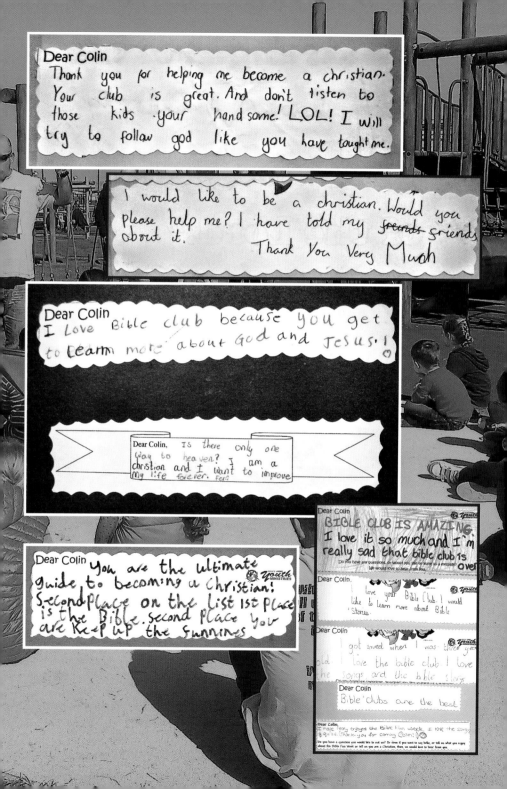

Dear Colin
Thank you for helping me become a christian. Your club is great. And don't listen to those kids .your hand some! LOL! I will try to follow god like you have taught me.

I would like to be a christian. Would you please help me? I have told my friends friends about it.
Thank You Very Much

Dear Colin
I Love Bible club because you get to Learn more about God and JESUS. ♡

Dear Colin, IS there only one Way to heaven? I am a christian and I want to improve My life forever. Fern

Dear Colin You are the ultimate guide to becoming a Christian! Second Place on the list 1st place is the Bible. second Place you are Keep up the funnines

Dear Colin
BIBLE CLUB IS AMAZING. I love it so much and I'm really sad that bible club is over

Dear Colin.
I love your Bible Club. I would like to learn more about Bible Stories.

Dear Colin
I got saved when I was three years old. I love the bible club I love the songs, and the bible stories

Dear Colin
Bible clubs are the best

Dear Colin,
I have realy enjoyed the Bible Fun week. I love the songs. Thank you for coming Colin!

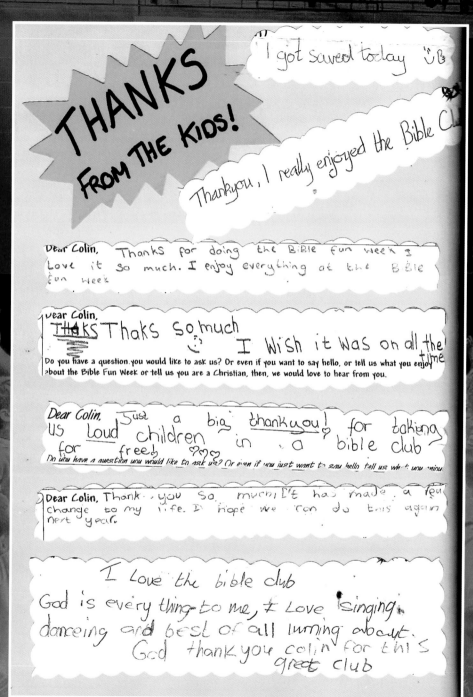

Dear Colin

I will miss you and Joanna so much. xox

Dear Colin

I'm in P.7 and I've been going to bible fun week since P.4. When I leave bible fun week on Friday I will be very upset!! Bible fun week is Awesome!!!

Dear Colin

- Can people be born in heaven?
- I love this bible club it is so fun!
- How was God created?
- I ♡ all the songs! ☺ ☺

Love

Bible Club!!

Dear Colin

IF you were a christian and you had been cheeky what would Happen

Dear Colin... Why have you Started to go to schools and teach about GOD!?

Dear Colin

I love the BIBLE club!

HOPE FOR Youth MINISTRIES

Dear Colin

I (Love) Bible club.
Thank you colin for teaching us about God and Jesus.

MINISTRIES

Dear Colin It is my last year in Pond Park and I have been coming to bible fun week for 3 years now and every year I've came it has been great so I hope for my last year it will be even better :)

I'll miss bible fun week and Pond Park

Do you have any questions, or would you like to leave us a message? We would love to hear from you.

HOPE FOR Youth MINISTRIES

Dear Colin I like your Teaching.
IT IS very good!!!
Thank you ☺ ♡OLin !!!
From. Talitha.

HOPE FOR Youth MINISTRIES

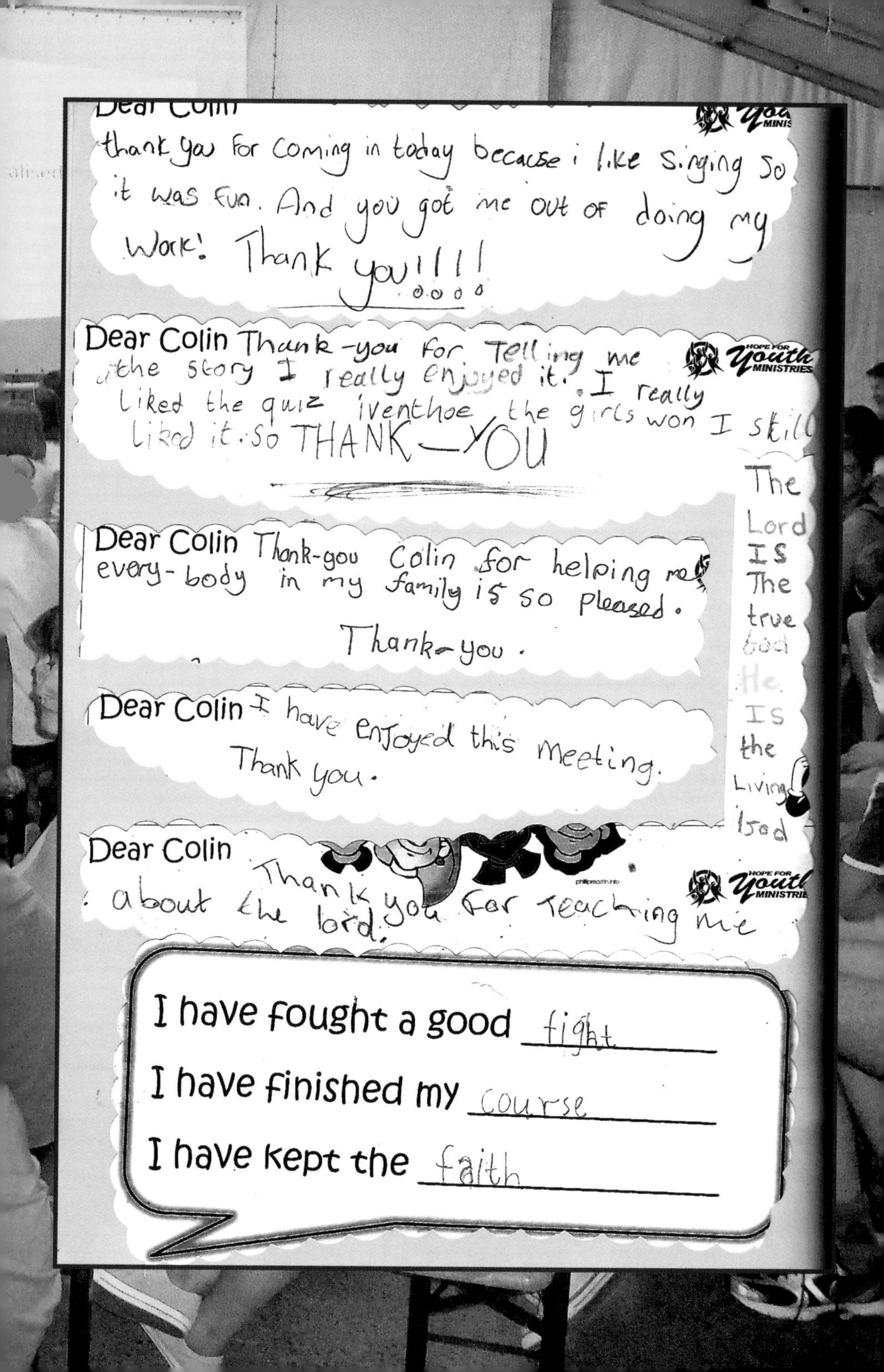

Dear Colin
thank you for coming in today because i like singing so it was fun. And you got me out of doing my Work! Thank you!!!!
Dear Colin Thank-you for Telling me the story I really enjoyed it. I really liked the quiz iventhoe the girls won I still liked it. So THANK-YOU
HOPE FOR Youth MINISTRIES
The Lord IS The true God He IS the Living God
Dear Colin Thank-you Colin for helping me every-body in my family is so pleased. Thank-you.
Dear Colin I have enjoyed this meeting. Thank you.
Dear Colin Thank you for teaching me about the lord.
HOPE FOR Youth MINISTRIES
I have fought a good fight
I have finished my course
I have kept the faith

"Love the Lord thy God with all thy heart"
Luke 10 verse 27

"Men looketh on the outward appearance, but the LORD looketh on the heart."
Samuel 16 v 7

"Love the Lord thy God with all thy heart"
Luke 10 verse 27

"I will go in the strength of the Lord GOD:"
Psalm 71 verse 16

"Christ Jesus came into the world to save sinners"
1st Timothy 1 verse 15

To Colin and team

You have taught me so so much and I whish you wern't going beacuse I never knew that learing about the bible was so so fun so Thank You

From Cameron ps

Happy Easter

Thank you For Every Thing COLIN

STORIES CHILDREN LEARN FROM THE BIBLE!

Stephen is stoned to death   The spread of Christianity

Stephen

Lord Please forgive them they don't know what thr

Stephen Has the 1st Christian Martyr

Feeding the 5000
A little boy and his lunch
(John 6:1-14)

Jesus heals the Ten Lepers   Luke 17:11-19

Dear Colin
You have really inspired me to become a chirstian.

Thank you Colin
From Annalee

Hope for Youth MINISTRIES

Dear Colin I love your missions they are really great

from Ben Blakely

★ ★ ★ ★

Hope for Youth MINISTRIES

I WILL REALLY MISS BIBLE Club

Do you have any questions, or would you like to leave us a message? We would love to hear from you.

Hope for Youth MINISTRIES

Thank you for teaching me about Jonah. I pray that God will help me be Strong and courageous when I tell people about Jesus dying on the cross for their sins.

This was my 1st time at camp + I have loved it. All the activities were really great fun but it wasn't just all about the games. The meetings/devotions gave me alot to think about. (Its all helped me So much)

Do you have any questions, or would you like to leave us a message? We would love to hear from you.

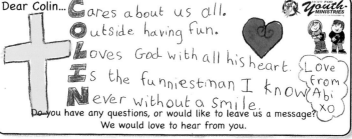

Dear Colin...
Cares about us all.
Outside having fun.
Loves God with all his heart.
Is the funniest man I know.
Never without a smile.

Love from Abi XO

Hope for Youth MINISTRIES

Do you have any questions, or would like to leave us a message? We would love to hear from you.

Have you called on Jesus to save you?

Dear Colin I like bible club and I have become a christian.

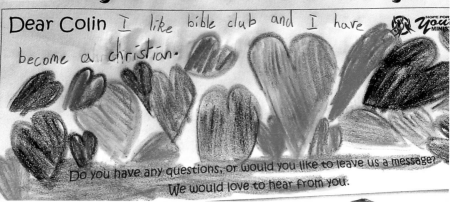

Do you have any questions, or would you like to leave us a message?
We would love to hear from you.

Dear Colin, When you ~~for the juggling~~ came 2014 I realised that God was important to have in your life and since then I have been a christan.

Thankyou colin... #your Book is EPIC

Do you have any questions, or would you like to leave us a message?

We would love to hear from you!

Dear Colin... I became a christian at your club last year. It really Inspired me that you are Inspiring other people to be a christian. Thanks for showing me how to let Jeseus into my heart.

Do you have any questions, or would like to leave us a message?
We would love to hear from you.

Dear Colin... Please come back I never belived in god but you have made me thank you

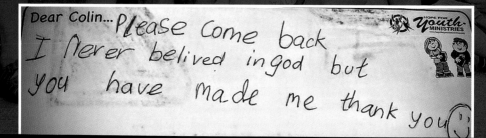

Dear Colin

I never want you to stop doing these Bible Clubs I really Like them I've got a book called "Walking With God" that Was wrote by you and it is very very good.

Colin Theese are my comments.

I love the Bible club and I don't want it to end,
I love getting soaked by the water pistle
I love getting out of school to listen to the word of God

Dear Colin...

I became a Christian after Bible club yesterday when I prayed with my Mum!
Thank You for all the worksheets, I love the activities

Do you have any questions, or would like to leave us a message?
We would love to hear from you.

Dear Colin...

I like you more than the Beano!

Do you have any questions, or would like to leave us a message?
We would love to hear from you.

Dear Colin...

Christ is forever
Open your heart
Love Jesus
Important to us
Never forget

FROM Abi x

Do you have any questions, or would like to leave us a message?
We would love to hear from you.

THIS IS THE LIFE STORY OF JOANNA TINSLEY

A professional and talented artist from Poland. Her story, as told in her book, is all about growing up as a child in Poland, how she longed and searched for God for many years before she found Christ as her Saviour. Joanna has been married to Colin for 20 years and together founded an amazing children's ministry reaching thousands of children with the gospel all over the world. Joanna is available to tell her story and even demonstrate her paintings.

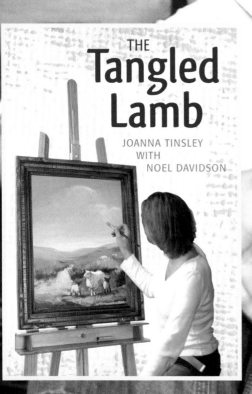

THE
Tangled Lamb

JOANNA TINSLEY
WITH
NOEL DAVIDSON

- When Jesus was in the tomb did he go to heaven or hell or did he do nothing for those three days?
- Is Jesus more powerful than God?
- Has anyone ever seen Jesus recently?
- When will Jesus come back to earth again?

Questions about being a Christian:

- How do you become a Christian?
- Does God love everyone or just Christians?
- What do I need to say to become a Christian?
- What happens when you ask the Lord Jesus into your heart?
- When you become a Christian will you feel different?
- If you do not believe in God will you still go to heaven?
- I am a Muslim – does that mean I cannot be a Christian?
- How does God clean our hearts?
- How does God take away sin?
- What do you mean when you said 'your soul will be in heaven?'
- I am scared to ask the Lord into my heart – can you give me any advice?
- If you sin as a Christian do you have to keep getting saved?
- Do you have to be baptised to become a Christian?
- If you have been good will God forgive you and still let you into heaven?
- How can I be a better Christian?
- I already am a Christian but when I do something wrong does that mean I still have sin?
- How do I get my friends and family to become Christians?
- I am a Christian but how can I serve God?
- How can I get my friend to stop saying bad words?

- What do you do when your friends laugh at you for being a Christian?

Questions about heaven:

- Where is heaven?
- How big is heaven and what is it like?
- Will we see God in heaven?
- How many people are in heaven?
- Who was the first person to go to heaven?
- Can people be born in heaven?
- What does God do in heaven?
- How does a Christian get to heaven?
- Do we become angels when we die?
- Will I still know my mummy and daddy in heaven?
- What will happen to the earth when the Lord Jesus returns?
- Do we have birthdays in heaven?
- Do animals go to heaven?
- How long will we be in heaven for?

Bible story questions:

- Why did God send a flood?
- Why did the people not believe Noah when he told them there was going to be a flood?
- Why did God close the door of the ark?
- How many animals were on the ark?
- How many dinosaurs were on the ark?
- Who was the oldest man to live?
- After the flood did God have to make things again?
- Why did God tell Isaac's dad to kill him?
- Why did Isaac not go and find a wife for himself?
- How did one little stone kill Goliath?
- Why was Daniel put in the lions' den?

- Why did the shepherds worship the Lord Jesus?
- Out of all the people that had sinned why did Jesus choose Zacchaeus?
- Why did the donkey not throw the Lord Jesus off?

General questions:

- What is sin?
- What is a spirit?
- Why are there bad people?
- Is Easter or Christmas more important?
- Does every individual person have a purpose on this earth?
- What food did they eat in Bible times?
- Why did Jesus choose regular people to be his disciples?
- What do you see when you die?
- If a baby dies as soon as it is born does it go to heaven?
- Is hell a real place?
- If you swear does that mean you go to hell?
- Did Judas go to heaven or hell?
- If you're a Christian does that mean you will never worry?
- Is it possible to see people who are dead?
- Do we all have an angel?
- Where do we find the Ten Commandments?
- How do you know Jesus answers prayer?
- How can I go to church if no one in my family goes?

As you can see, children love to ask questions. Perhaps the Lord will put our ministry on your heart and you will remember to pray for us each day as we seek to give biblical answers to such deep questions.

APPENDIX II

What the Volunteers Say

"I am so thankful to have been involved in a small way with Hope for Youth Ministries. From Tollymore camps to Bible Clubs and Mission trips to Poland – so many opportunities to serve! One special memory was during a youth weekend at Murlough House. I felt like Moses at the Red Sea with obstacles on every side and no way out! Everett brought a powerful message and I realised I needed God to roll the sea away and He did! Keep 'er lit! As a wise man once said, 'It's great to be in the work!' Amen."

David (Ahoghill)

"I met Colin shortly after I became a Christian on a mission trip to Poland. Since then, I have been on five mission teams with him and Joanna, including the best trip of my life to Kenya in Africa. Colin and his ministry has had a huge impact on my Christian walk. Through Colin I have learned that being a Christian is about grabbing every opportunity to serve the Lord and most importantly, to serve Him with joy in your heart! I wasted my teenage years when I walked away from God but Colin always encourages me by saying, 'It's not how you start, but how you finish!' Colin serves God joyfully with all of his heart, which has been an inspiration and blessing to me personally and also my wider family."

Julie (Portadown)

"I wasn't long saved when I first met Colin and Joanna, but after getting to know them I was soon helping out in children's Bible Clubs, summer camps and mission trips to Africa and Poland. Now, almost six years later, Hope for Youth Ministries still plays a huge part in my Christian walk and brings much encouragement into my life. 1 Samuel 12:24"

Jonny (Dungannon)

"Hope for Youth Ministries has challenged and encouraged me in the Lord's work. It has shown me that nothing is impossible with God and that time and time again, God answers our believing prayers! To God be the glory!"

Hannah (Antrim)

"Colin and Joanna have really inspired me by how they do everything in the Lord's work to a high standard and take every opportunity to further the cause of Christ. As well as helping locally, I have joined them on trips to Poland, Kenya and Asia. As I have volunteered with the ministry, I recognize all the work that Joanna and many others do behind the scenes. Dozens of volunteers, who are united by a desire to see children won for Christ, give their time, talents and energy to carry out peripheral tasks to help keep Colin on the frontlines reaching the children – whilst they are bound behind desks during school hours. Teamwork makes the dream work!"

Phil (Banbridge)

"Hope for Youth Ministries has been and continues to be a real blessing in my life. It has given me so many opportunities both here and in Poland to get involved with children's work. It's very encouraging to see the enthusiasm and passion Colin has for sharing the gospel with children all over the country. Keep up the good work and I pray God will give you much fruit for your labours. Thank you so much for all the opportunities to get involved."

Ruth (Saintfield)

"Colin has encouraged me many times in my Christian walk. He always has a big smile on his face, a good story to tell and plenty of words of wisdom. Volunteering with Hope for Youth Ministries has been a real blessing to my life."

Suzanne (Portadown)

"Colin and Joanna have been a fabulous help to our children's work by providing us with much practical help and invaluable encouragement. Their enthusiasm is infectious and the obvious vision and energy they possess for this work is inspirational. I have been so blessed in my own soul by their steadfast, unfailing and consistent dedication to the teaching of God's Word to the next generation. Their continued mentorship and exhortation of others to become more adept in this great work is unmeasurable."

Florence (Limavady)

"Colin is a man who makes an impact! His enthusiasm, joy and obvious love for the Lord, encourages many around him (myself included), to live life more radically for God. ...And I don't think he even realises it!"

Caroline (Newtownhamilton)

"I've been to Poland with Colin twice and the experiences completely changed my outlook on life as a Christian and how God can use me. Just spending time with Colin and the team gave God the chance to do an amazing work in my life."

Luke (Castlederg)

"I have been on three mission trips to Poland with Colin and Joanna and every time I was blessed in many different ways. Seeing children call upon the Lord for salvation by getting down on their knees and asking for forgiveness truly encouraged me. We often set out on these trips with the objective of being a blessing to the children and the leaders but they always bless the team even more! One night at the camp, a young girl called Veronika gave her testimony and told how she was saved and baptised a few months later. Immediately, I felt God challenging me to get baptised too. Unbeknown to me, two other girls on the team felt God telling them the same. The following day the three of us got baptised in the lake at the campsite. The feeling of God's presence was so real and I was really excited about returning home to see what God had in store for me. "The fruit of the righteous is a tree of life; and he that winneth souls is wise" (Proverbs 11:30).

Rebecca (Markethill)

"It has been a privilege to know and work alongside Colin teaching boys and girls the gospel at camps, Bible Clubs and in their schools. His tireless work and amazing enthusiasm is inspiring. May the Lord continue to bless Colin in his labours for Christ."

Rebecca (Lisburn)

"'Their soul is precious' (Psalm 49:8). I first met Colin when he was conducting Bible Clubs in Randalstown and the above verse was one he always quoted. Whilst volunteering with Colin I have seen for myself the redemption of precious little souls at Bible Clubs here in Northern Ireland and at Bible camps in Poland. Long may the Lord give Colin and Joanna health and strength to carry on this tremendous work of reaching children with the gospel."

Gary (Randalstown)

"Some of the most blessed and joyful times of my life have been my experiences with Hope for Youth Ministries. Telling boys and girls about the gospel from Portadown to Poland is something I would never have imagined myself doing a few years ago!"

Joshua (Waringsford)

"I have been truly blessed and privileged to share in the spread of Christ's kingdom with Colin in many places around the world. He has given me great opportunities to serve the Master and challenged me to live my life for the Lord. One memory that sticks out is when we were preparing for a Bible Club in my hometown of Markethill. Amongst all the preparations, Colin asked would there be helpers experienced in leading children to the Lord. This sums Colin up – he has a believing heart where he not only knows that God can save, but he truly believes that God will save children when the gospel message is proclaimed."

Paul (Markethill)

"The energy and drive which Colin always has is a blessing to any Christian. The heart he shows to see little children won for the Lord has always encouraged me to go that extra mile for God."

Mark (Rasharkin)

"Helping Colin and Joanna has been a great source of inspiration for me. Colin's mentorship, teaching and encouragement has been invaluable for my own spiritual development."

Calvin (Limavady)

"Very thankful for your friendship, help and guidance over the years. Not least as we've watched the work 'down on the farm' develop from our first Bible Club back in 2010, to a weekly Good News Club and then onto a monthly youth focus group. The kids of Duneane have been left with many precious memories. God is good!"

Helen (Randalstown)

"Colin's Tollymore camps were the highlight of my children's summer. Helping with the camps and travelling to Poland made me realise that serving Christ was what I wanted to do in life. I'm now full-time with the Faith Mission."

Robert (Augher)

"I have been serving the Lord through Hope for Youth Ministries for over six years now and have loved every minute of it! The opportunity to reach children with the gospel is life-changing – firstly, for the children who get to hear about Christ's love for them, and secondly, for the helpers who are blessed in serving. It is also a great way to meet other like-minded Christians for fellowship."

Paul (Randalstown)

"Colin has had a tremendous impact on my life. I have been given more opportunities to serve the Lord through Hope for Youth Ministries than anywhere else. I have been able to go on various mission trips around the world and experience many different forms of evangelism with people of all ages."

Alex (Loughgall)

"Thank you so much, Colin and Joanna for all your encouragement to us as a family. The farm mission was a really blessed time and will never be forgotten – to God be the glory, great things He hath done! Thank you for your constant enthusiasm to spread the gospel to all. The Tollymore camp is a time for the young ones to have fun, but to also grow spiritually. Thank you for your labours of love and dedication. Hebrews 6:10"

Rebecca (Ardaragh)

Colin and Joanna have been true friends in time of need as well as being continual encouragers and inspiring role models in the Lord's work. Their zeal for soul-winning is second to none. Only heaven will reveal how many precious souls have been won for the Lord. 'He that winneth souls is wise' (Proverbs 11:30). We wish you God's richest and sincere blessings."

Roy, Sharon and family (Rasharkin)

"Hope for Youth Ministries has provided me with many opportunities to reach local children with the gospel – children who otherwise I may have just passed in a local shop or playground. However, through helping at the Bible Clubs, I have had the privilege of witnessing to hundreds of children and leading some of them to Christ. 'Jesus said, Suffer little children, and forbid them not, to come unto me: for of such is the kingdom of heaven' (Matthew 19:14). Thank you for the opportunities!"

Cherry (Kinallen)

"Hope for Youth Ministries has been used by God in the Rathfriland area to reach children from all religions and backgrounds. The Bible Clubs have broken new ground for those involved with local churches. They have been a real encouragement and blessing to all my family."

Gary (Rathfriland)

"Through Hope for Youth Ministries, I get the opportunity to do what I love every week. It's a real blessing to go into many schools and tell children that they need to get saved. I love the ministry and am so thankful for every opportunity I get through it. Colin is one of the most gifted children's workers I've ever met. To work alongside him and watch what he does and to see the love the children have for him would melt your heart. I've learned so much about children's work through this ministry. To God be the glory!"

Cheryl (Randalstown)

"Reaching the children with the gospel is a really blessed work. I've helped with Hope for Youth Ministries for five years. I've been to many schools and caravan parks to bring the gospel to the children and I've been really blessed and encouraged doing so."

Stephen (Cookstown)

"Volunteering with Hope for Youth Ministries has provided me with numerous opportunities to serve God in a range of different missions and settings. It has been a blessing and encouragement to watch children come to clubs year after year with enthusiasm, questions about God and most importantly to offer their lives to Him."

Rachel (Banbridge)

"On a number of occasions I've travelled to Poland with Colin and Joanna and have been blessed to see the passion they have to reach and teach children about God. Both my teenage girls also served at these camps and they were inspired and motivated in their Christian walk. When I help in this ministry I know we're sowing the good seed of the Word of God into the lives of the next generation."

David (Moira)

"Over the last number of years, I have had the privilege of working alongside Colin and Joanna at home and abroad. They are a truly great couple who have fully grasped the Great Commission. Their tireless work preaching the gospel to children, delivering Bibles to persecuted believers and training young adults to carry on the work will no doubt earn them the great commendation from the Lord: 'Well done, thou good and faithful servant.' (Matthew 25:21)

P.S. There aren't many people who can carry around 70kg of Bibles in a backpack and make it look as easy as big Colin does! May God continue to bless you both as you labour for our Saviour."

Stephen (Lurgan)

"My first ever mission trip was with Hope for Youth Ministries to Poland. We had a real ball and witnessed tremendous blessing. Colin encouraged (pushed) me to speak and I surprised myself that it wasn't really that scary! It was really what I needed and since that trip, I have helped out at Holiday Bible Clubs and Tollymore camp. Every trip I have been on, I have seen God working and the best experience of my life was the first time I led a child to Christ. Volunteering has helped me grow closer to God and teach me how to show God's love to others in my own church."

Amy (Aughnacloy)

"What a privilege to spend last week with Hope for Youth Ministries telling boys and girls that Jesus died on the cross for their sins and rose again. Over five hundred kids were reached each day and more importantly, many of them were won for the Lord. Thanks for the opportunity Colin."

A keen volunteer

"Great night at the Hope for Youth Ministries' IMPACT devotion book launch. A real blessing listening to volunteers tell how God has worked in the hearts of kids and young people in this country. God is doing great things and greater things are still to come! Let's pray on for Colin and Joanna and this great work that they do."

An encouraging supporter

"This week has been brilliant helping with six Bible Clubs in Portrush. Best of all fifteen children got saved. I want to thank Colin and Joanna for giving me the opportunity to volunteer. Best week of the summer – I will never forget it!"

An enthusiastic volunteer

"I love you, a man of God and I have also started some Bible Clubs in my country. You have motivated and inspired me to do more!"

Ralph Baidoo (Africa)

"Guess what Colin? ...I was 'doing evaluations with kids at sports fun week and several kids told me they heard the gospel through you or else were led to Christ by you! One young girl said she had just got saved a few weeks ago in her home on the Friday night after a Bible Club but hadn't informed you!"

An encouraging volunteer

What Colin Says

Often children ask me personal questions about my life and ministry. Here is a selection of them and the answers I give.

What is your funniest moment?

I have literally had hundreds of funny moments but one that stands out was when I was nominated to drive the student minibus to church one Sunday when I was at Bible College. It was an old rusty bus that didn't go particularly fast and we were running a little late. As I swung into the carpark, the sliding door on the side of the bus fell off and landed in the middle of the carpark! Some old people stared at us in disbelief wondering where the rowdy bunch had arrived from. Imagine their shock when a few minutes later we all walked up to the pulpit to take their service! That was a service we will never forget as we giggled the whole way through it.

What is your favourite Bible verse?

I love the Bible and have dozens of verses that mean a lot to me for various reasons. If I had to pick one, it would be: "For whosoever shall call upon the name of the Lord shall be saved" (Romans 10:13). I love how the 'whosoever' opens the way and invites absolutely everyone to come to the Lord – regardless of age, size, gender or colour. It also includes the word 'saved' – the most important word in the Bible, which is when a person passes from darkness to light. By doing so, they exchange their sins for Jesus' righteousness and secure their eternal destiny in heaven.

Who is your favourite Bible character?

Whilst there are many fascinating Bible characters who truly lived for God, such as Moses, David, Gideon and Paul, the prophet Elijah is my personal favourite. This man inspires me with his fearlessness when he stood up against evil King Ahab and opposed idolatry. He even challenged the king to a competition to prove that the God of Israel was the one true God by calling fire down from heaven. After this spectacle, we read how he outran the king's chariot, which makes him even faster than Usain Bolt! Despite being extremely bold for God, there were also darker times in his life when he felt weak, scared and even suicidal. However, he still remained faithful and persevered for God. We read in 2 Kings 2 how he never died but went straight to heaven in a chariot of fire!

What country have you most enjoyed visiting?

We have visited more than twenty countries over the years and every one of them is unique in their own way but Jamaica was my favourite. We lived there for a year and it was where we got our first opportunity to pastor a church and speak to hundreds of children in public schools.

What is the worst thing about you?

I can be quite a stubborn person at times. Once I set my mind on something, it takes a lot of persuading to turn me around! It is not always a positive trait as often it is rooted in my pride.

What is your favourite part of the ministry?

My favourite part of the ministry is doing Bible Clubs in the schools, which happens to be where I spend the majority of my time. In contrast to church-based missions, many of the children we engage with have never heard the gospel message clearly before. As the Bible Clubs run every day for a full week, we build up good relationships with the children and give them lots of leaflets and worksheets so they can review what they have learned and ask us questions the following day. I believe the schools are where we make the greatest impact with the gospel as many children get saved. For those who don't, we believe we are planting seeds that will take root sometime in the future. What brings me the most joy is that many children tell me their favourite part of the Bible Club is the lesson, which is centred on the precious Word of God.

What is your favourite food?

I love pretty much every kind of food but Joanna knows whenever she makes Spaghetti Bolognese, I am a very satisfied man! The same goes for anything Italian.

Who is your favourite person?

My good wife, Joanna! We are best friends and have been married for over twenty years and share everything in life together. She understands me better than anyone else and is the most sympathetic, forgiving and compassionate person I know. She also is full of fun and enjoys a good laugh. We share many interests and passions: a love for the Lord and desire to do His work, travelling, volleyball and swimming to name a few. Most of all, she prays a lot for me and is someone I can share my personal concerns and burdens with. She also gets really excited and can't stop smiling every time I tell her that a child has got saved!

Which couple helps you the most in the ministry?

Many individuals and couples assist us in many ways, but Paul and Cheryl McIntyre from Randalstown are the ones who help us the most. Both of them have an intense desire to reach children for the Lord and are committed to helping the ministry in any possible way. They have endless amounts of energy, which inspires the children and other volunteers. If I am ever not able to fulfil a meeting or double-book myself, Paul or Cheryl are always willing to step in – sometimes with only an hour's notice! They are both naturally gifted at working with children and are equally as capable teaching Bible lessons to the masses as ministering to individual children. If there is ever anything practical needing done, whether it is giving us a lift to the airport or collecting equipment or literature, all we have to do is ask. As well as being fellow-labourers for the Lord, Joanna and I love their company and banter.

Do you have any regrets in life?

My greatest regret in life is that I didn't get saved until I was seventeen years old. If I had called upon the Lord when I was seven, I could have served the Lord for an extra ten years. However, the Lord is sovereign and knows that this regret motivates me to serve Him more now. God gives us an incredible promise through the prophet Joel: "And I will restore to you the years that the locust hath eaten…" (Joel 2:25) This is why I don't beat myself up over my past but rather focus all my energy on serving the Lord today and in the future, God-willing, as best I can.

What is your greatest ambition in life?

My biggest ambition in life is to complete at least one thousand missions and Bible Clubs for children. Although it isn't always about numbers, every child matters to God, so I challenge myself to reach as many as possible. These days, it alarms me how few children attend church or Sunday school and as a consequence, know very little about the Bible. Our objective is to introduce such children to God and the gift of salvation through Jesus Christ.

What is your favourite childhood memory?

I have so many wonderful memories. Every night at bedtime, my brothers and I had great fun wrestling each other just like the Wrestle Mania Royal Rumbles on TV. It amazes me that none of us ever broke a bone or sustained a serious injury! Another fond memory is the day Dad bought us a horse, who we named Silver. We used to love riding him around the fields, one after the other. Sometimes three of us would get on at a time but he didn't mind as he was quite strong and we were just little fellas. The poor horse hardly got a rest some evenings.

What is your worst childhood memory?

Thankfully I don't have too many bad memories, but one that still grieves me was the morning my mum caught me stealing money from her savings jar to spend in the school tuckshop. Getting caught and feeling Mum's wrath was little in comparison to the sad look on her face as she realised one of her sons was a thief. It will haunt me forever because my parents brought us up to keep the commandments and to honour the Lord and I let them down over a few sweets.

What is your most embarrassing moment?

I have a lot of these, unfortunately – just ask Joanna! If I have to pick one, it is probably the night I was attending a mission in Kilkeel and Pastor George McConnell was preaching on the Lord's return. Just a moment after he said the words, 'the Lord will return suddenly without warning', I leant back slightly in my chair and it snapped with a loud crack. Some of the people around me jumped, maybe thinking the Lord had returned! When the pastor mentioned me by name publicly I was very embarrassed, especially since it happened at such a pivotal moment in his message. Though, maybe it emphasised the point he was making!

What is your saddest memory?

I was distraught when Joanna lost our baby for the fourth time after three previous miscarriages. It is a natural desire for most married couples to become parents and raise children, so we were devastated. Having a baby was the one human thing we both wanted more than anything but we had to accept that God's plan for our lives wasn't going to involve raising our own children. It was a very difficult time for us, but the Lord carried us through and is healing the pain and hurt.

What is your happiest memory?

It would be the first time I saw Joanna, on the 10th September 1993. For the first time in my life, I fell in love with someone I had never met before. As crazy as it sounds, I looked at her and firmly believed she was going to be mine. It was a euphoric moment when I first fell in love and our love continues to grow deeper every day.

Do you have a favourite preacher?

There are many good pastors out there, but I am really blessed whenever I listen to the Rev Roger Higginson. He is full of knowledge and has a great gift for making the Bible come alive. Every time I listen to him preaching, it makes me think about the Lord, as well as encouraging me to love and serve Him more.

Does the ministry impact families?

Over the years, many families have been affected and encouraged by some aspect of the ministry. Once I spoke at a mission in The Commons Mission Hall, Carrickfergus. During the week, numerous children got saved, including two girls who were twins and their sister. I didn't realise it at the time but they were the children of a local pastor and naturally he and his wife were delighted at the news. Then five years later I was at another mission hall and that pastor was taking the meeting and his three daughters were up in the pulpit with him, singing as a trio.

Who has been the most practical help to you in the ministry?

That is hard to answer because dozens of people assist me practically. Here are some of the diverse ways that people help out:

Joe Costley sorts out all the printing of our literature – invitations, tracts, books, prayer letters, etc.

Richard Gilliland supplies me with the stickers for the big signs we use to advertise the evening Bible Clubs and also lends us a generator for Tollymore camp each summer.

Robert McMillan looks after the maintenance of the van and makes sure it is ready for its MOT.

Walter Watson provides us with minibuses to bring hundreds of children to the evening Bible Clubs each year.

These Christian men offer their talents, resources and time willingly and refuse to take any form of payment for their help. It saves the ministry thousands of pounds every year, which can be used to print more books or spent on diesel for the van to travel to more Bible Clubs.

Do you have a favourite book to read?

I am not a great reader as I'm easily distracted and not the most patient man in the world! I enjoy short missionary biographies as these men and women have 'been there and done it' and are a great source of inspiration and encouragement in the work. Most of them are honest and write about the opposition and trials they face, yet God always comes through in the end and works all things together for good. Overall though, the Bible is my all-time favourite book. I love to read about specific characters and see how they lived for God. Each one is unique and I look forward to meeting them in heaven someday. On the other hand, Joanna is the complete opposite to me in this area and reads one book after another and hardly sets a book down until she finishes it.

Which person has inspired you the most?

That would be a man called Peter Crory, who was the leader of the YMCA in Lisburn, which I got involved in shortly after getting saved. Peter took a genuine interest in my life and gave me many opportunities to work with young people. He was a great mentor and encouraged me to go on international mission trips to Holland and America. Above all, he taught me the importance of prayer and encouraged me to pray in public for the first time. He just said, "Will you pray, Colin?" I asked him, "Who to?" There was just the two of us in the room and I thought he meant at a meeting. Wittily, he smirked and replied, "To God obviously!" Like me, he enjoyed practical jokes which drew us together and gave us many laughs over the years.

Do you have a favourite book you have written?

The children's discipleship book called 'Stepping Stones' is my favourite because it has helped hundreds of children over the years in their walk with God. Many of the children we meet in the schools come from families who never go to church and this book is the only thing they have alongside a Bible to learn about God. In 2016 we translated it into Polish to help the children in Poland, where our mission partners Henryk, Pastor Pawel and Pastor Janek serve. Some of these kids live in orphanages and treasure their book as one of their most prized possessions. The next step with this book will be to translate it into Russian, following requests from Christians in Eastern Europe.

What has been the greatest change in the ministry over the years?

Without a doubt it has been the surge in use of the internet and social media. Whenever we started Hope for Youth Ministries, no one had a mobile phone or Facebook but nowadays nearly everyone has both. Such communications enable us to organise mission trips and form a team in a few days, whereas it could have taken months in the early days – along with lots of stamps and envelopes! Social media and group texting is also a fantastic means for giving updates on the work and requesting prayer for specific situations.

What is your favourite animal?

That would be my Golden Retriever dog, Tas. We got him when he was a pup and he is great fun at home and when we go for walks. When I am travelling around Northern Ireland doing Bible Clubs from early morning until late at night, he is great company for Joanna in the house. Whenever we are overseas, Tas gets a change of scenery too and stays at my parents' farm. It takes some persuading to get him to come back home when we return though! He loves Tollymore camp and has attended each one. The children love him and he is very gentle with them all.

What is the nicest thing someone has ever said to you?
One day after a school Bible Club, an eleven-year-old boy came up to me and quietly said: "Thank you for inspiring me to become a Christian." It was very touching and was a great encouragement to me. It made me realise how every minute of our lives are like living sermons and every word and action can either attract or repel others from coming to Christ.

Finally, here are some of my memoirs from recent years (in no particular order):

"Just home from a fantastic weekend in Dundrum we organised for fifty young adults from all over the country. It was great to see their hunger and desire for the Lord and His Word. Prior to the weekend, I travelled over one thousand miles this week doing three Christmas missions for children. I had the joy of seeing seven of them come to faith in Christ. This incoming week, we are missioning in Belfast to reach the children of the city for Christ. Pray for a great work to be done in their hearts!"

"Had an amazing week in the Isle of Man last week. With a team of ten volunteers, we held three missions and gave out over two thousand Bibles, creation books and tracts in eleven primary schools. To top the week off, TEN children put their trust in JESUS, the SAVIOUR of this world."

"Over four hundred people turned up for the gospel meeting at the barn in Rathfriland tonight. It has been an amazing week, with almost two hundred children attending every night and seventeen trusting the Saviour!"

"Just finished the busiest and most incredible year of ministry yet, which involved one hundred and twelve missions and Bible Clubs. Another eight children have trusted Christ this week in schools around the country. To see a principal's face light up when children told her they got saved was very touching. Several hundred children have trusted Christ this year and we are greatly encouraged to meet children who were saved in previous years and hear how they are progressing in their Christian walk."

"Powerful start to the Christmas Bible Clubs in Newry, Caledon and Aughnacloy. We had the joy of seeing twelve children putting their trust in the Lord Jesus this week. Speaking on the birth of Jesus led to the new birth in these children's lives. Next week we have another three clubs in Lisburn."

"This week the Lord's presence came down mightily on the children's mission in Limavady. On Thursday, the minister, his wife, the Sunday school superintendent and Cheryl McIntyre were all counselling children! On the bus home, two more children were led to the Lord as one child counselled the others. On the final night, Joanna spent the whole meeting speaking with the kids as one after another they wanted to get saved during the meeting. In total, eighteen children trusted Christ for salvation there. The workers have never seen anything like what they witnessed this week."

"Had a great night at the mission in Killyleagh last night as I taught how the apostles became filled with the power of the Holy Ghost and three thousand souls got saved in one day. Three children asked for help to get saved at the end of the meeting. It was very special. Imagine if Christians today had the same boldness to preach Christ as the apostles did, what could happen? Pray for an awakening – it could happen amongst the children!"

"A fantastic week in Cavan and Monaghan. We experienced another one of those strange times when the Lord's presence came down amongst the children. At one club it happened on Wednesday and at another one on Thursday. Children stood up one after the other and testified as to how and when the Lord saved them. When we arrived in Cootehill on Friday, the children were already in groups reciting the commandments and verses they had learned all week. They were so grateful for the Bible Club and one child wrote on his worksheet: 'Thank you for the Bible Club and telling us that Jesus is the only way to heaven.' Let's get on with reaching the lambs for whom Christ died. Next stop is the big housing estate, Steeple, in Antrim and then the farm mission in Randalstown."

"Another fantastic week completed with six souls coming to the Lord in Antrim and on the farm outside

Randalstown. The father of one little girl came to the farm this morning with a smile on his face and told us his daughter got saved before going to bed last night.

"Incredible week! Forty-one children have come to Christ in Portadown and Banbridge. Children got saved before, during and after the meetings. It cannot be controlled or organised but is the work of the Lord! On Friday evening in Banbridge, for twenty-five minutes children lined up to give their testimony in front of over two hundred other kids and thirty adults. Some shared how they got saved this week, others last year or a couple of years ago. I asked a little girl if she would change it for a million pounds. 'No way!' she replied. All the glory goes to God alone!"

"Another mother contacted me on Facebook to say how her little boy got saved after the mission in Magherafelt. That brings the number of souls saved to thirty-six this past week. These are great days for reaching the kids as there seems to be a real earnestness for seeking after the things of God – I'm keeping the shorts on and going vigorously after these little souls for whom Christ died. To Him be the glory!"

"Just finished another week of Bible Clubs in the Lisburn and Antrim areas. On the final day in Lisburn, nearly the whole time was taken up with testimonies and question time. Four teachers and the vice-principal were there to witness children one by one testify of God's salvation in their lives. Another seven children trusted in the Lord in Antrim."

"We have just returned from another summer camp in Poland. Again the Lord came down and moved in a miraculous way and saved many children. The breakthrough came on the Sunday night after the Word of God was preached. Seventeen children were counselled for salvation. There was much crying and brokenness amongst the children as they repented of their sin. To witness this again is a very touching thing. God continues to bless these camps in Poland one year after another. A teenager who Joanna led to the Lord eighteen months earlier at a winter camp was used to help counsel some of the children!"

"This past week has been the busiest week ever with seven Bible Clubs in Portadown and Richhill – reaching over a thousand children with the gospel. Most days we had no time for the quiz, as the kids asked dozens of spiritual questions. One eleven-year-old girl put her hand up at the back and said 'I don't have a question but want to tell you I got saved this week because you came to tell us we needed to!' They just love listening to the pure word of God broken down in a simple childlike way! Many of them say 'it's the best week of the year!'

"May is over for another year and we have had a brilliant month completing twenty-three missions and Bible Clubs. During June, some weeks we have six Bible Clubs in one week – an intense time of evangelism. God is continuing to bless us abundantly and we get much encouragement seeing little lives being changed by the truth of God's Word. On Friday, at one stage, five volunteers were counselling different children simultaneously! Throughout the clubs in Belfast, the children just kept coming one-by-one desiring to get saved. We are in the

Randalstown-Ahoghill area this week. Please keep praying as we reach the children – the adults of tomorrow, with the wonderful, life-changing message of the gospel!"

"Lift up your eyes, and look on the fields;
for they are white already to harvest" (John 4:35).

Acknowledgments

THIS AUTOBIOGRAPHY TOOK me just over three weeks to write. The majority of the chapters were written whilst on a mission trip delivering Bibles to persecuted Christians in Asia. Initially I envisaged it taking the form of a journal, but as it developed and I shared early drafts with a few friends, I was encouraged to publish it as a book. It has since taken much longer to edit, proof-read and publish.

I would like to acknowledge and thank the following people in particular:

Editing: Phil Buchanan, Jonny Ormerod, John McCreedy

Photos and design: Joanna Tinsley, Philip Topping

Publisher: Hope for Youth Ministries

Printer: JC Print Ltd

Thanks also to many other friends, far too many to mention, for their encouragement, dedication, wisdom and feedback when proofreading the book. Finally, I must acknowledge my gratitude to the Lord who saved me and gave me a story to write about. To Him be the glory, Amen.

Conclusion

THIS CONCLUDES MY book. I trust you have enjoyed and were blessed reading it as much as I was writing it. It felt strange writing my own story but it is something I have always wanted to do and I trust God will be glorified through it. As I look back over my life, I am honestly taken aback and humbled beyond words that God chose me and then took me on this extraordinary journey.

Colin Tinsley
4th November 2017